Black Days in Andaman and Nicobar Islands

The rocky shore off South Point
Background - Ross Islands

Black Days in Andaman and Nicobar Islands

Rabin Roychowdhury

Manas Publications
New Delhi-110 002 (INDIA)

Manas Publications
(Publishers, Distributors, Importers & Exporters)
4858, Prahlad Street,
24, Ansari Road, Darya Ganj,
New Delhi - 110 002 (INDIA)
Ph.: 23260783, 23265523 (O); 27131660, 27143052 (R)
Fax: 011-23272766
E-mail: manaspublications@vsnl.com

First published, 2004

ISBN 81-7049-183-5

Rs. 495/-

Typeset at
Manas Publications

Printed in India at
Nice Printing Press
and Published by Mrs Suman Lata for
Manas Publications, 4858, Prahlad Street,
24, Ansari Road, Darya Ganj,
New Delhi - 110 002 (INDIA)

Dedicated to my wife
Smt. Kamala Roychowdhury

A Japanese bunker

Preface

Writing a book on the history of a particular period on a specific class of people least concerned and the land less known is a very strenuous and dedicated job and it needs the writer's overall involvement. Even then it is impedial to perform while it lacks the support of sufficient records and documents. Above all, if the period is least traversed by others, there are possibilities that the book may be exposed to plangent criticism or benign euphoria. For me, it's a belated debut that awaits endorsement or suggestions from savants.

For the last thirty years I have been in the Andamans which all along attract me with her pristine beauty and enigmatic past. Being a student of history, it is but natural that I shall be inspired to study the less-known history of these islands. My area of study is the modern period so I paid intense attention to learn its history of last two hundred years since the visit of Archibald Blair in 1788 with special emphasis on the history of the Japanese regime in the Andaman and Nicobar Islands.

Close study of almost all the books available on the modern history of these islands reveals that most of the books have been written either in a biased way sitting far away without having any interaction with the locality, nay with the local populace and somewhat erroneously depending on the hearsays. What I believe is that facts must be interpreted in the aura of the then times and not in the light of present day perspectives. Moreover, these facts should be treated with a scientific acumen and arranged in a systematic manner. It usually happens, the more one moves towards the primordial times, the more one faces with a scarcity of source materials but in the case of these islands, it is just the reverse.

The more one proceeds towards the present times, the more one experiences the dearth of proper documents and records. Major reasons may be that the Britishers on evacuation destroyed all the existing documents and the Japanese before surrender incinerated all their records and reports etc. Last but not the least, the islanders were not at all conscious to preserve documents, relics, antiques and being terrified by the Japanese, they destroyed whatever historical evidences they still had. The natural calamities like the catastrophic earthquake of 1941 and the devastating fire in 1974 did the last act of perdition. Naturally I had to depend on the secondary sources. Of course I have spent several hours in recording interviews with the old people who are the living witnesses of the bygone days. These interviews helped me a lot to cross examine the facts.

In the course of my study, what pains me is the apathy on the part of the Andaman and Nicobar Administration to collect and preserve whatever written evidences are still available with the National Archives of India, National Library, Kolkata, Asiatic Society, Kolkata, British Library, London, Archives of Defence Ministry and so on. What is more deplorable is the lack of initiative on the part of the Administration even to procure the published reports including all Census Reports of the Government of India particularly those related to these Islands and preserve them scientifically. One most important document relating to the Administration of Japanese Military Authorities is still lying in the stackroom of the Ministry of Defence but it's not accessible to the public. Only the Andaman and Nicobar Administration can move officially to collect a copy of the File No. 601/7652H containing the report, "History of Japanese Administration in the Andamans". Besides, many important documents are still available in different State Libraries, especially in Pune, Allahabad, Lucknow, Meerut, and Delhi and they can easily be collected.

For public interest, the Administration should work out a plan to set up a historical Library cum Museum. In this matter, National Memorial Cellular Jail is the best site to materialize the idea. Shri Swapnesh Choudhury, Curator of NMCJ has already taken initiative within his limited means to develop its library as a proto – archive of books, records, old manuscripts, coins, photographs relating to the freedom movements. He has done a laudable job by procuring a number of micro-films of the records relating to these Islands from National Archives of India, New Delhi. I had the opportunity to study many rare photographs of the British period collected by him from the British Library, London. These photographs are so vivid and authentic that they bear the testimony of the British period.

However, I must say that among all the books dealing with the history of these islands, only a few deserves a mention. One of such books is "History of the Andaman Nicobar Islands (1756–1966)" written by L.P. Mathur, but sadder is the fact that the author seemed more dexterous to prepare his dissertation leading to his doctorate than devout to write a history of the islands in the true sense of term. Naturally it lacks the elements that make the subject interesting for intimate and comprehensive study. Moreover, the major lacuna of the book is the conspicuous absence of his deliverance on the history of the Japanese rule in the islands, though he has mentioned that the period under his study is from 1756 to 1966.

The other book to be mentioned is 'The Andaman Story' by N. Iqbal Singh. The title of the book itself suggests the contents of the book which contains 27 chapters of which only 3 chapters have been spent to deal with the period of the Japanese occupation.

Despite his utterance, " I must however hasten to add that whatever material I have used has full documentary support," a number of errors has escaped his vigil. Sometimes, his emotions have overshadowed the facts and at times, prejudice has surpassed the truth.

However, after going through all these books, it is felt that a book on the history of these islands may be written in a holistic manner for conceptual studies. During my long tenure, it is found that people as a whole know Andaman by the sobriquet, *Kalapani* and after visiting this place, their curiosity ends in awe and wonder. To the contrary, the people of these islands are strangely indifferent and complacent having no sign of inquisitiveness towards the past. This sort of inertness and quiescence on the part of people both within and without prompts me to write this book.

Indeed, *Kalapani* only amounted to social stigma without any limit of apostasy. It seems suspiciously like a snob symbol of those mortally afraid of the sea and perhaps invented to cover up their cowardice. Hence my venture is to wipe out the enigma and waive the stigma to establish the facts. To know '*Kalapani*', to feel the throbbing pulses of *Kalapani*, to understand the weal and woe of *Kalapani*, one should study history of this place. My purpose shall be served if and only if the readers become enthusiastic to study more about the land and people of '*Kalapani*'.

I admit that the popular area of the history of these islands is related to the aborigines and obviously the dictum, 'Jarawa' itself has become a saleable item. Similarly the word 'Cellular Jail' has earned the ingenious diction, 'Bastille' and in due course it has become a gambit of Island Tourism Department. With these trivia, one markets one's scribbles obviously in the name of history.

Hence in my venture, I have tried to overcome these stigmas and trances, and bring out the facts lying obscured beneath the shroud of oblivion. As the core area of my study is invariably the era of the Japanese occupation, out of 15 chapters, I have spared only three chapters to sum up the past history culminating to the outbreak of the Second World War and subsequent twelve chapters have been dedicated to give vent to the history of the Japanese rule and aftermath. My attempt is not only to give a detailed account of the political, social, economic conditions of the people of these islands under the Japanese rule, but also to emphasize on the strategic importance of this territory.

In fine, being an inmate of these islands I like to convey my great regards to Netaji Subhash Chandra Bose who hoisted first the tricolour here in the Gymkhana ground on the soil of 'Free India' on 30 December, 1943 while the rest of the country was still struggling for freedom and haggling for power. However, I have always dreamt to get the book released on 10 March as on that date the great heroes of the First War of Independence, 1857 stepped first on these islands and sanctified the soil with the spirit of struggle and sacrifice. Now a days, the 10th March is celebrated in these islands as the beginning of Settlement. However, whatever may be the date of release of the book, I pray, let it be consecrated with the blessings of those Great Heroes.

In conclusion, I prefer to quote from Nagavarma, an eminent Sanskrit scholar of the past—

"Owing to great haste, ignorance, faults of inappropriate diction if anything here becomes something different, let the greatly wise who are not envious and whose minds are free from malice, take it up and correct the faults."

Rabin Roychowdhury

The lonely grave of Zulfiqar Ali, in a corner of the Aberdeen Village

Contents

List of Illustrations

Special Insertion of Illustrations

Plate 1. Sher Ali who murdered Viceroy Lord Mayo at Hope Town Jelly in 1872.

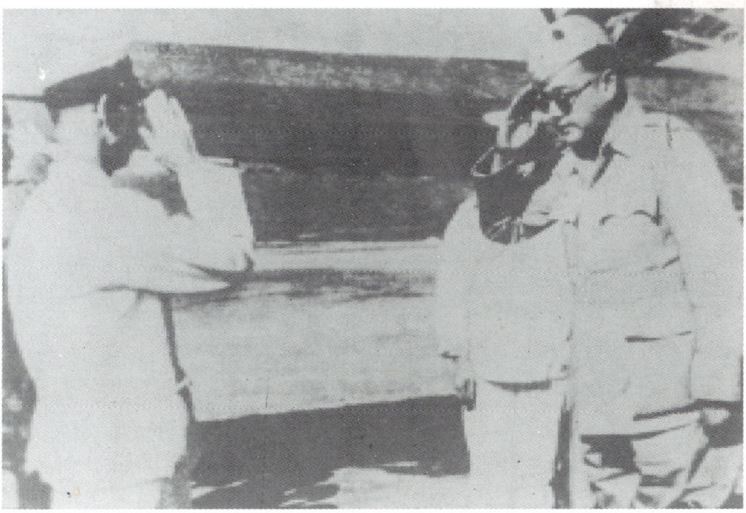

Plate 2. Netaji Subhash was received by Jap. Admiral at Lambaline Airport. Port Blair on 29 December, 1943.

Plate 3. Guard of Honour accorded to Netaji Subhash at Lambaline Airport on 29 December, 1943.

Plate 4. Netaji Subhash receiving a purse of Rs. 10,000/- from Ramakrishna in the dias in the Gymkhana Ground on 30 December, 1943.

Plate 5. Left: Netaji inside the Cellular Jail
Right: Netaji on the sea-shore behind the Celluar Jail.

Plate 6. Netaji Subhash at the gate of the Cellular Jail on 30 December, 1943.

Plate 7. Netaji Subhash along with INA officers and Jap. Officers in front of Chief Commissioner's Bunglow at Ross Island.

Plate 8. In front of Chief Commissioner's Bunglow at Ross Island.

Plate 9. Allied Bombardment at Chatham Saw mill.

Plate 10. After reoccupation, Viceroy Lord Wavell's Visit of Andaman.

Plate 11. Chatham Saw mill with cause way.

Plate 12. Netaji Subhash and Ananda Mohon Sahay at Gymkhana ground accompanied by the Japanese officials.

Plate 13. The British Chief Commissioner's bunglow where Netaji stayed during his visit to the Andamans from 29th to 31st December, 1943.

Plate 14. Japanese military personnels to run the administration in the Andamans.

Plate 15. Bridge over a stream at Ross Island.

1 Historical Background

Situated in the Bay of Bengal, a little over 1250 kms. away from the coast of India,193 kms. from the Cape Negrais in Myanmar (Burma) and about 550 kms. from the northern extremity of Sumatra, a tiny India is emerging from the blue spell of the emerald sea throbbing with life and vivacity. Andaman, once condemned as the dreaded destination for the expels or the infernal hell for the patriots, and queerly damned with a frightening sobriquet, '*Kalapani*', is aptly eulogized as the sylvan paradise of nature's bounty and beauty. After independence the land has turned to become an epitome of India as it reveals many a facet of modern India altogether different from what we have seen elsewhere. Here the people speaking different languages, belonging to different cultures, hailing from different parts of India ingenuously cultivate the spirit of Indianness defying diversities. Thus, spiritually united, [illegible]al, socially unique and culturally identical, the unique society of this land is a glaring example of national integration.

The Andaman and Nicobar islands, say the *AndaNico* constitute more than 570 islands, and form the remotest part of India. The inky blue waters of the Bay of Bengal and the Andaman Sea, and the overwhelming grandeur of vast cloud-ridden sky overhead brilliantly compose a domain of unsullied nature. The splendour and opulence of this land not only bespeak its glory as a tourists' paradise but also signify its efficacy as a shrine for sacrifice by the innumerable heroes of the freedom struggle.

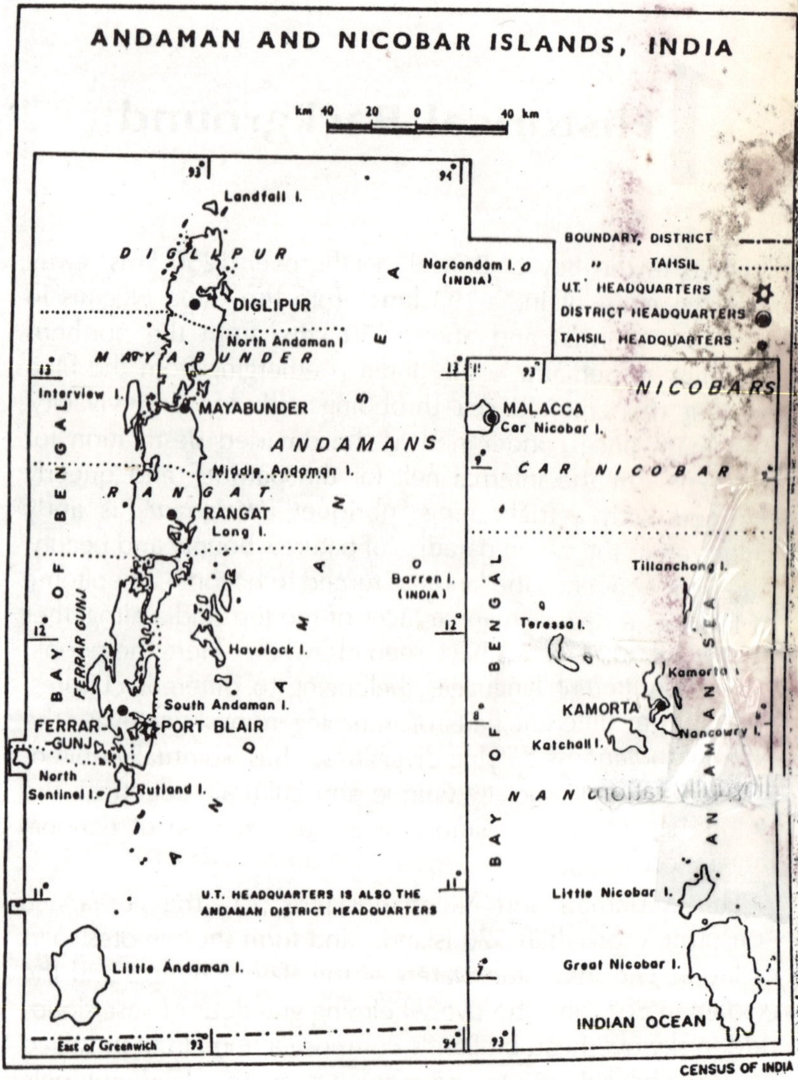
ANDAMAN AND NICOBAR ISLANDS, INDIA
km 40 20 0 40 km
BOUNDARY, DISTRICT
" TAHSIL
U.T. HEADQUARTERS
DISTRICT HEADQUARTERS
TAHSIL HEADQUARTERS
Landfall I.
DIGLIPUR
North Andaman I
MAYABUNDER
Interview I.
ANDAMANS
Middle Andaman I.
RANGAT
Long I.
FERRAR GUNJ
Havelock I.
South Andaman I.
FERRAR-GUNJ
PORT BLAIR
North Sentinel I.
Rutland I.
BAY OF BENGAL
ANDAMAN SEA
Narcondam I. (INDIA)
Barren I. (INDIA)
U.T. HEADQUARTERS IS ALSO THE ANDAMAN DISTRICT HEADQUARTERS
Little Andaman I.
East of Greenwich
NICOBARS
MALACCA
Car Nicobar I.
CAR NICOBAR
Tillanchong I.
Teressa I.
Kamorta I.
KAMORTA
Nancowry I.
Katchall I.
NANCOWRY
Little Nicobar I.
Great Nicobar I.
INDIAN OCEAN
CENSUS OF INDIA

HYDROGRAPHICAL CHART of the ANDAMAN AND NICOBAR ISLANDS

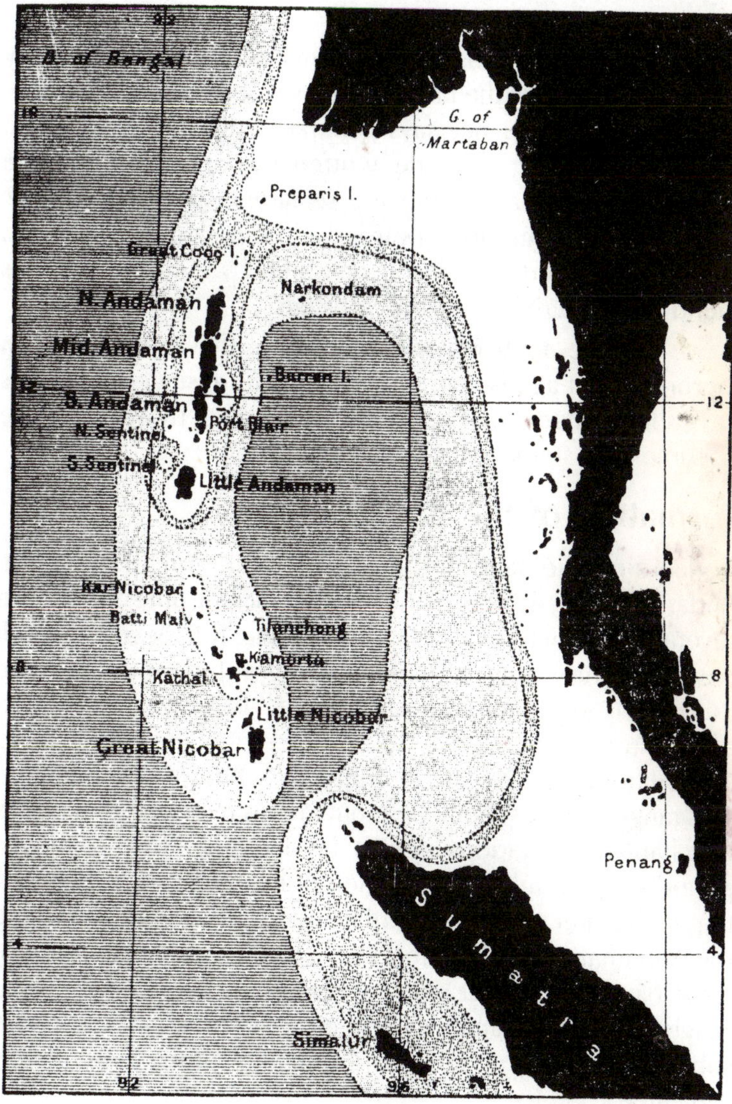

Depth of Sea less than 100 fathoms

" " 200 "

" " 1000 "

" more than 1000 "

The *AndaNico* stands with all its magnanimity and austerity as a mute witness of the past which is still shrouded in mysteries but the enumerous hearsays generate only misconceptions. Sadder is the fact that the written evidences, mostly the accounts of the traders and the seafarers, speak their views only of the 16th century onwards but the period anterior to it, is either obscured in oblivion or glared by cursory mentions found in the scribbles of the voyagers.

So, to trace a chronological history of the *AndaNico* from the primordial age is very difficult therefore, sincere attempts have been made in this book to arrange those available documents systematically as far as possible.

Formation of the Bay Islands

Concerning the facts for the geological formation of the Andaman and Nicobar Islands in the ancient times, there are several contradictory postulations. Colonel R.B. Seymor Sewell has explained in his book, "Geographic and Oceanic Researches in Indian Waters", that the *AndaNico* has formed a continuous range of lofty submarine mountains stretching in a curve from cape Negrais in Burma to Achin Head in Sumatra. This range of lofty submarine mountains is interrupted in places by channels of various depths formed prior to the Triassic period which marks the evolution of mammalia. It is believed that in the later part of the Tertiary epoch, the land constituting the Andamans first appeared above the sea as an extension of Cape Negrais and later became isolated by subsidence due to neighbouring volcanic actions or due to great cataclysm submerging a greater part of the land and getting these islands separated.

The Andaman Islands are of Tertiary formation and of geological structure similar to that of the Arakan Yome Range, the line of elevation connecting them with the Preparis Island.

Similarly the geological findings collected from the Nicobar Islands indicate more or less distinctly that they are also of

Young Tertiary age. In "Geology of the Nicobars", F. Von Hohstetter[1] writes, "We find a repetition of the geological condition of the Nicobars on the southern coast of Java and the south–west coast of Sumatra".

Botanist Sulpiz Kurz and geologist R. D. Oldham[2] studied the geological features of this archipelago in 1866 and 1884. They considered the Andamans as residue above water of submarine subsidence which was still continuing. Portman[3] also believed that in the immediate past there had been subsidence at certain places in the Andamans.

Bonnington[4] viewed that the rising and subsidence in the various parts of these islands were purely of a local and superficial character and were mistaken by Kurz and Oldham.

Of course, C. Boden Kloss[5] after a detailed study of the avifauna of the regions, mentions that there had never been any surface connection between the Andaman & Nicobar islands and the Asia continent, for the most characteristic species of the Arakan Hills were absent in these islands and the latter exhibited a great number of distinct and indigenous specimens completely unknown to the former.

However, the different theories about the surface connection of the Bay Islands with the Asia continent are somewhat based on inferences. If it is to believe that there was land connection at all, it might have existed at an immensely remote past. At a later period, the Andamans were cut off from the continent and the Nicobars have been separated since long. The process by which they have been disconnected among themselves is a phenomenon of comparatively recent past.

Origin of the Names

Andaman

The name, 'Andaman' is said to owe its origin to the *Ramayana* in which *Hanuman*, played the most vital role. The Malayans who knew the islands from time immemorial and exploited them as a base for their piracy, would call them 'the islands of Handuman' which seems a corrupt form of *Hanuman*. Thus, transcription of *Hanuman* to *Handuman* eventually became Andaman.

But Sir Henry Yule[6] suggests that the origin of the name, *Andaman*, may be traced to Ptolemy, the great Geographer of the Roman Empire, who in his map in the 2nd century located a group of islands in the South East Seas under the name of "Islands of Good Fortune" or "Insulae Bonae Fortunae" which had been converted into "The Angdaman Islands". With the passing of time Angdaman evolved to Andaman. So this may be considered as the first known report of the Archipelago.

According to Portman[7] the Andamans were perhaps called after the name of Agathodaemon, a Roman mathematician of the 5th century who drew the maps of the world in accordance with the exploration of Ptolemy. Marco Polo passed these islands in 1290 and located them as 'Angamanian'.

As to Portman[8] a Chinese traveller I' Tsing referred to the Andaman Islands as *Andabain*.

Though it seems very difficult to trace the origin of the name, 'Andaman' accurately, it was however very old and widely known to the seafarers.

Nicobar

The origin of the name, 'Nicobar' appears to be somewhat less mysterious because throughout the historic times, the Nicobar islands have often been referred to as the land of the naked people in the accounts of the voyagers.

The earliest mention of the Nicobars may be traced in the geographical works of Claudius Ptolemy who marked two islands as the islands of the naked (nanga) and Barussea as mentioned is possibly Teressa Island of Central Nicobar. Ptolemy propounded another reference to the Nicobarese by 'Satyorum Insulae Tres' as the people who have tails.

I-T'sing[9] a Chinese traveller described the Nicobar islands as *Lo-Jen-Kuo* which means the land of the naked people.

The Arab travellers namely Abu Zaid Hasan and Sulaiman came in contact with the Nicobarese during a voyage to Southern China in 850 A.D. They mentioned in their accounts the Nicobars as *Lakhabalus* or *Nagabalus* or *Langabulus* which also means the land of the naked as the people went naked except that the women achieved modesty with 'big leaves'. Perhaps, *Nagabalus* is a mistranscription of some form of the Nicobars.

Only in the Tanjore inscription of 1050 A.D. for the first time there is almost a clear mention of the name, 'Nicobar' as *Nakkavaram* or *Naccavarum* which also indicates the land of the naked. According to this inscription, the Chola King, Rajendra Chola established his hegemony over Car Nicobar on way to a naval expedition to Malaya.

Since long the name, 'Nicobar' has been mentioned almost in all accounts of the voyagers as to their own pronunciations. Marco Polo's (1292 A.D.) *Necuveran*, Rashiuddin or Rashiduddin's (1300 A.D.) *Nakawaran*, Friar Odorie's (1322 A.D.) *Nicoveran* etc., all obviously precede Portuguese '*Nacabar*' or *Nicubar* which is ultimately deduced to modern '*Nicobar*'.

Natives of the Bay Islands

Andamanese

It is a matter of great controversy to establish the origin of the natives of the Andamans as they are morphologically and culturally widely different not only from all the inhabitants of the Asia continent but also from the natives of the Nicobars who are immediately contiguous to it.

The most popular theory is that early in the 16th century, Portuguese ships, laden with slaves from Mozambique had been wrecked and cast on the shore of the Andamans and the present Andamanese are the progeny of such ship-wrecked human cargoes. As it is stated, "The manner in which these islands were peopled is a matter of mere conjecture. We are told that when the Portuguese had a settlement near Pegu, two of their ships, with cargoes of slaves on board, amounting in number of men and women to 300,were cast away there, and as the inhabitants are of the *Coffree* caste, probability favours this opinion or conjecture. They are a strong, robust set of *Coffrees* and in their appearance and mode of living resemble much what Cook describes to us of the inhabitants of South-West part of New Zealand[10]..." But this conjecture is grossly erroneous because the Andamanese are known to have been dwelling in these islands long before the slave trade started and it bears the evidence from the accounts of the Arab travellers of the 9th century which are long anterior to the navigation of those seas by the Europeans for slave trade.

It is presumed that in the very early stage of human civilization, a *nigrito* race dwelt in an enormous extent of this region. In the remote past, due to natural calamity, subsidence or great cataclysm had separated the branches of the race dwelling in the Andamans which in due course developed in different parts of these islands as distinct isolated tribes. The remnants of that original race are now found pure only in the Andaman Islands, and of course, until recently in the now extinct Tasmanian tribe, nearly pure in the Aetas of the Philippines and in the Semang of the Malaya peninsula.

As to the ethnographic study[11] it is contented that the *Bushmen*, the dwarf tribe of Congo forest and other *Nigrito-African* tribes do not belong to the same race as that of the Andamanese who are not *nigros* but bear *nigrito* consanguinity.

Nicobarese

Till yester years the Andamanese were nomads but the Nicobarese lived in huts and did the plantation. They belong to the Mongolian race. Their physical features, way of living, language, social and economic organizations are completely different from those of the Andamanese. Even the Shompens, though of Mongolian stock, are quite distinct from the Nicobarese. In comparison with all these tribes of the Bay Islands, the Nicobarese are more progressive and virile than other tribal people. The religious beliefs of the Nicobarese are animistic in which spirit worship, animal sacrifices and witch doctors dominate their rituals.

There are several legends about the origin of the Nicobarese. All the legendary tales are somewhat imaginary and highlight the fact that they, though primitive but unlike the Andamanese, were migrated and domiciled here from the South East Asia and have been inhabiting in these islands since the remote past.

In one tale, it is said that once upon a time, a Burmese princess was banished by her father for her unnatural relationship with a dog. Being driven by the wind and waves, she landed on the shore of Nicobar and gave birth to her son.

In due course, for the urge of procreation, she married her son and the Nicobarese are said to be the scions of these parents.

There is yet another legend about the origin of the Nicobarese to the effect that the first stranger on Nicobar found some ant-sized people moving around the shore. He brought them up to the size of common men and women. It is said that they are the ancestors of the Nicobarese.

According to another story, once there was a great cataclysm that inundated the entire land. When the flood water receded, only one man could survive as he had taken shelter on a big tree and was astonished to find a bitch atop the branches of the tree. He, however, rescued the bitch and made her his wife.

They lived together and the procreation started and surprisingly they were all human beings. The Nicobarese are said to have descended from them.

It seems no wonder as during celebration, the *Nicobari* males wear a tail-like loin cloth, a 'Kisat' and fasten a two-horned head-dress, 'ta-chokla'. From these practices, one may consider that these are symbolic of the canine origin. However, it is interesting to note that the Andamanese and the Nicobarese have some similarity in their legends about the origin of their respective races. Both of them believe in the tale of a great deluge and trace their genesis to the cataclysm which engulfed the islands and separated the people even creating a natural barrier between the Andamans and the Nicobars.

Historical References

The existence of a chain of islands from Cape Negrais of Burma to Achin Head in Sumatra was known even in the 2nd century as identified by Claudius Ptolemy and demarcated in the maps drawn by Agathodaemon in the 5th century in accordance with the description of Ptolemy. In the maps, the island of Buzacata is laid down and we are not sure that the name was attributed to identify the Andamans. Moreover, we have no other information else than the remark, "it produces quantities of shells and the inhabitants go naked and are called Agmatae".

Gerini would identify Ptolemy's Maniola as Car Nicobar but exact identification of the Nicobars from the writings of the ancient geographer remains uncertain. Only we can assume that Ptolemy placed certain islands in the sea where the *AndaNico* is situated and further it is believed that these islands were somehow known to the maritime world at that time.

According to Portman, Ptolemy had identified 1400 islands on either side of the Malaya Peninsula including the Andamans as the habitation of Anthropophagi which can be traced also in his so called maps.

Others believe that Ptolemy's 'Insulae Bonae Fortunae' was suspected of having been converted into Agdaman, Angaman and finally Andaman. The name is, however, not distinctly recorded before the 9th century.

According to Chinese annals, it is said that old Chinese navigators had records of the Nicobars for a thousand years or more.

Fa-Hien sailed from India to China in the 6th century A.D. and probably passed through the Nicobars.

In 607 A.D., a Chinese envoy to Thailand is believed to have reached the Nicobars and reported about them.

The credit of next reference to these islands goes to I–T'sing or I-Ching, a Chinese traveller who sailed in a Persian ship on a voyage to India in 671 A.D. He studied Buddhism in Sumatra and then took another ship which is supposed to have anchored somewhere in the Nicobars and finally reached India in 673 A.D. He referred the Andamans as *Andaban* and described the inhabitants as *cannibals*. He mentioned the Nicobars as *Lo-Jen-Kuo* which means the *land of the naked people*.

According to the travel accounts of the Arab merchants, it is learnt that the Nicobarese brought ambergris and coconuts to the visiting ships in exchange of iron. The Nicobar island were no doubt used as halting stations by the ancient mariners voyaging from the different Indian ports namely Tamralipta (Bengal), Palura (Ganjam, Orissa) and other ports near Masulipattam 10th century onwards.

In due course, the Chola kings took keen interest to exercise their power over the sea spreading between the Nicobars and the Malaya. Rajendra Chola I even sent a naval expedition across the Bay of Bengal about 1125 A.D against the *Sailendras*, the dynasty ruling over Malaya and other neighbouring countries.

However, the first distinct mention of 'Andaman' is found in the early Arab notes on India and China. The Arabs perhaps undertook their voyages eastward and passed by these islands, probably the Nicobars, sometime in 871's. Their descriptions about the people though alarming, are somewhat tolerably correct. They write, "Beyond these two islands lie the sea of Andaman. The people (Andamanese) in this coast eat human flesh quite raw. They are dark, have fuzzy hair, frightful faces and eyes, enormous feet almost a cubit in length and they go quite naked". Even in the first millennium A.D., the Chinese and the Japanese knew the islands as *Yang-t'amang* and *Andaban*.

In the Tanjore inscription of 1050 A.D. the islands appear to be mentioned under the translated name, *Timaillivu* which means 'the islands of impurity',considering perhaps the cannibalism among the natives.

Another traveller who passed by these islands but perhaps never visited them, was Marco Polo, a citizen of Venice. He set out on his odyssey along with his father Nicolo Polo and crossed these islands sometime in 1290 A.D. They were the first travellers to trace a route across the whole longitude of Asia and were warmly welcomed by Kublai Khan, the Chief of the Mongols in China. He returned to Venice in 1295 A.D. and wrote an account of his voyage. In this account, he refered the Andamans as *Angamanain*[12]

Sir Henry Yule who wrote a commentary on Marco Polo, has suggested that *Angamanain,* the name used by Marco Polo is in Arabic dual signifying two Andamans, the great one and the little one.

Marco Polo comments, "Angamanain is a very long island. The people are without a king, are idolaters and no better than wild beasts. And I assure you, all the men of this island of Angamanain have head like dogs, teeth and eyes likewise, in fact, in the face they are just like big mastiff dogs...They are a most cruel generation, and eat everybody that they can catch, if not of their own race. They live on flesh and rice and milk, and have fruits different from any of ours"[13]. The whole account is based evidently on hearsay being utterly incorrect and absurd. Unfortunately, we had to depend on such accounts being the source of most of our information regarding the Bay Islands till recent times.

Henry Yule has mentioned another interesting story in his commentary on Marco Polo. He recalled that once Abraham Rogers had told him that the Coromondel Brahmins believed in the presence of *Rakshasas* or demons in the islands of Andaman lying in the sea route from Pulicat to Pegu and they were man-eaters. He comments, "This would be very curious if it were a genuine old Brahminical Saga but I fear, it may have been gathered from the Arab seamen."

Similarly, regarding the 'Narkandam' Island,[14] "some Brahmin saint Brandon recognized in it the mouth of Hell" as that of the *Rakshasas*. In reality, 'Narkandam Island' is a volcanic cone of an once active volcano situated to the north of the Andaman sea. Actually, the Andamans were a trade rendezvous for pirates who wished to enjoy monopoly in the trade so they spread wild stories only to dispel other intruders in the exploitation. Henry Yule concluded that the Brahmins might have heard the name 'Narkandam' and applied their wits to manipulate the name and came to a conclusion that 'Narkandam' means 'Narak Ka dham' but this is nothing but a paradox out of a fancy defying the fact.

Friar Odorie, a European traveller passed the Andamans in 1322 A.D. but never touched the shore. He remarked that the people were 'dog–faced and cannibals'.

It is possible that the cruel practices of the Andamanese having the custom of cutting the corpses of their dead enemies, into pieces and burning them off perhaps motivated Friar to consider them cannibals. Moreover, the cannibalism of Battas of Sumatra in the proximity of the Bay Islands might have inspired him to conjecture.

Another voyager, Nicolo Conti[15] who on his way to Indo-China from Damascus visited the Andaman islands in 1440 A.D. and mentioned them as 'Andamania' which means 'Island of gold', contrary to the contents of Tanjore inscription of 1050 A.D. explaining the Andamans as the islands of impurity because of the hostilities of the tribals supposing them being cannibals.

In 1566 Caesar Frederike[16] touched one of the islands of the Nicobars. He also mentioned the Andamanese as cannibals and the following extract is taken from his book:

"Eighteen years' Indian observation", bearing his observation, "From Nicobar to Pegu is as it were, a row or chain of islands, an infinite number, of which many are inhabited with wild people, and they call those islands, the islands of Andemaon and their people are savage or wild because they eat one another".

It is evident that very few of these voyagers ever visited the Andaman islands. What they remarked, were based on hearsays or wild rumours current in the neighbouring countries. Obviously, to spread the tales of cannibalism was the interest of the Malaya pirates who had been exploiting these islands since long and wanted to keep other adventurers away.

Indeed, besides getting safe shelter at all times of the year and running trade in shark's fins, edible bird's nests and tortoise shells the most important to the Malayas was to capture and sell the Andamanese as slaves to the Raja of Kedar, King of Siam and others.

After the discovery of the Cape of Good Hope, the contact between Europe and the Bay islands became frequent. By 1497 A.D. as the Nicobar islands fell en route, European expeditions were more numerous.

The voyager Barbosa[17] visited the Nicobars and in his book, "East Africa and Malabar", he remarked that the Nicobarese were "Gentiles, poor people".

Captain John Davis[18] on a voyage to the East Indies, touched at the Central Nicobar in 1599 and wrote, "The people are most base, only living upon fruits and fish, not manuring the ground and therefore having no rice".

In 1601, during the reign of Queen Elizabeth I, James Lancaster[19] on his voyages to the Spice Islands, paid a visit to the Nicobar Islands. In the chronicle Mr. May, one of his officers says that the natives were (in religion), Mohammedans. Lancaster's account is really interesting because it expresses his own experiences. He also observed, "The people of these islands go naked, having only the privities bound up in a piece of linen cloth which cometh about their middles like a girdle and go between their twist".

The next traveller was Keoping,[20] a Swede who touched at one of the islands of the Nicobars in 1647 A.D. but his observation was incorrect and based on wrong information. He perceived that the Nicobarese were the people with tails like those of cats. They were cannibals because a boat's crew of five men went ashore and never returned but next day their bones were found strewn over the beach.

In 1669 A.D. during his voyage from Malacca to Madras, Dominic Fernandez,[21] a Spanish missionary visited the Nicobars. He repeated the same myth that the Nicobarese were cannibals. He also heard of the gold producing quality of the water of a well somewhere in the island. If the water were sprinkled on metal, it would turn into gold. At that time, stories of 'Island of Gold' was very popular among seafarers.

We have a very exhaustive account of the Nicobarese by Captain Alexander Dampier[22]. In 1688, during a voyage round the world aboard the privateer, 'Cygnet of London', he was forced to land on the shore of Nicobar following a mutiny against Captain Read. Along with some fellow crew, he toured the islands. Boden Kloss opines, "Dampier's account of the Nicobars is by far the most full that we have of the islands in past times." Indeed, his estimate of the character of the Nicoabrese is very unbiased as describing them honest, innocent and submissive. He has further recorded that, they lived "under no god, equal without any distinction, every man ruling in his own house."

In 1695 A.D. John Francis Gemmeli[23], an Italian doctor landed somewhere in the Nicobars while voyaging round the world. About the Nicobarese, he writes, "The island (Nicobar) pays an annual tribute of a certain number of human bodies to the island of Andemaon, to be eaten by the natives of it. These brutes rather than men, use when they have wounded an enemy, to run greedily to suck the blood that runs."

He also believed in "a report spread abroad that there was a well in that island (Nicobar) whose water converted iron into gold and was the true philosopher's stone..."

This report of the gold producing quality of water led to the Dutch expedition towards the end of the 17th century. Such gold haunt legends led to Dr. Helfer's unfortunte ventures to the Andamans in 1839.

However, this myth of island of gold expired very slowly and existed down to the end of the 17th century. No gold was found on the Andaman islands nor it was discovered anywhere in the Nicobar islands.

In 1778, Dr. I.G. Koenig[24] a Danish Doctor on voyaging from India to Siam spent several hours in Car Nicobar. In his Journal, he has described Car Nicobar as 'Kare Nequebar'. He was moved by the natural bounty of the sylvan beauty.

During that period, a Dutch adventurer, William Bolts[25] hoisted the Austrian flag and took possession of the islands in the name of the Austrian Empress, Maria Theresa. He spent five months there and erected a fort on the island. He had been able to persuade the Austrian Government to form a company to trade between Madras, Pegu and the Nicobars. For the outbreak of war in Europe, the plan was cancelled.

Following the instances of William Bolts, the Danes sent another expedition in 1784 A.D.

This too met with little success in setting up colonies in the Nicobars. Only a guard was posted there for almost fourteen years.

Taking advantage of the Napoleonic wars in Europe, between 1807 and 1814, the English traders from India made ventures to establish trading centres at these islands and ultimately occupied the Nicobars. But while the wars in Europe were over, the British had to hand the islands back to the Danes.

In 1831, the Danes made another attempt to set up permanent colonies in the Nicobars. Pastor Rosen[26] was sent there . He spent three years at Nancowry and Trinkat. But he could not bear with the inclement weather and returned to Europe in 1834. Ultimately, the plan of establishing colonies was abandoned.

Then came the French Jesuists,Supries and Galabert[27] in 1836. They lived with the Nicobarese but could not be successful in converting any one of them into Christianity.

They were followed by two more French missionaries of the Catholic Order. They arrived at Car Nicobar in 1842 from Malacca and lived on Teressa and Camorta Islands. In the same year, one of them, Beaury[28] (Borie) died of fever and Father Chopard was left alone to continue the missionary activities.

In 1843 Father Renier[29] came to join but Chopard had never been in good health so he was sent back to Moulmein for treatment. Chopard returned only to die eventually in a hut at Teressa on 23 June, 1843. This was the last of the series of missionary attempts to establish colonies with a view to converting the natives.

In 1845, Mr. Mackay, Danish Consul at Calcutta made a voyage to the Nicobar islands in search of coal but the attempt was futile.

In the same year, Mr. Busch arrived at these islands and raised the Danish flag, both in Great Nicobar and Little Nicobar in the name of King Christian VIII of Denmark.

Next year Captain Steen Bille[30] on his voyage round the world aboard a Danish War- vessel, 'Galathea' arrived and took control of the central group of the Nicobars. This expedition was very significant not only for the detailed survey of the coasts, it performed, but also for its attempts to explore the islands for coal and other minerals. It is very interesting to note that the principal river of Great Nicobar was named 'Galathea' in memory of the 'Galathea (ship) expedition'. According to Greek mythology, "Galathea was a nymph, whom Polyphemus made love to, but she preferred Acis to him. Therefore he made away with by crushing him under rock, and in consequence of which the nymph threw herself into the sea. Thus Galathea died down into the sea".

In 1858, the Austrian appeared again and undertook the survey works of other parts of the Nicobars. As a result, valuable information concerning geological and ethnographical conditions of the islands was obtained.

In 1868, Franz Mauer, a Prussian officer, planned to occupy the Nicobar islands but the scheme was not approved by the Prussian Government. Finally, in 1869 the British took possession of the Nicobars and a settlement was established at Nancowry islands to check the piratical activities and give shelter or provide safe harbour to her ships during monsoon onslaught.

Similar decision was taken in the case of the Andamans. At the close of 18th century, in 1788, under Colonel Colebrooke and Captain Blair, a historic expedition was sent to the Andamans to explore the potentialities to establish a British

Settlement there. Eventually, the British Government occupied the islands for obvious reasons and a settlement was established in 1789 in the name of the then Governor General, Lord Cornwallis and the site was named as 'Port Cornwallis'.

The British ruled over the Andaman and Nicobar Islands till independence (in 1947) continuously except for a short period from March 1943 to October 1945, when the islands were under the Japanese occupation.

However, trustworthy history of the Bay Islands begins with the inception of the British Rule in 1898.

Notes

1. F.V.Hohstetter – 'Contribution to the geological & physical geography of the Nicobar Islands, vol 2, p59 – 73, 1869
2. R.D.Oldham : Notes on geology of Andaman Islands, vol.xviii, p 135, 1885
3. M.V.Portman, 'A history of our relations with the Andamanese' London 1899.
4. M.C.C.Bonnington : Officer in charge of the Andamanese in 1903, ex-officio Supdt of Census Operations, 1931, 'With the aborigines of the Andaman', vol 57, p 264- 67, 1931
5. C.Boden Kloss : visited the Anda Nico in 1901. 'In the Andaman & Nicobar – the narrative of a cruise in the Schooner Terrapin', London 1902, p 167-68
6. Sir Henry Yule : Famous interpreter of Ptolemy's accounts and commentator on Marco Polo.
7. M.V.Portman, 'A history of our relations with the Andamanese', vol 1, p 50.
8. Ibid
9. C.Boden Kloss, 'The Andamans and Nicobars', p 208
10. Published in The Calcutta Monthly Registrar, November, 1790
11. Census Report 1966.
12. M.V.Portman, p 52.
13. M.V.Portman : 'A history of our relations with the Andamanese', vol I, p 52
14. M.V.Portman

15. M.V.Portman ' A history of our relations with the Andamanese', vol I, p 53
16. C.Boden Kloss ' The Andamans and Nicobars' p 177
17. C.Boden Kloss – ibid, p 210
18. Ibid
19. Ibid
20. Ibid
21. M.V.Portman : ibid
22. C.Boden Kloss : ibid p 254

    Dampier, an English navigator, published 'Voyage Round the World', Once Alexander Selkirk accompanied him. (The Nuttall Encyclopaedia)
23. Ibid, p 178
24. C.Boden Kloss – ibid p 213
25. M.V.Portman - ibid
26. Ibid p 213
27. M.V.Portman
28. C. Boden Kloss
29. M.V.Portman
30. C.Boden Kloss : ibid, p 214

2 Advent of the British

British Operation in the Andamans (1788–1796)

Until the penal settlement was established in 1858, the Andaman and Nicobar Islands remained unnoticed to the outside world. Certain information regarding the Bay Islands would have been brought to notice only when any vessel on way to the South East Asian countries was compelled to take shelter in order to escape the fury of the monsoon or forced to anchor in search of fresh water or fuel.

However, by the middle of the eighteenth century, with a view to exercising hegemony in the Deccan Plateau and monopolizing the trade route through the Bay of Bengal, the British Government took some interest to take possession of the Andamans. While her attempts to establish a harbour in the island of Negrais in 1752 failed, attention of the British was diverted to the Andamans again.

John Ritchi, who had been assigned to do a survey of the Bay of Bengal in 1777, was the first man to emphasize on the importance of the islands. He submitted a report to Warren Hastings, the Governor General explaining 'The Great utility' of occupying them.

It is interesting to note that even in 1783, Thomas Forrest felt the necessity to establish contact with the aborigines of the Andamans and expressed his intention to proceed to the

Islands if the Governor General would approve, but it was not paid any heed to.

Five years later, in 1788 Captain Buchannan visited the coasts of the Andamans and explained the importance of the islands to the East India Company. He even suggested for a thorough survey of the islands so that the Company could explore and exploit the potentiality of the place.

Besides all these reports, what made the Company worried, was the information of increasing number of Malaya piracies and gruesome experiences of the ship-wrecked crews in encounter with the aborigines.

It was only during the administration of Lord Cornwallis, the then Governor General of India, the Company decided to send a survey team, under Lieutenant Archibald Blair of the Indian Navy to the islands. Two ships – '*Elizabeth*' and '*Viper*' were put under his command and Lieutenant Robert Hyde Colebrooke of the Bengal Engineers was asked to accompany Lieut. Blair.

The Governor General in his letter dated 19th December, 1788, expressed the very object of the survey, "The material object of the survey is to ascertain in which part of the island there are good harbours and which it would be most for the Company's advantage to project one"[1].

Lt. Blair was also instructed to maintain a friendly relation with the aborigines of the islands following " conciliatory means certainly without bloodshed. It is, therefore, recommended to you to endeavour by persuasion, presents and other allurements but not by force or deceit[2]" to maintain an amicable relation. At the same time, Lt. Blair was directed to obey the instructions of Commodore Cornwallis, C-in-C. of His Majesty's Squadron in India. On 20 Dec. 1788, Captain Blair along with Lt. Colebrooke left Calcutta and reached the Interview Island on 29 December 1788. During the sojourn in the islands, they were busy in completing an exhaustive survey of the islands and collecting all necessary information. Captain Blair returned to Calcutta and submitted his report on 9 June 1789, which created a deep impression on Lord Cornwallis, the Governor General of India. He suggested that the best site for the harbour would be at the Chatham island[3].

Hardly a few days passed, in the meeting of the Governor General in Council, it was decided to take possession of the islands in order to establish a safe harbour to provide shelter to the British fleet in the event of war or during the fury of monsoon and to protect the islands from the predatory activities of Malaya and Chinese pirates.

On being assigned to set up a colony, Captain Archibald Blair left Calcutta on 17 September 1789 accompanied by some artificers, labourers and soldiers, and reached 'Chatham Island' on 28 Sept. 1789 on the southeast bay of the Great Andaman now, called Port Blair but then called *'Port Cornwallis'* after the name of the then Governor General, Lord Cornwallis. As to Blair, 'Port Cornwallis' *was* the best site for the harbour as well as settlement. Although some convicts were sent there to render thèir labour in the development of the settlement, primarily it was not the intention of the East India Company to establish a penal settlement in the Andamans then and there.

On 25 Oct 1789 after clearing a portion of the island, he hoisted the British flag to mark the beginning of the British Settlement. He fixed on *'Chatham Island'* his Headquarters to run the Administration and conduct the development work[4].

However, on the 13 April 1790, Blair had reported that North – East Harbour (in Diglipur) was "deserving the attention of the Governor General" for its advantageous position to start settlement work. After visiting this harbour in November, 1790, and on receipt of the report of a special survey performed by Blair, Commodore Cornwallis also wrote to his brother, Lord Cornwallis, "I think North – East Harbour vastly superior for a fleet of Man–of–war to Port Cornwallis..." He further recommended the removal of the colony from Chatham Island in the southern harbour to the new harbour in the Northeast Island and it was approved by the Government.[5]

But on 19 March 1792 Blair reported that the life in the settlement was quite peaceful and healthy "both from a sanitary and from a political point of view. The natives were perfectly inoffensive as friendly relations had been established with the least possible trouble and bloodshed",[6] Inspite of it on 16 October, 1792, the final orders were issued for the shifting of the settlement and Blair was briefed with the object of the settlement that a naval arsenal was to be developed following the instructions of the Commodore.

On 5 November, 1792, the Governor General while praising the role of Lt. Blair, nominated Captain Alexander Kyde of the Bengal Engineers, the Superintendent of the new settlement and Lt. Blair was instructed to effect the shifting of the colony till Kyde took over charges of it.

The new harbour of North Andaman (Diglipur) was again called Port Cornwallis' after the abandonment of the former one in the South Andaman. While Captain Kyde joined his duties, Lt. Blair was relieved on 5 March 1793[7]. Lt. Blair had taken with him two of the Andamanese, probably Jarawas to Calcutta when he left Andaman.

On 13 June 1793, the news of the outbreak of war in Europe spread and Kyde took necessary steps for the defence of the Settlement. He selected a site on an Island, also called '*Chatham*' for fortification. In order to provide protection to the vessels and safety to the women and children at the moment of emergency, he proposed for a detachment of European artillery, sufficient mercenary power and arming of the vessels attached to the Settlement so that "it will no doubt, hereafter be the Company's principal maritime rendezvous in the Bay of Bengal.":[8] Though all his recommendations were accepted by the Government, the reinforcements were not dispatched immediately and delayed till the end of the year.

Instead for the first time five European convicts were transported on punishment to Andaman but Kyde declined to accept them and they were sent back to Bombay. Perhaps considering the gravity of the fact that the presence of the European convicts would only act upon the morale of the British Officers, the Governor General approved the action of Kyde and decided not to send any European convicts to Andaman in future.

Captain Kyde[9] was very optimistic of the bright future of the new Settlement, which was started with all enthusiasm in bringing turtle from Diamond Island, rice and livestock from Achin, and coconuts from Car Nicobar. Even fruit trees were imported from Sumatra. But with the passage of time, the condition of the new Settlement deteriorated because of insalubrious weather and incessant growth of mortality rate. Moreover, full dependence of the Settlement on the government supply proved too expensive.

On 14 May, 1794,[10] the Governor General in Council observed, "... the situation of Port Cornwallis has of late proved very unfavourable to the health of the settlers..."[11]. Indeed the condition of the Settlement was getting disastrous and health of the colonists continued to be worsened. Sadder is the fact that even Surgeon Raddich, incharge of the Settlement expired on being terribly sick.

Apprehending the impending consequences, on 8 February 1796, the settlement at Port Cornwallis was abandoned. In the Minutes of the Board, it was stated, "Considering the great sickness and mortality of the Settlement formed at the Andamans, which it is feared, is likely to continue, and the great expense and embarrassment to Government in maintaining it, and in conveying to it supplies at the present period, it appears to Governor General in Council, both with a view to humanity and economy, prudent to withdraw it.[12]"

Thus, the first Settlement in the Andamans was finally abolished in May 1796. Besides, the insalubrious weather and huge pecuniary burden, the immediate cause for this disastrous end primarily owed to the hasty decision of Commodore Cornwallis and hence the shifting of site of settlement from South Andaman to North Andaman proved fatal[12].

Of course, the Commodore advised the removal of the site from the South Andaman to the North Andaman considering only the strategic importance of the latter. However, according to C.Boden Kloss, "The new settlement proved so unhealthy, that after an existence of four years its abandonment was decided on. The prisoners were transferred to Penang and the troops returned to Bengal".

Period of Isolation (1796–1857)

After the abandonment of the first settlement, it was a period of isolation for sixty years from 1796 to 1856, when we had only stray references and sporadic mentions in the notes and reports of navigators while crossing the Bay Islands. During this period, a number of ships wrecked on its coast, the Malaya pirates resumed their slave–trading from the islands, the British remained busy with some other exploits in some other regions and the accounts of other European voyagers are inconclusive and somewhat concocted.

However, various notes and correspondences made by some of the ship–wrecked crews drew the attention of the British Government on many occasions. But for obvious reasons, the islands remained untenanted for several years by foreign elements. Its isolation was broken only when Sir Archibald Campbell commanding the British fleet carrying army to Rangoon, was directed to visit 'Port Cornwallis' in 1824 before proceeding to take part in the first Burmese War.

On 12 November 1825, Lieutenant James Edward Alexander, attached to the British Envoy at Tehran on way to

England via Madras visited the islands. He gave an interesting account of his experiences in Little Andaman and of his encounter with the aborigines.

We have some more records of the visits by travellers like Piddington, John Malcolm etc. While ascertaining the mineral possibilities of the islands, the murder of Dr. Helfer, a Russian Scientist employed by the British Government to hunt for gold, created some stir in 1839 but what made the British Government extremely perturbed, were the simultaneous shipwrecks and horrible tales of the crew. At last on 11 November 1844, two troops – ships, 'Briton' and 'Runneymede' drifted by a hurricane, were flung right over the reef. Though hardly a life was lost, being deprived of every provision, pestered and panicked by the savages, they somehow passed fifty-four days in the islands. This incident created a tremendous commotion and forced the East India Company to take decision to resettle there for the salvage of the ship and her crew.

Meanwhile in 1847, all rights over the Nicobars were abandoned by His Majesty of Denmark and the British became the ruler of the islands.

But before the Andamans became the field of British activities again, some unofficial but futile attempts were made to establish colony in the Coco Island because of plenty coconuts and no savages. However in 1855, the Council concentrated to think out a plan to stop the savagery of the Andamanese. Two years later, coincidentally the Great Indian Revolt broke out which compelled the British Government to chalk out a plan to set up a penal settlement in the Andamans as early as possible in order to pacify the aborigines as well as to punish the mutineers as the British termed them.

In 1857, the great patriots had waged the first war of independence and shook the very foundation of the British Raj. Though the revolt was quelled by force, it infused a sense of terrible panic and fear-complex in the mind of the British. Hence, to segregate the rebels the British Government selected these far away, forlorn islands of the Andamans for banishment.

Of course, the original object of the undertaking was to set up a commodious harbour on the East side of the Bay so that during the onslaught of the tumultuous North East monsoon, safe shelter could be given to His Majesty's ships. But on the suppression of the revolt, it seemed to the Government very urgent to establish a penal settlement in these far off islands to exile the rebels. Moreover, the outrageous attitude of the tribes of the Andamans had made it imperative that the islands must be occupied to stop savagery and to develop friendly relations with the natives. This would have been done sooner had the revolt not broken out.

Further, as to the report of Mr. Haughton,[13] it was anticipated that the Burmese were intending to find a colony in the Andamans. He also commented on the careless navigation of the Chinese which made the Andamanese desperate to give a fierce fight lasting for three or four hours to baffle the evil intention of the Chinese to kidnap the Andamanese.

All these factors contributed a lot to motivate the British Government to complete the formal possession of the Andaman and Nicobar Islands by the middle of 1857. The Andaman Committee consisting of Dr. F. J. Mouat, Inspector General of Prisons, Dr. G. R. Playfair, Surgeon of Royal Army and Lieutenant J. A. Heathcote, I. N., was formed and ordered on 23 November, 1857 to proceed to the Andamans to select the best suitable site for the establishment of a penal settlement.

Beginning of Penal Settlement

On the recommendation of the Andaman committee, the proposal to set up a settlement at the old harbour in the South Andaman, earlier planned by Lt. Blair, was finally approved and named after him as Port Blair. Subsequently, Captain H.

Man was directed to take possession of the Andaman Islands and to develop a penal colony.

In the letter of C.Beadon, Secretary to Government of India to Captain H.Man, (No87, dated 15 January, 1858,) the instruction was self explaining "It may be assured that the class of rebels and mutineers who are sentenced by the Civil and Military Tribunals to the secondary punishment of transportation or to imprisonment will not include any of the worst offenders and therefore, that the convicts with whom you will have to deal in the first instance will for the most part, be men who have been led to the commission of crimes against the State by the example of others and not men of a desperate or unmanageable character.[14]'

Thus, the Bay Islands were again the hub-nub of the British activities. Dr. James Pattison Walker, who had much experience and reputation as a jail Superintendent, was appointed the first Superintendent of the Penal Settlement at Port Blair. On 4 March, 1858 with 200 convicts of the revolt of 1857, a native overseer, two Indian doctors and a guard of 50 Naval Brigades men under an officer of I.N., Dr. Walker left Calcutta. Thus, the first batch of great heroes, the freedom fighters of 1857 arrived at Port Blair on 10 March 1858. Hence '10th March' is a very significant date in the history of the Andaman and Nicobar Islands and regarded as the beginning of Settlement.

Of course, in due course, started the transportation of hardcore criminals who had been sentenced to life imprisonment to Andaman for murder and robbery. Immediately on arrival, the first task for the convicts was to clear Chatham Island but due to inadequate water supply, some convicts were sent to clear Ross Island where the sources of water seemed perennial. Though the settlement started, the freedom fighters of the revolt of 1857 resented the punishment of transportation as it inflicted a sense of exile from their motherland. Indeed, transportation was itself a technique of segregation removing specific categories of people from the rest. So, transportation was seen as being more painful and more deterrent for Indians as it was for English criminals who were shipped to Australia during the same period. (Martin Wiener, in "Reconstructing the Criminal-Culture, Law and Policy in England, 1830– 1914"). Due to its isolation from the mainland and agony of long sentences, the penal settlement in the Andamans had greater demographic stability than most prisons in British India. Under this deliberation, the success of the Andaman as a Penal Colony can be assessed.

However, since their arrival at Andaman, the convicts commenced to flee away. At that time, the guard was insufficient and that too inspired them to run away. Moreover the convicts had the wrong impression that the landmass of Burma was very close to the Andamans so by swimming across the sea or by running through the jungle, they would reach the other part of land and escape. So the cases of escapes increased day by day.

To prevent it, the naval guard was doubled and a surveillance corps was formed. Though the punishment to the captured ones was very severe, cases of escape continued. During March and April 1858, as many as 258 escaped, of which 88 were recaptured. Though two were forgiven, 86 run away convicts were executed in one day under the order of Walker. His treatment with the convicts was so oppressive and outrageous that he was under constant threat to his life from the convicts. Once it happened on 1st April 1859, nearly 200 Punjabi convicts conspired to capture power by murdering Walker. One Punjabi convict, Moti Ram intimated Walker of the plot. Inspite of all precautionary measures taken, Walker had to run away to save his life. This too, led Walker to take even more savage measures to deal with the convicts.

However, Walker took certain steps to tackle the problem. To him the position of Ross Island looked not only strategically important but also very safe from the point of view of security. So he proposed to set up the Headquarters of the Settlement on Ross Island instead of Chatham Island and it was approved. Thus, Ross Island became the seat of Administration till the Japanese occupation on 23 March 1942.

On 8 October, 1858, a small island in front of Port Blair was also occupied and developed quickly as the first open air prison in the Andamans. It was named as Viper Island in memory of the first British ship, '*Viper*' of Lt. Blair's fleet that reached Andaman but unfortunately wrecked. By choosing that particular name, '*Viper*', Walker had the ulterior motive to incite a terror-phobia among the convicts.

Moreover, to appease the less hostile convicts, Walker planned to set up thirty-two villages between Port Blair and Port Mouat to accommodate 421 convicts. He further advocated the plan to accommodate 1684 convicts in all 64 villages. He also encouraged these convicts to get their wives and families down here from the mainland. As to his plan, the convicts would not only be busy with their family but also act as a safeguard against the savages. Thus towards the close of the years, the number of escapes considerably decreased.

Besides all these problems with the settlement, what made the British worried, was the frequent skirmishes with the Andamanese. Whenever they found that there were only a few guards, they suddenly attacked the convicts while they were digging wells, clearing jungle or cooking, and carried off tools, clothes, cooking vessels, iron junks etc. Among all the attacks two were very serious and worth mentioning.

On 5 August 1858, during ambushed attack, Lieutenant Templer, I. N., with eight armed guards chased the Andamanese and in disgust burnt their huts and killed some of them. But the Governor General did not approve of the action and strongly remarked, "on this occasion, as it appears from the paper, our people were the assailants." In that letter no. 1079, dated 12th ultimo, Walker was further requested 'to adhere strictly to the conciliating line of conduct' and 'to absolutely prohibit any aggression upon them'.

Despite all these cautions, the most fierce attack, known as the 'Battle of Aberdeen' took place on 17 May, 1859. Had the British not been warned timely by a run away convict, Dudhnath Tewari by name, very serious damage might have been caused to the British camp.

Dudhnath Tewari a life convict, no 276 had escaped[15] to the jungle almost immediately after his arrival at Port Blair on 23 April 1858 but was captured in miserable condition by the Andamanese who spared his life and took him in confidence. Dudhnath lived with them for a year and 24 days, and married an Andamanese tribal woman named Leepa. One day observing their movements and preparations, Dudhnath came to know of their plan to attack the British camp. He somehow managed to flee away to inform the British of the plan of the Andamanese. Only due to the timely warning, the attack was encountered ruthlessly and the plunder of the tools on a large scale was prevented at the cost of life of many aborigines whose primitive weapons, bow and arrows, could not match with the bullets. The concerted attack on the British camp at Aberdeen, by the Andamanese came to be known as the 'Battle of Aberdeen' which took place on 17 May, 1859.

British policy towards the tribals

After the Battle of Aberdeen, the British Government started to think more seriously about the relations with the tribes of the Andamans. The impact of the Battle of Aberdeen, if any, was to force the British to realize the gravity of the question of their survival what for they had fought to the last. Since the coming of Archibald Blair, encroachment and infiltration by the outsiders in the tribal territory made the Andamanese vindictive. Though in paper, the British followed the policy of conciliation, yet in reality, it was just the reverse and Walker was responsible for it. After his departure in 1859, Captain Haughton became the Superintendent of the Settlement. He was liberal and tried to pursue the policy of tolerance to establish friendly relation with the Andamanese.

Besides, gift dropping and hospitality towards the captured ones, a Christian priest, Corbyn took initiative to establish Andaman Home at Ross Island with a view to civilizing the aborigines. Owing to goodwill ventures by Tytler, Homfray, Stewart, Portman etc. sincere attempts were made to maintain cordiality with the natives. Some other too zealous administrators set about civilizing the aborigines overnight. In pursuance of their impractical provocations, the Andamanese had to leave their jungle habitat to adopt clothes and to eat strange foods contrary to their own natural habits. By this civilizing mission, the British might seek consolation but the natives were only exposed to exotic as well as endemic diseases, particularly veneral diseases which ultimately resulted in sterility and infant mortality. In contact with the civilized people, the Andamanese developed the addiction towards opium, tobacco and liquor. Thus by taming them, they were engaged in catching run away convicts and in punitive raids against the Jarawas. Over the decades, the pendulum of British policy for the tribals swang awfully.The policy of punishments as well as blandishments was pursued as to the need of the authorities so the welfare of the natives was always denied.

The more the contacts with the outsiders increased, the more the question of survival of the Andamanese became jeopardised. Actually in the long run, both Indians and Europeans with good or bad intentions, deprived them of their land and livelihood, undermined their culture and infected fatal diseases. Thus, the so-called civilizing mission dragged them to the limit of disastrous end.

After independence, unrestricted flow of population disturbed the whole eco-system of the islands. In the name of development, the Andaman Trunk Road was constructed passing through the dwelling areas of the Jarawas. On the plea of further settlement, reclamation and rehabilitation started in the habitation of the Jarawas and the Onges. Indiscreet encroachment, reckless poaching and desperate interference made the tribal people more hostile and antagonistic. The government took no measures to stop the influx of population. Ultimately, the number of population has crossed the limit of bearing capacity of the islands and due to reckless felling of trees and random encroachment, the area of forest had receded to 60% instead of 80% which is a must to maintain favourable eco -system. Hence, indifferent or immutable policy of the government and lukewarm or phlegmatic attitude of other organizations lead to the devastation of eco-balance of the Andamans.

Of course, the government has enacted the Tribal Act of 1956 for the protection of the tribals of the Bay Islands. Simultaneously, the habitation of the primitive people has been declared as reserved area and a contingent of Bush Police has been raised to look after the interest of the tribes and protect the villagers. As a part of philanthropic measures, Tribal Welfare Department has been formed and Andaman Adim Janjati Vikash Samiti has been constituted in 1976. Among the 'Nigritoes', the Great Andamanese and the Onges became friendly with us but the Jarawas remained hostile till recently and the Sentinelese are still very ferocious and confined to the North Sentinel Island so no contact has been made fruitful.

Several lacs of rupees have been spent to befriend the Jarawas. Sardar Bakhtawar Singh has been conferred Padmashree for his distinguished service in the sphere of tribal welfare and for his success to win the confidence and friendship of the Jarawas. But inspite of all these achievements, the eventuality only threatens the very existence of the Nigritoes in the Andamans. On the eve of Penal Settlement in 1858, the number of the Nigritoes was roughly 4800 and by the turn of century in 1961, the number declined terribly and it is now hardly 300 in all.

Who is to be blamed for this disastrous end? The Britishers or we, the Indians? Undoubtedly, so-called conciliatory policy of the British was guided only by their needs, not for the interests of the Andamanese. Civilizing missions pursued by the British bore no meaning to the Andamanese. Even Portman attached less value to the Andaman Homes than his predecessors. Bonnington, a British officer incharge of the Andamanese in 1893 was more critical to express his views, "the well-meaning attempts to civilize the Andamanese were contrary to the experience". He further commented, "local history and general experience elsewhere clearly showed that once a contact with civilization is established, the dying out of a primitive race like the Negrito is apt to follow in due course."

After reviewing the existing position, the British Government framed a new policy towards the Andamanese with specific guidelines:-

(a) to avoid the contacts of the natives with the convicts.

(b) to follow the simplest ways to educate them.

(c) to allow them to continue in their habitat attempts to change and, reform them should be made with extreme caution.

(d) to let them be isolated in reserved areas.

However, the British civilizing measures only exposed them unfortunately to the curses of civilization. After independence, with more enthusiastic means, we have followed the same policy of gift dropping, introducing bra and panty, skirt and *lungi*, giving shelter in artificial houses, *AdiBasera*, supplying cooked food etc, etc, and thereby, we have made them more dependent on us. Contrary to their age-old habit of taking protein-rich food, we have forced them to eat carbohydrate

– rich food i.e. cooked rice, boiled rice and pulse mixed. Besides other reasons, this civilizing mission alarmingly acts upon them physically and genealogically and leads them towards biological extinction. There is little hope for the revival or regeneration of the race. Today, they are just the lively puppets in our hands to experiment with or to entertain the V.V.I.P's and tomorrow they may be arrayed as showpieces in the museum to boast with. Unfortunately, this may be their destiny.

Notes

1. National Archives of India, Secret Department, Proceedings Volume, 22nd December 1788, p 4788-4808.
2. Ibid
3. Ibid, No. 6-29, 30th December 1789.
4. Census Report, 1901, p. 358.
5. Source: The Madras Courier, 22nd Dec 1790.
6. M.V.Portman : 'A History of our Relations with the Andamanese', Vol I, p 84
7. National Archives of India, Home Deptt, Public Branch, O.C. No. 4, 1st Feb 1793
8. Source: Calcutta Gazette, 13 January 1791.
9. Ibid
10. Minutes of the Board, 8 February 1796
11. NAI, Home Deptt, Public Branch, O.C. No. 7-15, 7th Oct. 1793.
12. Ibid, No.5, 8th Feb. 1796.
13. M.V.Portman : ibid p 187, 188, 197
14. N.A.I. Home Deptt. Judicial Branch, O.C.No. 21, 15th January 1858.
15. N.A.I. Home Deptt. Judicial Branch, O.C. No. 39, 5 Oct.1860

3 Growth of the Penal Settlement

British Penal System

After the retirement of Dr. Walker on 3rd October 1859, Captain Haughton took over the charges as Superintendent of the Settlement. Under his administration the British policy towards the convicts had become more reformative than repressive. The same milder policy was followed by his successor, Colonel R.C. Tytler. During his regime from 1862 onwards, transportation of female convicts to the Andamans started and weddings between these women and male convicts who were awarded the credit of 'Self-supporters' after their term was over, were encouraged through marriage parade by the female convicts.

Once life-term prisoners were released, they became free settlers, known as 'self-supporters'. When a convict was declared as 'self-supporter', he was allowed to live in the society where female was counted as the most enviable property. As to ratio, at that time there was one female for seven males. Naturally, very few could marry and due to allurement or some other charms, at times, even married woman would indulge in entertaining more males. This sort of debauchery was an open secret and very few bothered for morality. Sometimes, the affairs would go to that extent as one resorted to further murder or fatal conflict.

However, out of all odds, with the passing of time, a unique society evolved in the Andamans and the descendants of these convicts live with all graces and glories in communal peace and harmony.

During the tenure of Colonel H. Man, the Nicobar Islands were brought under control of the Superintendent on 16 April 1869. Mr. Man introduced a set of rules for the convicts, which were followed till the abolition of the Penal Settlement in 1945. After Colonel Man, Major General D.M. Stewart became the Superintendent of the Settlement on 15 July 1872.

From 29 July 1872, the designation of Superintendent was changed to Chief Commissioner and Stewart became the First Chief Commissioner of the AndaNico Islands. During his administration, one very significant event happened and that was the murder of Lord Mayo, the then Governor General of India. Lord Mayo had a very keen personal interest in the maintenance of the Penal Settlement and decided to visit Port Blair. Emotionally, he was involved in the upbringing of the sick convicts and decided to select a site for a sanatorium. He, although, climbed up Mount Harriet to have a personal knowledge of the site. He was so moved by the panoramic beauty that he spent there a couple of hours. On his way down the hill it grew dark. All of a sudden he was attacked and grisly murdered at Hopetown Jetty by a Pathan convict, named Sher Ali on 8 February 1872. After a brief trial, Sher Ali was hanged in the gallows of Viper Island.

Maulana Mohammad Jafar Thanesari who was a transportee being convicted for his involvement in the revolt of Wahabi was an eyewitness of the execution. In his autobiography [1] he writes, " On going up the scaffold, he (Sher Ali) turned to other convicts and shouted loudly, 'Brothers, I have killed your enemy and you are my witness that I am a Muslim'. And then he started reciting the *Qalma* and died while doing so".

After this murder, special attention was paid to the administration of the penal settlement. J. Scarlett Campbell, Home Secretary to the Government of India was sent to Port Blair to review the penal system. He recommended that classification of the convicts should be made as to the seriousness of their crimes and their behaviour. Fourth class or 'Gaol Gang' was the lowest. They were put to the strictest gaol discipline, employed on hard extra-mural labour and low diet, and immured to solitary cells. Those who were well behaved and submissive were kept in the first class. They were entitled to remain in the barracks, to receive dry rations and payment from Rupee one to two per month. Among the convicts of this class, only a few were granted 'Self-supporter' tickets, and allowed to marry and live in the society as to their own. From 3rd class and 2nd class, convicts after satisfactory service in the penal settlement for five years, might be transferred to higher class if the Jail Officers recommended so.

In May 1874 Major General Sir Henry Norman visited Port Blair and found that on 11 June 1874, there were 7820 male, 895 female life convicts, 888 term convicts, 500 married couples with 578 children and 1167 free ticket holders. Among them 476 were women.

Norman recommended certain changes but the most striking ones came with the visit of C.J. Lyall and A.S. Lethbridge, Inspector General of Jails. They submitted their report on 26 April, 1890. They were in favour of settlement of convicts in the Andamans rather than sending them back to mainland. They wanted that penal transportation should be truly penal i.e. a deterrent. To increase the severity of punishment, confinement in solitary cells was recommended in their report.

Nearly forty years after the penal settlement, the British felt the necessity to erect a jail complex; so the proposal of the Cellular Jail was sanctioned. The construction was taken up in 1896 and completed in 1906. It was 'a city within a city, and a prison within a prison'.[2] There was a similar jail in London's Pentonville which was built half a century before the construction of the Cellular Jail. Like Pentonville, the Cellular Jail was designed to function as a machine in the process of punishment and reform but in reality for punishment alone and to inflict a sense of horror and terror. It was diabolically planned so. Within the jail complex, the gallows, the flogging stand, blood squeezing workshop for coir pounding and oil grinding, dingy solitary cells and condemned cells–all were accommodated in the same compound with a view to create panic among the convicts, breaking their spine and throttling their spirit.

Construction Of Cellular Jail

Though the revolt of 1857 was suppressed, yet the unquenchable thirst for freedom and indomitable urge for achieving martyrdom could not be subdued. The brave heroes of Wahabi Movement, Mopla Revolt, Manipur Uprising, Tharawardy Rebellion, the Rumpa Revolt etc. all were transported to Andaman. Thus the Penal Settlement started growing with the arrival of all these freedom fighters along with thousands of dreaded criminals. Though attempts were made to accommodate all the convicts in different stations of the Andamans i.e., Viper Island, Navy Bay, Phoenix Bay, Brichgunj, Dundus Point etc, the British authorities found it extremely difficult to enforce discipline and ascertain safe custody of the convicts. So, it was decided to construct a jail complex, self-contented and self-dependent.

A committee headed by Charles J. Lyall and Surgeon Major A.S. Lethbridge, recommended the construction of the Cellular Jail which started in 1896 and completed in 1906 on the basis of the Settlement Order No. 423 dated 13 September, 1893 issued by Col. N.M. Honsford. The main idea behind the construction of the Cellular Jail was to keep the largest number of revolutionary elements and hardcore criminals condemned to long-term imprisonment at a minimum cost and to run by only a few personnel with maximum efficiency.

The jail was originally designed for confinement of 690 prisoners and the estimated cost was then Rs. 5,17,352. The name 'Cellular' was derived from its unique feature that it had only Cells, 698 in all and no dormitories. The Cellular Jail was designed like a gigantic starfish with seven massive tentacles or wings fanning out from a central hub. Each wing is a three storeyed structures with long rows of dingy cells, each measuring 13′5″ x 7′ with a ventilator of 3′ x 1′, nearly 10′ above the floor at the back and having an iron grilled door in front. The design is so unique that a lone sentry at the Central Tower can keep watch and control of the cells. The jail has been so tactfully constructed that the front of each wing faces the back of the other. Hence, the degree of segregation has become terribly unbearable.

The life convicts were kept into the Cellular Jail for six months to undergo severe confinement with strictest discipline. Then they were transferred to other penal stations for 18 months to undertake hard work. For the next three years, they were allowed to live in the adjoining labour barracks. In this way after spending ten years in imprisonment one could get 'ticket' to live as a 'Self-supporter' only on recommendation of the Jail Authorities.

Living condition of the Inmates

Life in the Cellular Jail was so dreadful and nightmarish that in every moment, some horrible experience awaited even the innocent. This became worst because of the arrogant attitude of Mr. Barry who joined the Cellular Jail in 1910 and was the most notorious jailor. On receiving the freedom fighters at the gate he proclaimed that he was the only mortal God in that God-forbidden land and only his orders were to be followed there as rules and no other rules got any meaning there. So, to defy him meant to entertain death. This was not merely a haughty utterance but it was a crude reality. His rule caused the death of so many, resulted insanity of many more, and provoked general strike by many others. The Cellular Jail was the mute witness of all these atrocities.

Nand Gopal, a Punjabi Kshatriya, was the Editor of the '*Swaraj*' of Allahabad. He defied the Jail authorities by his unique attitude of passive resistance. He decided not to work in the oil-mill, as it would not suit him. His attitude led to the outbreak of the first hunger strike of the political prisoners in the Cellular Jail in 1933.

In other incident, Indu Bhusan Roy, a young revolutionary of Bengal could not bear with the humiliation and inhuman torture in the jail. One night he tore his shirt, made a rope and hung himself from the skylight. He committed suicide out of exhaustion and frustration.

The case of Ullaskar Dutta was much more tragic and pathetic. He could not withstand the barbaric torture. The oil machine to which Ullaskar was yoked was like the one that only bullocks can rotate. Even the robust and strong fellows got prostrated and exhausted in turning the wheel of oil-mill. As a result of hard work, torture and insults, Ullaskar became seriously ill and insanity developed. For the rest of his life, he had to spend his days in lunatic asylum. All these cases are the burning examples of the bestial treatment meted out to the inmates of the Cellular Jail.

With the fall of night, even the political prisoners were compelled to be confined inside the dingy cells and were exposed to all sorts of nightmarish experiences in combating bugs, centipedes, scorpions, mosquitoes and snakes. And with the break of day they were handed over to the warders of working gangs for all sorts of laborious and blood-squeezing jobs, which were usually allotted to hardcore criminals. Operation of coconuts, turning the oil-mill, making *Thukka* shells, coir pounding and weaving, hill cutting, swamp filling, crashing the boulders, clearing the jungles etc. etc, were the types of hard work which even the political prisoners were subjected to, though they were not at all accustomed to these sorts of physical labour. Cutting trees in the jungle, constructing roads, preparing bricks and lime in the kiln under the scorching sun were so terrible that very often the convicts ran away in fright and many committed suicide. On an average, three prisoners in the jail committed suicide every month. This was simply because of brutal torture and inhuman treatment of the British towards the convicts.

Since the first War of Independence in 1857 down to the revolutionary movements of early twentieth century, innumerable freedom fighters from Bengal, Punjab, U.P, Bihar, Assam, Madras who were dedicated to the cause of making India free from the bondage of British rule, were deported and exiled in the Andamans. Since 1909 to 1921 and 1932 to 1938, in these two phases, majority of the revolutionaries, incarcerated in the Cellular Jail, were of Bengal and Punjab.

Besides, Fazal Haq Khairabadi (Friend of Mirza Ghalib), Maulana Liakat Ali, Sheikh Formud Ali, Madhu Malik, Maulvi Ahmedullah, Syed Allabadi all great heroes and followers of the first War of Independence of 1857, a there were many other charismatic personalities like Savarkar Brothers, Vaman Rao Joshi, Sohan Singh, Barindra Kumar Ghose, Ganesh Ghose, Bhai Permanand, Trailokyanath Chakraborty, Mohit Moitra, Gurumukh Singh, Loknath Bal, Ananta Singh, Baba Prithvi Singh Azad, Nand Gopal, Ladha Ram etc. etc. Most of the freedom fighters passed away unsung and remained in the abyss of oblivion even after the independence. During long imprisonment, they had to bear with savage treatment from the British and many of them had to face gallows and bullets. The gallows of the Viper Island and the Cellular Jail still bear the witness of this diabolical tyranny and perpetual atrocities under the British rule.

Era of hunger strikes

The unbridled reign of terror was let loose by the British against the revolutionaries whom they condemned as indisputable criminals. The treatment meted out to them was intended to drag them to slow but sure and agonizing death. On protest against the British barbarism, the desperate freedom fighters resorted to all sorts of defiance and resistance, and went far beyond any reconciliation. Ultimately the hunger strike was declared on 12 May, 1933. In reply to their demands, J.W.Smyth, the then British Chief Commissioner remarked, "I shall not budge an inch. Let their dead bodies be floating on the ocean". When a month passed on hunger strike, the jail authority felt that the thing had gone too far and the settlement with the strikers seemed expedient. The Govt. of India demanded from the Chief Commissioner to explain why three lives, of Mahavir Singh, Mohit Moitra and Mohan Kishore Namadasa passed away within a month on hunger strike. The Inspector General of Prisons of the Punjab, Col. Barker was deputed to meet the strikers and find out ways to end the strike.

But when he met the strikers, he concealed his real purpose. He talked to the four strikers in yard no 7 with an innocent smile, "so you have started your old game". Instantly they reacted, "As long as your treatment would be based on inhuman principles, within the jail walls there shall be no peace". Immediately, he ordered drinking water to be stopped. The condition of some of the strikers was already precarious and some of them were removed to the hospital in an unconscious state but the strike continued. At last Col. Barker realized that nothing would deter the strikers and only way left was to offer honourable terms. Thus, Government of India yeilded and the strikers triumphed in their cause.

The strike lasted for 46 days and tolled precious lives of three patriots – Mahavir Singh, Mohit Moitra and Mohan Kishore Namadasa. They all died because of the drastic attempts of forced feeding by the British agents. The jail authorities were so frightened that their dead bodies were thrown secretly in the sea and the last rites had not been observed. Only the blustering waves embraced the immortal heroes into their watery graves. The martyrdom of the three dedicated strikers and the heroic struggle of the others created a wide spread commotion and excitement throughout the length and breadth of the country. Even Rabindra Nath Tagore being emotionally upset, sent a telegram imploring the strikers to call off the strike with the message, "Your motherland will never forget her full blown flowers". Of course, the strikers were aptly inspired but because of the adamant attitude of the British, they could not terminate the strike at that moment.

At last the British Government was compelled to concede to the demands of the freedom fighters and the strike was called off on 26 June, 1933 on the forty-sixth day of its inception. Now the political prisoners got substantial relief, of course, at the terrible cost of three precious lives. However, their main demands were accepted and they were allowed to mix among themselves and provided with study materials, newspapers, magazines and books. Lights were provided in each cell at night. Facilities were extended also for indoor and outdoor games such as caroms board, chess, playing cards, Ping Pong, foot ball, volley ball etc. They were allowed to conduct musical and other artistic performances for their recreation.

Revolutionary University

As to the agreement, they were assigned with lighter works for shorter period of time. To exhibit their triumph over the British – devil, for the first time, Durga Pooja (Worship of Goddess Durga) was performed inside the jail complex. Now, at the initiative of veteran freedom fighters, a new study centre, in fact, a revolutionary university was organized inside the jail. From the very outset, the History drew the greatest attention. Classes were held on the World History with greater stress on the modern period, on diplomacy relating to strategy and tactics. On Economics, James Huxley, Karl Marx, Gean, and on Science, Marconi, Einstein, Darwin were the favourite authors. Book reviews were done by capable comrades and excerpts of newspapers, magazines were read out in the form of broadcast of news. Afterwards a 'School of Journalism' was opened with the publication of a hand written magazine 'CALL' which had its English and vernacular sections. Ten fortnightlies were brought out in Bengali and one in Hindustani. This enthusiasm in studies made the prison life a little more tolerable and inspired the internees to prepare themselves for a greater movement.

Second hunger strike

Though the political prisoners were enjoying a lot of relief, their living in the prison was not easy going. The jail authorities were always resorting to all heinous ways to deprive them of every facility. So the clashes were going on and the situation was aggravated with the arrival of a new Superintendent of the Cellular Jail. Gradually, all facilities remained for namesake. With the enactment of the Government of India Act, 1935, the Congress leaders demanded univocally with the political prisoners in Andaman for their repatriation.

Since, the first hunger strike was called off the political prisoners tried to draw attention of the British Government to their demands regarding repatriation and uniform classification. The representation was submitted on 28 April, 1936 to the Home Secretary to the Government of India, Sir Henry Craik who ironically described to a group of Simla Journalists that Andaman was a 'Prisoners' Paradise'. On the contrary, the political prisoners expressed their grievances and anguishment to the Secretary of the State on 13 October, 1936 that Andaman was not a 'paradise' but "a prisoners' hell" because of repression and oppression metted out to the patriots by the British. In their representation, they demanded immediate repatriations to the mainland. Further, they moved for immediate introduction of uniform classification for all political prisoners. But the British Government did not pay any heed to. So on 25 July, 1937, they started the second mass hunger strike. Out of 290 political prisoners, 230 had joined and the news spread like wild fire. With the passing of time, while the number of strikers was increasing, their general condition was getting worse. Due to sheer weakness, several strikers became unconscious and number of serious cases increased day by day. So the jail authority resorted to forced feeding. When the orgy of feeding started, ordinary prisoners refused to join the feeding gang. They were full of sympathy for the strikers.

The news of mass hunger strike in the Cellular Jail leaked out. The political demands of the strikers gave a new impetus to the democratic movements in other jails and camps in the mainland. The political prisoners of Alipore, Deoli, Berhampur jails also started hunger strike in support of their compatriots in the Cellular Jail. Thus, the whole country rallied behind them. In reality it had become a mass movement for the repeal of repressive rule and in support of repatriation of the exiled prisoners, and extension of civil liberties. Thus, the revolutionary prisoners transformed the Cellular Jail from a place of suffering into an active centre of the political movement.

Repatriation

The hunger strike lasted for 35 days and everybody became worried about the health of the strikers. The Congress leaders also expressed their resentment and demanded immediate settlement with the strikers. Jawaharlal Nehru, Fazlul Haque, Bhulabhai Desai, Satyamurti sent telegrams to the strikers with the request to call off the strike for they were negotiating the matter with the British Government in their favour. On behalf of Rabindranath Tagore, Gandhiji sent cables on 28 August, 1937, appealing them to suspend the strike and assuring them the redress of their demands. To honour all these appeal, the hunger strike was called off. As a result of intervention of national leaders British Government agreed and repatriation started on 22 September, 1937 and completed with the last batch that left Port Blair on 18, January, 1938. Thus, a very significant chapter in the history of the Andamans, though abominable on the part of the British yet glorious on the role of the political prisoners, ended.

Remembering the contributions and sacrifices of the political prisoners of the Cellular Jail, one can very well be amazed. What a great sacrifice was made at the altar of liberation! What draconian atrocities, oppression and repression was faced by the valiant freedom fighters! What a glorious chapter of freedom struggle was written in blood, sweat and tears of the patriots on the walls of the Cellular Jail! The Britishers condemned them as despicable criminals but in the hearts of the masses, they were the most venerable heroes and martyrs. They were honoured as self-sacrificing patriots. To free their motherland from the British yoke they started their perilous journey along a path in every bend of which lurked persecution, danger and death. By their glorious examples of martyrdom, they succeeded in instilling in the hearts of the people, the spirit of defiance against the mightiest empire of the world.

Spell of Horrors

Though the saga of sacrifice and resistance of the freedom fighters glorified the Cellular Jail, it still remained dreaded and harrowing to the other convicts. In the days of the British Raj, the very utterance of the name 'Cellular Jail' would create horror, funk and phobia even in the mind of the most hardcore criminals. Thus it earned the blood curdling odium – '*Kalapani*'.

Though the British reformers like Samuel Romilly asserted that "solitary confinement drove prisoners to madness". (Webb and Webb, English Prisons pp 93), the prison authorities resorted to cellular punishment frequently. Even when the plan of Cellular Jail was under consideration, Col. T. Cadell, the Superintendent of Port Blair expressed his grave concern that 'It might prove injurious in the case of men already suffering from mental depression on first arrival in the settlement'. (Webb and Webb, English Prisons) but his opinion was denied. History only speaks the truth. Like Ullaskar Dutta, hundreds of them languished in isolation and expired or resigned into the lunatic asylum.

Not only the British but also the Japanese exploited the sinister infamy of *Kalapani* and defiled the hallowed Cellular Jail, the shrine of freedom struggle by converting it into a torture-house to punish the innocents arrested on false charges of spying in favour of the British. The oozing blood of these helpless people, however, sanctified the arena of the AndaNico and their glorious sacrifice is yet to be written with honour and reverence.

Netaji Subhash Chandra Bose as the Head of the *'Azad Hind Government'* visited the Cellular Jail on 30 December 1943 to pay his tribute to the firebrand heroes of Mother India. But the functionaries of *'Azad Hind Government'* stationed at Port Blair could not bring forth much effective change because of the utter reluctance of Japanese Military Authorities and quick reversal of the war scenario.

Only after re-occupation by the British, the Penal Settlement was abolished in 1945 and on 11 February,1979 the Cellular Jail was dedicated to the Nation as a National Memorial by Shri Morarji Desai, Prime Minister of India. Now it stands with all grandeur as a mute witness of agonies and ecstasies of the olden days.

Notes

1. Md. Jafar Thanesari : 'Kalapaniya – Tawarik –e- Ajeeb' in Urdu, wrote after 18 years of penal servitude in Andaman since 11 January 1866.
2. Dr. Satudru Sen, 'Disciplining Punishment', Oxford, N.D. p10

4 Strategic Importance of the Bay Islands

Geo-political location

The history of the Andaman and Nicobar Islands does not end with the abolition of the Penal Settlement in 1945. The annals of fears and tears still remain untold. The facts about the foreign domination over these islands do not cease with the termination of the British Rule but there are scintillating episodes of another foreign regime when these islands were under the Japanese occupation.

From the time immemorial, the pristine glory and sylvan beauty of these islands with her enumerable myths and ghastly tales have always been alluring the foreigners to settle there. Before the advent of the Europeans, these islands were a trading and treading ground of the Mongolians, especially of the Burmese, the Malayasians, the Indonesians and the Chinese. Its geological location at the cross-roads of the Bay of Bengal and the Indian Ocean strengthens the facts that over the centuries, these islands have played a very important role as a witness to the vicissitudes of the region. Because of their topographical advantages, their excellent natural harbours have served as a refuge in the furious monsoons and as a place to replenish fuel, water and to collect valuable marine and forest merchandise including shark's fins, edible bird's nests, tortoise shells, trepang etc. Once slave trade was the most lucrative one mainly run by the Malayasians. Indeed, Malaya pirates treated these islands as their Headquarters and their regular visits were for obvious reasons. Even in 1974, it was found that some Thai families had settled in some areas in the Nicobars and of course, these foreign squatters were turned out. Also in 1981, some 70 Malayasian families were ejected after several months of their stay at Tilangchong in Nancowry Island. On the other hand, Myanmar (Burma) always had imperialistic design and tried all along to occupy these islands. It has already established its control over Coco-Island, which is very close to India's Landfall Island of the AndaNico.

Considering its geo-political position and its strategic location, these islands enjoy an advantage to keep vigilance on the naval movements of any country in the Bay of Bengal or the Indian Ocean. Ignoring its constant surveillance, nothing by air or sea can penetrate into the defence of India. These islands can even act as bases to counter any threat from Burma or to foil indirect intrusion of China through its presence in Coco-Island, where it has already established a naval base in intrigue with Myanmar.

In the past, except some sporadic and abortive attempts to colonise these islands, this territory was largely overlooked by the colonial powers. Of course, Rajendra Chola, conquered 'Naccaveram' or Nicobars but never tried to set up his own colony. Since long, enumerable sea-farers, travellers, traders and adventurers usually passed by these islands, and even if landed, never tried to develop their own establishments. The only reason for this reluctance or setback was that these islands had never earned any fame for their natural resources. Hostility of the aborigines and inhospitality of the climate always refrained them from settling there. Only in the 18th century the imperialist countries began to consider the importance of its location with a view to protecting their trade and trading vessels, lives and cargoes. But the strategic importance of these islands was, however, ignored even during the British regime till the first half of 20th century. Otherwise this territory would have been the sole bastion guarding the gateway of India from the East or the South East through the Indian Ocean or the Pacific Ocean.

In 1777, John Ritchie first drew the attention of Warren Hastings on "the great utility" of these islands. Even Archibald Blair in 1788 stressed on the strategic location of these islands. The British Government had the knowledge of Burma's design to settle in these islands and of Malayasia's desire to set up colonies in the Nicobars. It is obvious that their nefarious presence would create obstacle to the movement of the British fleet. All these factors compelled the British Government to occupy these islands. Their only objective was to exercise maritime hegemony over the Indian Ocean. Though the first settlement was established in 1789 and withdrawn in 1796, only in 1858 after the Great Revolt, the Penal Settlement formally started at Port Blair.Even then the British paid no attention to the strategic importance of the islands. On the eve of independence, no leaders of National Movement bothered a fig for the fate of these tiny islands. It was only due to timely interference of Lord Mountbatten and Jawaharlal's insistence that the AndaNico was neither partitioned despite Jinnah's obdurate attitude to secure a share of this territory for Pakistan, nor submitted to the evil wills of Wavell to establish a naval base for U.K.

The Japanese invasion to India utilizing these islands as a launching base for air and seaward attack was the *raison d'etre* for Nehru to evince India's stand and to convince Admiral Mountbatten to settle the transfer of these islands in favour of India and not to accede to Wavell's proposal to retain them as a British Ocean territory. Only luck bestowed and the circumstances favoured, otherwise these islands could have been another 'Diego Garcia' of the East.

In fact, the political situation of pre-independent India was quite different and all the movements, within and without, were terribly anti-British. Even the global war scenario was against the British interest. After the Second World War, the Labour Ministry of Great Britain expressed assent to wind up her empire and concentrate to make good of her great material loss to achieve victory in the war. So, Britain agreed to concede India's Freedom. Moreover, the international support was also in favour of India. What had been possible in the case of Mauritius, could not have repeated in India. Hence, with the Independence of India on 15 August 1947, this territory became an inseparable part of Independent India.

Trends of India's defence policy

What is a matter of great concern, is that even after the re-occupation by the British, these islands remained unconcerned of British colonial rule in the Indian sub-continent. This territory had been so long used only for the penal settlement and its strategic location was simply ignored. So the British met with disastrous consequences during the Second World War. The British never felt that only owing to their naval supremacy, their maritime colonial empire had been built up but surprisingly enough no attempts were made to develop any naval base in these islands rather it always ventured to evolve as a land power. This faulty trend in the British military policy enabled Japan to occupy these islands easily for there was really no defence. Despite her cognition of strategic importance of the islands, Japan, too could not develop a naval base in these islands because she was doggedly busy in building up fortifications there as quickly as possible.

Even after independence, India paid no attention to the strategic importance of these islands. In the early years Indian Navy was the Cinderella child of the Defence Ministry. Only the smallest portion of the total defence budget was allocated for the Navy. On military development and security of these islands, there was low priority or no priority in Indian perspective planning. In the late fifties modest expansion of Indian Navy began, which however was condemned by an article published in *The Economist*[1] as such "Asia appears to be giving birth to an embryo super-power with expansionist ambition". Only in 1957–58, the Navy performed the hydrographic survey and sheer navigational charts of certain islands of this territory were prepared. But what actually made India indifferent and apathetic to consider the strategic importance of these islands cannot be discerned and why India remained unconscious of her sea-ward defence is beyond understanding. While most of the littoral countries have been building up very sophisticated naval power, India remained unconcerned.

Obviously her conflicts on her territorial borders with China in 1962 and with Pakistan in 1965 and 1971, made India more concerned of her land manoeuvre. The continuing threat from these quarters forced India to be more alert of her border defence. Only after her defeat against China, defence budget was multiplied. While Army and Air Force got a lion's share, Navy was neglected. Only after Indo–Pak war of 1971, India's naval awareness, strategic perception of the Indian Ocean and her future policy in South East Asia underwent a radical change. The dramatic expansion of Indian Navy in 1970's and 1980's for her territorial security and protection of her economic zone around her coasts proved India's deep concern to grow up as a maritime power.

The policy of sea control of the Bay of Bengal was instituted in 1971 at the AndaNico as a forward base for fuel, victuals and maintenance. Sea denial was also exercised by conventional submarines operating from these islands particularly in the absence of nuclear propulsion. In 1945, K. M. Panikkar, an eminent historian rightly pointed out the importance of the Indian Ocean, "while to other countries, the Indian Ocean is only one of the important oceanic areas, to India it is a vital sea. Her lifelines are concentrated in that area. Her future is dependent on the freedom of that vast water surface. No industrial development, no commercial growth, no stable political structure is possible unless the Indian Ocean is free and her own shores are fully protected." [2]

However, to go deep into the matter, we must take into account the reasons of India's inability and international interference as well. Despite the importance of the Indian Ocean to India's security and economic growth, in the fifties and sixties, India remained unconcerned and paid more attention towards border security because Pakistan's obtrusive activities on the west and China's offensive design on the north and the east, had created acute border problems. Naturally, the earlier objective of India's defence policy was to equip her as a major land power, so her Navy remained neglected.

Only in mid-sixties, India witnessed the beginning of the Super Power Naval rivalry and the bone of contention was of the possibility of the deployment of Polaris SLBM in the Indian Ocean by USA. In 1963, the rendezvous of U.S. Naval fleet only goaded the situation. Though India was not the target of any of the Super Powers, their ominous presence made us conscious of the importance of sea-ward surveillance and utter necessity of a strong Naval Force. Confronted with the growing presence of foreign naval forces in the Indian Ocean, India had no alternative but to strengthen her Naval defence and resist any attempt to undermine her independence or to deride her integrity from the direction of sea.

After independence, from the Hydrographic study, India came to know that Burma had already constructed a light house and stationed a battalion of Burmese Army at the Table Island in the North Andaman and consequently to appease them India had to accept the Burmese right over the Table and Coco Islands. Even then we did not try to develop a kith and kin relation with Burma whereas China took advantage to exploit the situation and developed consortium with Burma.

K. M. Panikkar once cautioned us with his postulation, "The defence of Burma is in fact the defence of India"[3] and that is why Burma should have been made a buffer state between India and China to prevent conflict and to stop supply of arms to the terrorists through Burma, but still it is not given priority and India's security is yet affected seriously by border problems.

At the time of transfer of power, we inherited an army with a legendary reputation. We also had the nucleus of an Air force as old as that of some European countries of yester years. But the British never wished to share the maritime power with India, so she still enjoyed naval supremacy.

After independence, the Indian Government emphasized on investment of all available resources only in the development schemes without thinking that investment in development alone cannot strengthen the country's defence so India failed to repel China's attack in 1962. India, of late realized that issues of development for prosperity may be considered on priority only if security against external attack is assured. Nevertheless security does not depend on Army alone, so our emphasis on land manoeuvre failed to dissuade the foreign aggression.

Hence, development and security should walk hand in hand. Development of a vast country like India has multi-faceted dimensions – sociological, ethnic, environmental, economic, political, etc. Above all, development in defence sector deserves priority to assure security. To consider the gravity of the issue, we must review the whole situation.

India is a sub-continent as well as peninsula having coastline of 76000 kms. Adjoining these, there is a vast continental shelf where economical marine assests are being created at an enormous expanse. Within and beyond the limit on both sides of the peninsula, lie 600 odd islands of our country composing of the Lucca and Minicoy Islands and the AndaNico. Among them strategic location of the Andaman and Nicobar Islands is very significant pertaining to the defence of India. Hence, to protect these islands and to safeguard the vast coastline, a strong Navy must be built up.

Because of conspicuous activities of Super Powers in the Indian Ocean, sometimes the security of India seems to be threatened. The military activities of America such as presence of U.S Naval base at Diego Garcia, her command in Malacca

Strait, her strongholds in the Pacific Islands etc. or growth of China and Japan as potential naval powers also poses a threat to peace and stability of the region, in and around the Indian Ocean. Establishment of a naval base at Coco Island by China, rapid growth of pro-China sentiment in South East Asia and continuous detrimental tensions of Indo–China relations since the outbreak of Indo-China war in 1962, have only endangered the situation. Indonesia's claim over the Nicobars and growing up relations between it and Pakistan during and after Indo–Pak War of 1965 have intensified the problem. Military insurgency in Myanmar, political uncertainties in South East Asia and infiltration of L.T.T.E. in the region – all these contributed to the threat-perception of India and have a direct impact on the security of these islands.

Under this circumstances, India is to build her own sea power for offensive and defensive manoeuvres and to strengthen her strongholds in these islands. As to the definition, sea power is the totality of nation's fishing fleet, merchant fleet and military fleet, the sophistication and efficacy of its communication system and finally the R&D apparatus accompanying all these. The plan for a balanced all–round development of Indian Navy should encompass the parallel development of other components of sea–power.

Indian Ocean – A Zone of Peace

Since long India and other third world countries have been endeavouring to convince, U.N.O. to declare the Indian Ocean free of military activities. In the U.N. General Assembly Session of 1971, the Indian Ocean was declared as a zone of peace but in reality it has always been ignored and defied by the Super Powers. Besides, India has always propagated the idea that the Indian Ocean as a zone of peace should be conceived in true spirit of disarmament and collective security which is denied too.

In 1977, in the International Conference of Sea Laws held in New York, it was decided that from the actual coastline, a distance of 19.31 kms in the sea shall be treated as the territorial limit of a country and a distance of 320.9 kms will be considered as Exclusive Economic Zone (EEZ). In that conference, Shri H.R. Gokhale, the Law Minister of India proposed that the A&N Islands should be conferred with the status of Archipelago but it was opposed by the Big Powers and the proposal was turned down on the ground that this group of islands has got no separate entity as it is a part of India.

In the third United Nations Conference of the Laws of the Seas (UNCLOS) held at Geneva in 1980, it was resolved that outside the territorial water, rights of exploitation over vast resources of the sea in E.E.Z. and also in the vast continental shelf will be enjoyed by all littoral states. Henceforth, the sea around these islands happens to be a playground for poaching, so careless navigation has become enormous and thereby aggravates the tension of the region.

To calm down the tension, India has to depend on the regional co-operation within the gamut of developmental strategy in the maritime region of the Bay of Bengal and the AndaNico Islands will play a decisive role in that development based national security strategy. India's maritime code act of 1976 defines the importance of the Exclusive Economic Zone (EEZ) encompassing an ocean area of some 2.5 million sq. kms. It proclaims, "... its sovereign rights for exploration and exploitation of the living and non-living resources as well as for other economic uses and exclusive jurisdiction to authorize, regulate, conduct and control scientific research and take measures to preserve and protect the maritime environment."

But by mere proclamation of sovereignty over the immense reserves of the undersea food and mineral wealth, the rights cannot be exercised, so the sovereign rights have to be protected by might and means. Security of these assets in the deep sea means augmentation of India's Naval power. The primary condition of over all security is to maintain peace and create an environment of amity and mutual progress among the neighbouring littoral states.

To the neighbouring states, India is dubiously considered a colossus, which would bestride over her neighbours and impose her will on them. Hence, to remove their fear-complexes and susceptibilities, India extended her goodwill mission to settle her maritime boundaries with all her South East Asian neighbours.

Hence, besides SAARC, BIMSTEC (Bangladesh, India Myanmar, Sri Lanka, Thailand Economic Cooperation) and ASEAN (Association of South East Asian Nations) these two agreements were signed in 1997 to appease the members and pacify the tension among themselves, so that cordial and co-operative attitude may be developed for peaceful co-existance and prosperity.

With Indonesia, the first agreement was signed in 1974 to settle the boundary between the Great Nicobar and Sumatra. In 1977, the boundary line was extended both into the Indian Ocean and into the Andaman Sea by another agreement. An agreement between India and Thailand was signed in June 1978 to settle the boundary in the Andaman sea.[4] The maritime boundary agreement with Burma was confirmed in 1987 [5]. A maritime border between India and Bangladesh is yet to settle. Though the naval strength of any of the littoral states does not pose a direct threat to India, the situation will be subversive to India if any of them is instigated either by China or by Japan to estrange relation with India to cut her to size.

Between 1968 and 1971 India opposed the establishment of any military bases of any country in the littoral and hinterland states, and campaigned to declare the Indian Ocean as a Zone of Peace. Lusaka Resolution of 1970 and U.N. Resolution of 1971 endorsed the India's stand. But in reality instead of being a zone of peace, the Indian Ocean has become an arena to exhibit strength by the Super Powers.

Hence, it is rightly felt that an appropriate policy must be followed in consonance with all other littoral states, since all of them will suffer if the Indian Ocean is allowed to be used as a playground to exercise the military excellence of the Super Powers. Deployment of nuclear submarines and other sophisticated weapons in the Indian Ocean helps America target southern reaches of Russia, China, Iraq, Afghanistan or any belligerent country and hence it only aggravates the situation and spoils the peace.

Gnashing of dragon of China

From early times, the dragon of China has been gnashing its teeth and sharpening its claws to extend her hegemony over the whole South East Asia and build an empire to be dominated only by the Mongolians. The same thing happened when Hitler dreamt to own a vast land to be inhabited only by a race of pure Aryan blood and to fulfil his dream, he attacked Russia. Thus, the Chinese design can easily be perceived and naturally the AndaNico will come under her sphere of influence. Hundred years back, C. Boden Kloss commented, "Doubtless the Chinese knew of the group (AndaNico) in comparatively early times for they have records of the neighbouring Nicobar Islands going back for more than a thousand years." [6]

He has further mentioned certain incidents when the Chinese were found to spend several months in the Nicobars. From many evidences, it is proved that the Chinese would come to these islands frequently for poaching, forceful trading and other predatory activities. From Captain Hopkinson's letter, it is noted that the Andamanese had never allowed any outsiders to do any mischiefs to them. Once they gave a fierce fight lasting for three or four hours to resists the Chinese kidnapping the Andamanese and those who were captured, were brutally butchered by the Andamanese.However, the British decided to lease out lands in the Nicobars to the foreign settlers. In 1874 lands in Nancowry were leased free to the

Burmese and Chinese labourers on condition that they would not encroach into the land of the Nicobarese but this attempt of colonization failed. Again in 1882, the Chinese were preferred for colonization in the Nicobars and the scheme was sanctioned by the British in 1884. Fifteen Chinese families were chosen for settlement on Camorta and their cost of passage from China was borne by the government. Even a dole of daily ration of rice and salt-fish was sanctioned. Though the settlement was made in December 1884, it was abandoned in 1885 due to lack of interest among the settlers.[7] After all these futile attempts, the British Government dropped the idea of colonization of foreign settlers in the Nicobars, otherwise, India would have faced a critical ethno-political threat in these islands as it happened in Hong Kong.

Ethnically it has been proved that the Nicobarese belong to the Mongoloid race and genealogically it has been discerned that in them there flows a mixture of blood of the Chinese, the Burmese and the Malayasians. Sir Richard Temple,[8] after studying the habits, customs, rituals, concludes that the Nicobarese seem to be descended from the Indo-Chinese race. Even at the present times, the Chinese influence on rituals is the most common in the south and in some parts of central group of the Nicobars where most of the trade had been carried on by the Chinese in the past.

Whatever may be the outcome of anthropological researches and ethnological investigations, it is widely accepted that the Chinese were the frequent visitors to these islands from very early times and because of their racial affinity, China puts forth its claim over these islands and it still instigates the warlords of China to accomplish their rights. So, real threat lurking over the AndaNico may come from China, or any of the Super Mongolian powers.

The heightened and enlightened sage of India, Swami Vivekananda made a prediction as early as 1898 when he said, "If and when British leave India, there is every possibility of China invading India".

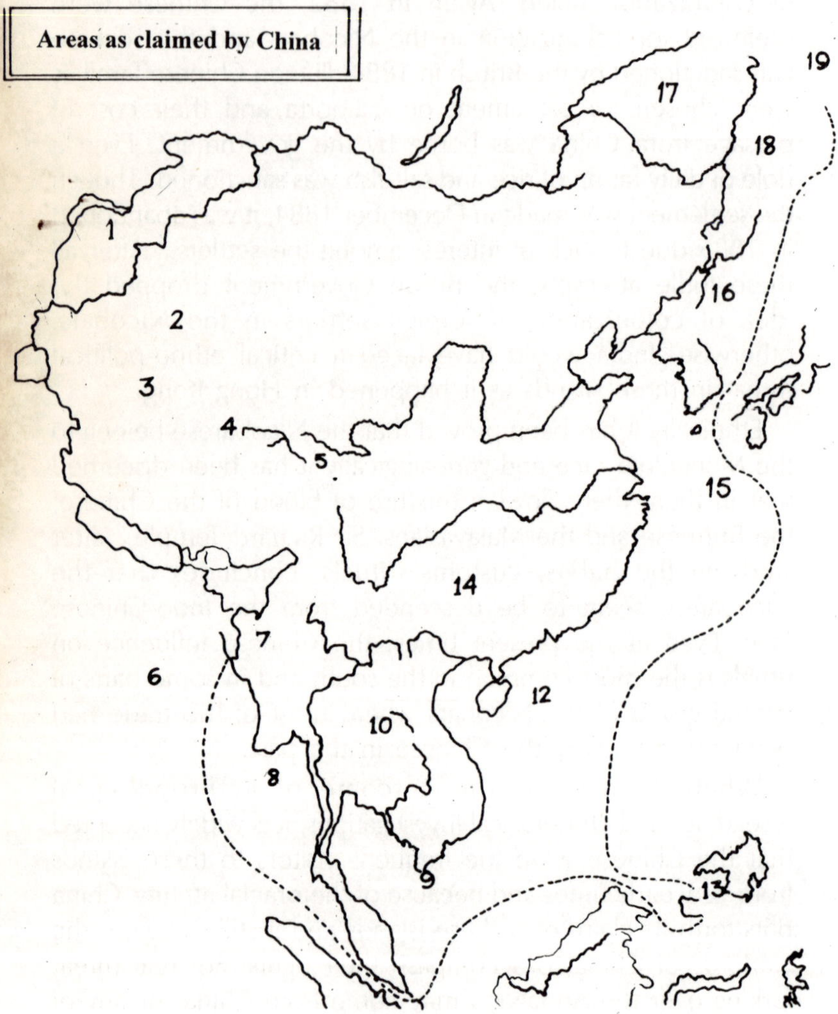
Areas as claimed by China
1
2
3
4
5
6
7
8
9
10
12
13
14
15
16
17
18
19

The Map in the book showed the territories which the Chinese claim as their own and which according to them was seized by the Imperialists during the first period. The translation of the text in the map (reproduced here) shows the nature and extent of China's expansionist ambitions. The legends from 1 to 19 suggest:

1. The Great North-West, according to the Chinese text in the map, "was seized by Imperialist Russia under the Treaty of Chuguchak, 1864". It covers huge segments of the present day Soviet Republics of Kazaghastan, Kirghizia, and Tajikistan.
2. The Pamirs was "secretly divided between Britain and Russia in 1896".
3. Nepal "went under the British after 'Independence' in 1898".
4. *Che-Meng-Hsiung* (i.e. present-day Sikkim) was "occupied by Britain in 1889".
5. *Pu-tan* (i.e. the whole of Bhutan) "went under Britain after 'Independence' in 1865".
6. *Ah-sa-mi* (i.e. the whole of Assam) was "given to Britain by Burma in 1826".
7. Burma "became a part of British Empire in 1899".
8. The Andaman Island "went under in Britain".
9. *Ma-la-chia* (i.e. the whole of present-day Malaya) was "occupied by Britain in 1895".
10. *Hsien-Lo* (i.e. the whole of Thailand) was "declared 'Independence' under joint Anglo-French control in 1904".
11. *Annam* (covering the present day North and South Vietnam, Laos, and Cambodia) was "captured by the French in 1885".
12. Taiwan and Penghu Islands were "relinquished to Japan in accordance with the Treaty of Shimonoseki in 1895".

13. Su-Lu-Island was "occupied by the British".
14. The region where the British crossed the Border and Committed aggression.
15. Liu-Ch'iu (i.e. Ryukyu Island) was "occupied by Japan in 1910".

17 & 18. The Great North-East, covering a huge area of the Soviet Far East, "as given to Russia under the Treaties of Aigun (1858) and Peking (1860)".

19. K'ui-Ye (i.e. Kurile Island) was "divided between Japan and Russia".

His political idealism or his proper understanding of Chinese past history has been proved true to the test of time when China invaded India in 1962. Vivekananda's vision and political sagacity was derived from the fact that the modern Chinese satrapy is nothing but descendants of Changis Khan and Halaku, the mass murderers of their times. Long before the Indo-China war of 1962, an official map appeared in a book namely, "A Brief History of Modern China",[9] published in March 1954 and written by *Lin Pei Hua* following Maoist design of making a modern China. The book contains the provocative map highlighting 'the Chinese territories' occupied by other imperialist countries in the old democratic revolutionary era (1840 – 1919) and China's claim over those territories has been propagated both through the text and the map of that book. It is reiterated in the book that China should wage wars against all those imperialist powers to reoccupy her so far lost territories.

However, the map simply foreshows the motive of the Chinese leaders and reveals the geo-political policy of the Communist Party of China. The nature and extent of the map bear the proof of China's expansionist ambition, which arouses suspicion and generates anxiety in the mind of the people of these countries whose areas have been demarcated in the map. There are reasons to be worried because in the map, even these islands have been separately located in 'block 8' as a lost territory of China which "went under Britain" and China claims her rights over these islands through that map. China's aggressive policy in the Central, South and South-East Asia is as old as the Han race. After independence in 1949, China's only contemplation is to reoccupy her lost territories and to fulfil her lust for land and power.

To achieve that goal, she did not spare even Myanmar (Burma) which was ironically the first country in the world to recognize the People's Republic of China and in return China reinforced her Red Army in 1951 all along the borders of Burma to exert military pressure on her. Compromising with the neighbouring countries is not the motto of China but circumstances forced her to do so. The failure of the communist insurrection in Burma on the one hand and China's success to stage a showdown against India in 1962 on the other hand prompted Beijing to change her tactics and compelled her to settle the border disputes with Burma but not with India. Though she fought small wars against India and Vietnam, and forcibly occupied Aksai Chin of India and the Paracel Islands of Vietnam with impunity, she realized that it would be suicidal to fight against the then Soviet Russia single-handed to reoccupy her lost territory. So China for the time being receded from her policy of aggression and proceeded with the policy of regression to build up her military strength to be at par with other Super Powers. For her policy of hibernation, she earned the glorious sobriquet as "the land behind the iron curtain." During this period of recession, she silently ventured to provoke a war between USA and USSR, and to intensify her entente with the U.S. with a view to launching a common war against Soviet Russia.

But by the turn of fate, the USSR fell flat and was disintegrated. On the contrary, China became a permanent member of the Security Council. Obviously, her politico-military policy has been drifted towards a new strategy to consolidate her power by developing herself first and then evolve a new foreign policy of aggression and accession.

Establishment of a naval base at the Coco Island of Myanmar is a clear indication of her ulterior motive. Indeed, China being a delayed but very rapidly growing naval power is vastly superior to the Indian Navy both in number and also in Weapon–System. While she was having 6 submarine depot – ships for their 115 submarines, India possessed only 17.[10] China is also involved in the clandestine trade to transfer vast quantity of weapons to India's belligerent neighbours and to supply arms to the insurgents and terrorists in India. China did not only supply naval equipments to Indonesia but also inspired her to support Pakistan during Indo–Pak War in 1965.

M.L. Sondhi of Indian Council of Social Science Research and Ashok Kapoor of University of Waterloo, Canada have rightly opined, "China has special ties with Pakistan, Iran, Nepal, Myanmar and it appears to have a plan to create a wedge between South East and South Asia through Myanmar and to maintain access to the Arabian Sea through the Karakoram highway and a new port being built in Pakistan under Chinese auspices."

"China has different policies for her neighbours. She strengthens Pak military to contain India and seeks to do the same through her activities in Nepal, Myanmar, Bangladesh and her missiles cover all major Indian cities. She has a policy for the development of naval bases for her uses in Myanmar and Pakistan so her India-related policy has a naval dimension which eventually also affects South East Asian countries and the U.S. and her allies in Asia".

A few years ago, *Jane's Intelligence Review* referred to a remark made in 1993 by Director of the Chinese Academy of Military Sciences was, "China can't accept India's naval expansion and we are not prepared to let the India Ocean become India's Ocean." Hence, China is busy in upgrading Myanmar's naval facilities. These include at least four electronic listening posts along the Bay of Bengal and in the Andaman Sea: Man-aung, Hainggyi, Zadetkyi and Coco Island, located about 23 nautical miles off Landfall Island in the Andaman and Nicobar Islands. According to *Jane's Intelligence Review*, the base in the Coco Island, "would be ideally situated for monitoring Indian Air and Sea movements in the eastern part of the Bay of Bengal as well as intercepting telemetry associated with Indian Missile tests over the Bay."

It is no doubt, strategically significant to ponder over the crucial remark made by Brig. Darshan Khullar in his book, 'Security, Peace and Honour' that China has been assiduously cultivating Myanmar with arms and economic aid. Its objective is to gain a foothold in the Indian Ocean and use Myanmar (which is only 100 kms. from Indian Islands of Andaman and Nicobar) as a spring board for military action against India when the need arises.

Pakistan's Air Marshal, Ashgar Khan[11] disclosed in his autobiography that Sukarno had offered her help to divert India's attention from Pakistan by occupying the Andaman and Nicobar islands. Even Jakarta sought permission from Ceylon to use her airports to transfer some military aircrafts to Pakistan. Indonesia also lent a flotilla of Russia built sea crafts to Pakistan. During Indo-Pak war in 1965,Jakarta also put forth the bogey of the "Indonesian Ocean" and even claimed that the Nicobars were a part of the Indonesian archipelago. During the days of sixties, India has passed through the phases of inimical relations with the littoral states.

At times it was felt that the threat to India might come from forces operating beyond South – East Asia and it actually happened in late forties. What remained confined in the intention of China and expressed in her harangues or likewise through the map of the said book, became a reality while Japan, another Mongolian country occupied the Andaman and Nicobar Islands on 23 March, 1942. Though Japan had surrendered, danger of foreign invasion never ceases.

Who knows when and in which form, a foe will strike. Suspicious activities of some foreigners in these islands raise the questions of their intents and purposes. How did an Australian got permission to undertake an aerial survey of every nook and corner of the Nicobar Islands in the pretext to search for his missing son. Of course, he was remanded later while he was taking notes of the coastline and sketching a coastal map.

A few years ago, two Japanese entomologists as they claimed, were interrogated for their sinister activities on the sea-shore of Chidyatapu in South Andaman. Apparently, they were collecting butterflies but their doubtful movements did not support their statement. Who knows how many foreigners are coming in some sort of disguise to serve their hidden purposes.

Defence built–up in Bay Islands

All these overt and covert actions, though added stress to tensions yet perpetrated as an eye opener for New Delhi that at last felt the necessity to augment naval defences in these islands and to follow up an appropriate need-based defence policy for the safeguard of India. But the process was slowcoach and the development was deterrent. After independence, importance was given to the growth of Army and since independence it took three decades to build up the Navy to cope with a conventional conflict. In the 1950s, the Navy acquired its Fleet Air Arms, a modest beginning culminating in the commissioning of a Light Fleet Carrier. The next decade saw the accretion of the Submarine Arm, a potential conferring the capability to undertake underwater operations. The 1970s ushered in yet another vital development with the acquisition of missile–bearing naval craft and the prospect of strengthening the sinews of the Fleet in a surface action.

Considering the gravity of the situation, the Coast Guard establishment with its Regional Headquarters at Port Blair was pressed into action since 1 February, 1977, as a part of Navy.

In August, 1978, it became independent not only to protect 6083 kms long coast line of the mainland and that of about 2000 kms of these islands from poaching and infiltration, and to safeguard nearly two million sq.kms of her exclusive economic zone but also to thwart militant groups from using scattered and desolate islands for nefarious activities. Hence, the Coast Guard with a surveillance and armed reconnaissance capability has been pressed into duty without disturbing the regional balances. In due course, several naval bases at Port Blair, Campbel Bay, Rangat, Long Island, Diglipure, Camorta and CarNicobar have been set up to carry out the responsibilities more successfully. District Headquarters were set up at Campbell Bay in Nicobar district and at Diglipure in Andaman district.

After the Indo – Pak war, positive steps have been taken to strengthen the Naval base in these islands. Already *INS Jarawa* and, *INS Utkrosh* at Port Blair and *INS Kardeep* at Camorta are set into action effectively. During emergency, a verified Fortress Command, FORTAN (Fortress Commander, Andaman & Nicobar), the highest Defence Authority at these islands, stationed at Port Blair, will be the most effective trip-wire for defence and deterrence, and can oversee the busiest choke points in the world, the Malacca Straits as also the Ten Degree Channel. The Preparis and the Coco channels which are the gateways to the India Ocean for the East and can be crucial choke points both in war and peace. The Indian Navy provides sea and air defence to these Islands. Actually, the mission of safeguarding over 572 widely scattered islands is a Herculean task, which the Coast Guard is entrusted to discharge.

Lately, the Government of India and the Naval Headquarters thought out the plan to develop a station for third fleet of the Navy under a separate Command to be positioned in these islands. Though the naval bases of India have been stationed mostly on the eastern coast, the first line of India's maritime defence obviously has to be located in the AndaNico Islands.

In 1963-64 *INS Jarawa* was set up and the Naval Garrison with facilities for moving to various islands on patrol was stationed at Port Blair. In 1969 it was decided that facilities for Naval Air should be provided in these islands and logistic facilities were planned to implement in the AndaNico Islands. In 1970, the naval establishments were put under the Flag Officer Commander – in-charge of Eastern Command and the Nancowry Island was selected as an ideal place to develop the advanced Naval Base. On 11 May, 1985, *INS Utkrosh*, the first Naval Air station in these islands, was commissioned. Indeed Amphibious Forces are needed to ensure proper protection of these islands. Of course, Indian Navy works, in unison with Army and Air Force and United Fortress Command at Port Blair with communication bases, airfields, radar surveillance, store and victualling yards and the engineering units can oversee the busiest choke points in the world, the Malacca Strait, the Preparis and Coco Channels which are the gateways to the India Ocean from the Pacific outlets affecting India's defence.

Considering the geo-political location and strategic importance of the AndaNico, India Government had already decided for positioning a third fleet of the Navy under a separate command at Port Blair to act as frontline of maritime defence, to protect the immense marine wealth and prevent any foreign infiltration or poaching. In near future, it was so planned that these islands should have defence facilities upgraded to the highest level with modern naval ships and sophisticated Naval Air elements. Otherwise, what had happened during the Second World War, may repeat as the experts on defence strategy always emphasize that the threat to India is always lurking from forces operating from behind South-East Asia and obviously from a Mongolian Super Power. As Japan ventured first, the next attempt may be of China being the most ambitious country with numerous advantages.

With the turning out the last century, Asia's geopolitical condition has changed rapidly and radically, and the changes have increased India's strategic importance particularly to the United States despite U.S.'s involvement in Indo-Pak war against India in 1971. Undoubtedly, there is a triangular rivalry among the US, Russia and China in Eurasia. Although the US is presently the only Super Power that alone can project power globally but experts like Zhigniew Brezezinski and Henry Kissinger observe that the hegemony of US is temporary, so repositioning of Indo-US relation reflects new realities which are the outcome of the turning phases in global economy and international relations. These developments clearly indicate that the repositioning by India and the US vis-à-vis each other has a deep and broad Asian geo-political framework.

These changes make China calculate that even if she increases the size of her nuclear and missile arsenal against India, India can match the increase primarily if her security remains undisturbed and its economic growth keeps progressing unhindered. Presently, China has military advantage over India and in the foreseeable future, she intends to confuse and distract the thought–processes of the Indian political class by creating border problems or instigating Pakistan and others. Naturally, India becomes suspicious of China's activities.

Of course, in Asia-Russia, China and India are regional great powers. Possibly India was encouraged by Russia to join the coalition with China and Russia to subside US influence and challenge. The US might pre-empt this possibility so has ventured to improve relations with India to win her confidence.

Historically, India is a rival of China and civilizational differences along with her (China's) ambitious military policy have stimulated the rivalry, further attack on India in 1962 and forcible occupation of Aksai Chin and more deliberately fanning the jingoism of Pakistan against India are clear testimony of China's inimical attitude. So, India leans towards the U.S. without declaring that the common ground is China

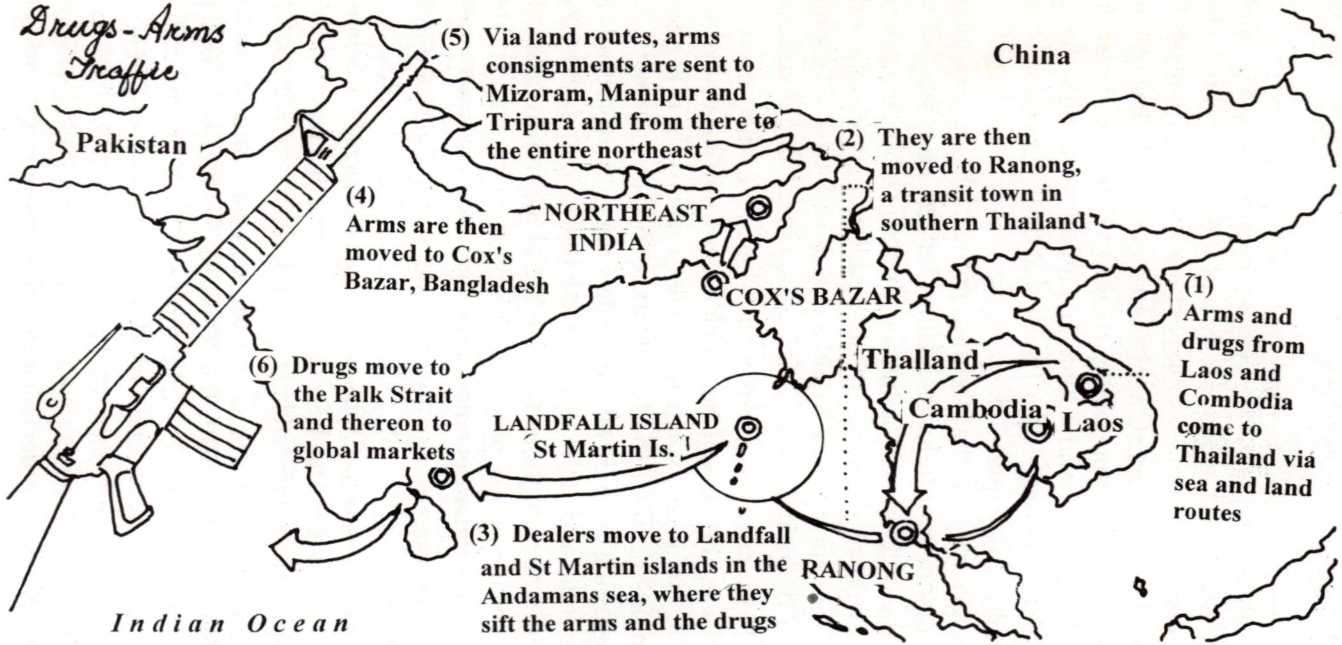

Drugs-Arms Traffic
Pakistan
China
(5) Via land routes, arms consignments are sent to Mizoram, Manipur and Tripura and from there to the entire northeast
(2) They are then moved to Ranong, a transit town in southern Thailand
(4) Arms are then moved to Cox's Bazar, Bangladesh
NORTHEAST INDIA
COX'S BAZAR
(1) Arms and drugs from Laos and Combodia come to Thailand via sea and land routes
Thailand
Cambodia
Laos
(6) Drugs move to the Palk Strait and thereon to global markets
LANDFALL ISLAND
St Martin Is.
(3) Dealers move to Landfall and St Martin islands in the Andamans sea, where they sift the arms and the drugs
RANONG
Indian Ocean

in addition to the attraction of the market-place and twinning of two democracies. The Sino-Indian rivalry is reinforced by China's policy of armed support for Pakistan as a threat to India during warfare and moral boosting to Pakistan to spread insurgency in India even when there is preposterous peace.

Just before 2003 dawned, Bangladesh signed a defence pact with China. Pakistan and Myanmar are already in China's pocket. Nepal is under the spell of maoist insurgence. Even America asked India to reduce her non-military presence in Afghanistan just to satisfy Pakistan. Once Nixon declared, "The integrity of Pakistan is the cornerstone of American foreign policy." America needs Pakistan now not to block Russia's advance in the Indian Ocean but to facilitate a stable South Asia for constructing an oil pipeline from Central Asia. Similarly, China needs Pakistan as a second front against India. China's hegemonic mindset still dictates the need of a Pakistan hostile to India. More interestingly, America overlooks India's security concern in defence to China and ignoring India's interest exercises indulgence towards Pakistan. This complex situation directly affects the security and defence of the AndaNico Islands as the territory is at bay.

Hence, the repositioning is not a passing flirtation; rather it is grounded in new realities. Geo-politics and not simply global economy is the new game in many Asian and Western capitals. The Indo-US realignment may be emphasized to overcome China's threat., But Dingle Shen,[12] Deputy Director at Fudan University's Center for American Studies, Shanghai, has pointed out that recent development of relations between India and US raise some very pertinent questions: Is India getting too close to the US? Too fast? Are Washington and New Delhi warming up to each other to contain China? Obviously these perceptions are gaining currency in India, China and else where, making it only natural to stoke suspicion in China about New Delhi's and Washington's intentions.

All along China remained a long term problem for the US and thenceforth the growing entente between Russia and China contributed tension for America. With the turning of time, cool relations between the US and Pakistan over Pak support for Taliban and Islamic forces, and China's non-conformity, there would likely foresee a possibility for ensuring a natural affinity between the US and India in the strategic and other spheres. Of course, India must be critical and conscious to analyse the eventuality and follow proper policy suitable only for her defence and security.

Arms and drugs traffic

Apart from all, what is the most baffling is the recent trend of India's defence policy that appears to be a matter of great anxiety for the security of the islands. Due to slackness in surveillance of the defence look out and leniency towards the Myanmarese rebels as well as the LTTE, the seas off the Andamans are not only being used in the drugs-arms trade but also the deserted Landfall Island and St. Martin Island of the Andaman group are obtrusively misused as two main transit points in the trade. It is surprising to note how this sort of nefarious activity is being ignored and how the order of the Defence Ministry, 1998 for free use of the islands is being manipulated by the militants to serve their own purposes. (Source: *Outlook*, March 26,2001)

Now the clandestine practice is that the LTTE ships that carry arms and narcotics separate at Landfall and St. Martin Island with the arms going northwards towards Bangladesh on their way to Myanmar and northeast India. Obviously, Ranong Island off the coast of Thailand is the staging point for arms shipments that originate from Cambodia and take the sea-route through the Andamans to the major receiving point at Cox Bazar in Bangladesh. The route covers Thailand, the Andamans and the land track via Myanmar and Bangladesh before ending up in the hands of the northeast insurgents. (See map, exhibit No.5).

Though the route has been used by arms dealers and their end–users for several years, recently it has come to the notice of the army. In December, 2000, Lt. Gen. T.S. Shergill, the General Officer Commanding,3 Corps based off Nagaland's Dimapur town briefed to the Press in Agartala, "we have information that this arms consignment worth $ 750,000 which comprises AK series rifles, mortars, landmines, stenguns and high powered explosives, is coming into the northeast from Cox Bazar."

The duty of the army is to prevent ingress of arms consignment meant for various insurgent groups in the northeast. Despite having advance knowledge of such frequent operations through the Andamans seas, the armed forces are unable to stop the shipments in the high seas because of the express order from the Defence Ministry. In February, 1998, a tri-services operation, Operation Leech had sought to put a stop to all these. But it is said some order from the Defence Ministry put a stop to any precipitate action against the gun-runners on the plea that it violated their human rights. Hence, the arms reached Cox Bazar unhindered. (source: *Outlook*, 26 March, 2001).

It is assumed that the LTTE is deeply involved in drug and arms trafficking and that too is through the Andamans seas. The unwholesome entente with the LTTE clears the path of clandestine trade. The evidence against the Tigers is said to be overwhelming and clear. Says an intelligence source, "The LTTE is directly involved with the Myanmarese drug mafia in making and distributing heroin". In July 1998 The Indian Navy had to refrain from intercepting ships suspected of carrying illegal arms to the Tamil Tigers. Later, it was instructed to Indian security forces to downgrade patrolling of the PalkStrait.

All these signify a sudden change of defence policy but it is not clear that at what cost and at the risk of security of the Andamans what objective of the Defence Ministry is to be fulfilled. The army officials in the northeast always wish that the arms-drugs route through the Andamans must be stopped for the sake of India's defence and it will be possible only if the Andamans seas are kept in strict vigilance of the Navy and the islands of this archipelago must be prohibited to be used by any foreign agents otherwise the defence of India as well as the security of these Bay Islands will be at stack. No doubt the pressure on those fighting insurgency around the border shall be considerably reduced if the arms supply to the various groups is sealed.[13]

Considering all these serious aspects, the defence facilities of the country should be upgraded to the highest level with modern naval ships and naval air elements. In these islands, the Aerial Bay of Diglipure Island and Nancowry in the Nicobars are undoubtedly the best sites to develop naval bases. Port Blair and Car Nicobar airstrips can be innovated properly to entertain the most sophisticated war-planes. And South Andaman and Campbell Bay are the proper area to accommodate Army regiments. If adequately developed, the AndaNico can certainly serve the purpose of becoming potential strategic location to perform its crucial role as the first line of India's maritime defence in the South-East.

FORTAN at Port Blair boasts of the only unified inter service command in India but it needs to be strengthened as to the proper plan of need based defence mechanism and the policy of offensive tactics. Indian Government has realized the strategic importance of these islands only after the victory of the Indo-Pak war in 1971 when Indian Navy's aircraft carrier *INS Vikrant* was stationed in the Andaman seas and deployed to conduct a counter-operation to foil Pak attacks. In that war, even America dispatched her taskforce headed by the U.S. Enterprises in support of Pakistan. But for the benign presence and determined action of *INS Vikrant*, the U.S. fleet had to recede. India's victory was so significant that it could create a deterrence for rest of the world and acted as an eye-opener for India's Defence Ministry. As a result, FORTAN was formed and now acts as the only unified inter service command in India.

On 8 October, 2001, the Andaman and Nicobar Command consisting of three services—Navy, Army and Air Force, besides Coast Guard has come into action under Vice – Admiral Arun Prakash being its first Commander-in-Chief. The formation of tri-service Command for the islands underscores its strategic importance and ensures impregnable surveillance and security in the region. The new Andaman and Nicobar Integrated Command assumes great importance in view of global problems of terrorism, narco-terrorism, drug-trafficking, arms-running etc. during peace time. Besides, the AN Command can properly take care of the region's vulnerability in times of war. Moreover, it can protect the economic and commercial interest of the country by its constant vigilance in the territorial water as well as the Exclusive Economic Zone (EEZ).

Hence, Andaman and Nicobar Command (ANC) must be all set to ensure undisrupted international shipping traffic, especially in the vicinity of Malacca Straits, off the southern tip of Indira Point in Campbell Bay. The formation of ANC is a positive step towards the defence and security of these islands in particular and the nation as a whole.

Notes

1. 'Imperial India' published in *The Economist* (London) April 15, 1989 p 16-19
2. K.M.Panikkar, 'India and the Indian Ocean, An Essay on the Influence of Sea Power in Indian History' (London, 1945, p96-7)
3. ibid
4. S.P.Jagota, 'Maritime Boundary (Boston, 1985), p79. P. Chandrasekhara Rao, 'The New Law of Maritime Zones With Special Reference to India's Maritime Zones' (New Delhi, 1983) p153-54
5. Salamat Ali, 'Hands Across the Sea : India and Burma Ratify a Maritime Agreement" *Far Eastern Economic Review* (Hong Kong) 8 Oct.1987,p52
6. C.Boden Kloss:'The Andamans and Nicobars',1971, p177

7. National Archives of India, Port Blair Branch. Aprogs. No.20 Oct, 1882 p no.54, Oct 1885.
8. Census Report, 1901, p 199,200
9. *The Link*, Feb 25,1979, p11
10. The Military Balance 1989-90 (The International Institute of Strategic Studies, London,1989)
11. Prof.Raju G.C.Thomas, 'India's Security Policy' (Princeton, 1986) p152, 153
12. Article written by Dingle Shen, pub. in *Outlook*, Feb.18, 2002, p38
13. An Article by Nitin A. Gokhale, pub. in *Outlook*, 26 March, 2001, p38.

5 Prelude to the Japanese Occupation

Munich Pact and its Impact

War begins with glory and ends in dismay. Pride of war-mongers is always proclaimed and cry for justice is usually denied. War is the outcome of conspiracy and it breaks out to satisfy the ambition of the collaborators. Indeed, it happened on the eve of the Second World War.

On 29 September, 1938, a quadruple alliance was formed out of a historic conference held at Munich and on 30 September an agreement was signed by Adolf Hitler, Mussolini, Chamberlain and Daladier. That infamous agreement bears the testimony of the worst act of appeasement conformed ever in the history of mankind. It was really a shameful act of betrayal to Czechoslovakia while her fate was dictated by Hitler and assented by other Allies without paying any heed to her cry for justice. Through this Munich Pact, the other Great Powers, Britain and France only paved the path for the growth of Fascism. The signatory countries agreed only to propitiate Hitler.

In an article heading, "On the Brink", Jawaharlal Nehru condemned the act of appeasement in his unequivocal words, "It was the rape of Czechoslovakia by Germany with England and France keeping her forcibly down". H.G. Wells sarcastically mentioned the incident when British Prime Minister, Chamberlain on his arrival to London airport, waving a piece of paper signed by him and Hitler along with others, exclaimed joyfully, "I believe, this is peace for our time". Indeed, the agreement was a denial of peace and betrayal of justice. It's rather a premonition of a global war.

The Munich Pact not only gave vent to Hitler's unleased yearning for supremacy but also kindled the fire of longing for power in the mind of the warlords of Japan and Italy. Harvesting the situation, Germany's thirst to establish a worldwide empire was not quenched by annexing only Czechoslovakia. It was just the beginning of bloodshed and tyranny to fulfil his desire. His sudden attack on Poland on 1st September, 1939 was just an eye-opener of the contenders and eventually compelled Britain to break off the cocoon of appeasement and declare war against Germany. Hence, on 3rd September 1939, the Second World War broke out.

Imperialistic design of Japan

The Munich Settlement had been synonymous with capitulations, appeasement and treachery to small allies. Its impact upon Japan was phenomenal. Since its rise during the first decade of the twentieth century, its growth had never been halted. All along Japan followed a policy of expansion and aggression to materialize her imperialistic design on South East Asia. When other parties of the Triple Alliance, Germany and Italy were exploiting the weaknesses of Britain and France, when the chariot of fascism moving triumphantly through Berlin – Rome-Tokyo axis was flagged off indiscreetly by the Allied Powers in September at Munich, Japan began her southward march in the same month, September. Japan's invasion started with the seizure of Canton and Hong Kong. Her intention was to seize the strategic points in the China sea. This was the prelude to her involvement in the South East Asian gamble.

In November, 1939, Japan invaded Kwangsi province to occupy the city of Nanking and China's strategic road leading to French Indo-China. The global situation favoured Japan and seemed propitious for a bolder venture. The rise of Hitler absorbed the attention of Europe. Anti-Comintern Pact encouraged the Allied Powers to extend active support and Non-Aggression Treaty inspired Russia to extend passive support to the Axis Powers. Besides, the Neutrality Act passed by the USA in 1935 announced America's policy of isolation. All these factors favoured Japan to follow a forward continental policy to fulfil her ambitions in the Asiatic region. Consequently, after the accomplishment of the Tripartite Axis Pact with Germany and Italy, Japan now felt politically bold and militarily very strong and dominating. Due to concentration of the Western Powers in Europe to cope with Germany and Italy, the colonies of France, Holland and Britain in South East Asia seemed almost defenseless. This opportune situation excited Japan to occupy these territories and secure the grateful support of the native populations of Japan's own race, Mongoloid being freed from their European rulers. This created an atmosphere to propagate a Greater East Asia Co-Prosperity Sphere duly dominated by Japan as the champion of East Asia Brotherhood against Western imperialism.

After strengthening her position in these areas, in July, 1941 Japan occupied Vietnam and after the fall of France to Hitler's greed, the whole of French Indo-China came under the Japanese occupation. On 7 December, 1941, all of a sudden Japan attacked Pearl Harbour and inflicted upon America one of the most disastrous defeat, she had ever sustained. Only three days after the attack on Pearl Harbour, Japan sank two British warships, *Prince of Wales* and *Repulse*, and appeared as an overlord of seas possessing overwhelming naval supremacy in the Pacific and the Indian Ocean. Thus, Japan's offensive went ahead with breathless speed.

Within five months after the attack on Pearl Harbour, Japan completed its mission by occupying most of the "Greater East Asia Co-prosperity Sphere" around the Pacific as well as the Indian Oceans. The undaunted Japanese Army had been able to terminate the colonial supremacy of the western powers from the region of South-East Asia and the era of western dominance in Asia seemed a reality of yester years. Because of racial semblance, Japan appeared to be the champion of

Mongolian affinity and tried to infuse a parochial feeling of racialism and a spirit of commingleness among the fellow people of the region.

But in reality the Japanese war cry "Asia for the Asians" did not win the support of the people because they became suspicious of Japan's dubious role. Of course, Japan's swift progress in the South East Asia multiplied the anxieties of the Allies particularly of Great Britain who had been ruling in the region specially Burma and India including the Andaman & Nicobar Islands since long. When on 7 March, 1943 Japan's victorious army had occupied Rangoon and the whole of the vast oceanic area had come under the Japanese occupation, the danger of Japanese attack to India became imminent.

Japan's interest in the Islands

During the early years of the war, the condition of the AndaNico Islands was very precarious. Since the beginning of the penal settlement, the British neither paid any attention to build up defence of these islands nor realized their strategic importance being the gateway to India. Indeed, the British was compelled to realize the strategic importance of these islands only when they were forced to counter the Japanese attack, but it was too late and they had no other go but to retreat. At the meeting of the Chiefs of the Staff Committee on 31 January, 1942, the British first admitted that the fall of these islands would only beget the early attack to India as the Japanese army would make use not only of these islands as their launching station but also of the convicts as their stooges for propaganda purposes and fifth column activities.

What the British felt only after retreating from their south –east strongholds, had been realized long ago before the outbreak of the Second World War by Japan and hence the attack on the AndaNico was superbly planned and executed accordingly. To the Japanese, the AndaNico Islands had never been a strange land. It was always to them a well-known destination. Since long they used to come to these islands apparently for fishing or collecting shells but later it was revealed that their activities were not as innocent as it seemed to be. They would usually come in their own boats with valid licenses from the British Administration and regularly went away to do their 'jobs'. Marine or Police departments never bothered to challenge them as in papers, everything was perfect. But there are reasons to believe that among these innocent fishermen, there were naval personnels in disguise. They visited these islands with the ulterior motives to survey the coastlines and to collect strategic information.

Certainly, they had their regular contacts with local persons. Actually, very few Japanese lived at Port Blair but no body knew when and where they had come from. In Aberdeen Bazar, Foko Moto ran his dental clinic with the help of his wife. B. Konishi managed his studio with his wife. Iwasaki, a photographer lived in Aberdeen Bazar. All these foreigners were arrested and deported to Calcutta on the eve of the Japanese attack. But the purpose of the Japanese had already been served so when the occupation forces landed at Port Blair, they had dossiers of each and all. Moreover, they had a detailed map with clear indication of all important places and indices of the coastlines for safe landing and defence fortification.

To go deep into details of the Japanese movements prior to the attack of these islands, we can have an idea about the massive activities of the Japanese forces for offensive purposes in the Bay of Bengal and in the vicinity of the littoral countries. Due to frequent aero-cruising of the Japanese fighter-planes around the islands and the strict surveillance of the Japanese battleships, it became impossible for the Allies to approach the Bay of Bengal. The Indian Navy had already lost a number of warships i.e. *HMIS Sophie Marie* blasted on being struck by a mine and on 28 January 1942, the paddle '*Idar*' was sunk being hit by a Japanese submarine.

The intermittent attacks of the Japanese forces, their reconnaissance activities and frequent pounding and sinking of British ships bore the testimony of the Japanese phenomenal success. The sky and the sea was completely under the control of Japan,being the overlord of South-East Asia. The regular shelling by the Japanese naval ships and offensive air–raids were making the situation worst day by day and it became evident that the Japanese invasion to the AndaNico Islands was imminent in the next few days.

On 1 February, 1942, the Japanese bombers first dropped bombs targeting *Aberdeen Jetty* but failed. On 5 February, 1942 *HMIS Ramdas* sank being attacked by the Japanese gun-boats. At least four merchant vessels met the same fate of watery grave. Singapore was occupied on 15 February, 1942 by the Japanese. Next day after the fall of Singapore, Burma Army Headquarters was informed by a telegram that Port Blair had been raided by three Japanese bombers for 65 minutes. Ground defences and aerodrome were the targets but the damage was negligible.

On 7 March, 1942, when the victorious Army of Japan occupied Rangoon, the whole of oceanic area went under its domination and the war scenario changed quickly in favour of Japan. When it seemed impossible to hold back Rangoon, the Allied Forces relinquished the plan to defend and decided, rather to quit Rangoon. At the same time, apprehending dangers and damages, the British decided to evacuate Port Blair because to them, security of India was more important than the defence of such tiny islets.

Evacuation by the British

To emphasize the significance of the fall of Rangoon, the eminent historian, S. Woodburn Kirby wrote in his book, "*History of the Second World War*", "One of the repercussions of the loss of Rangoon was the evacuation of the Andaman Islands. These islands had considerable strategic importance for they flanked the approaches to Rangoon."

In the islands, earlier there had been only one British Company which was, in January, 1942, replaced by a battalion of Gorkhas. After the fall of Rangoon when the Japanese invasion to these islands became imminent and there the defence mechanism was reduced to no-defence, the British realized that their existence was synonymous with the safety of India. On 1st March, 1942 following the order of General Wavell, the Gorkha battalion was withdrawn and the islands were abandoned leaving all the helpless islanders at bay. Before evacuation all offices, officers and their families were shifted from Ross to Aberdeen. Since then Ross Island remained neglected and deserted. Its past glory vanished very quickly into a state of decay.

However, evacuation started and the Europeans began to leave these islands in a frenzy. The last ship left Chatham Jetty on 13 March. Those who could not be accommodated, were asked to wait for the next sailing. Unfortunately, the ship on her return voyage was sunk by the Japanese submarine and further evacuation was suspended.

Actually, the Europeans were so panic-stricken that four of them consisting of Deputy Commissioner, the Harbour Master, Superintendent of Police and Jailor stealthily left the islands on a motor boat driven by the sarang Ashraf Ali and the engine driver Sewa Ram. After a long and perilous journey, they reached Madras safely. When the Gorkha battalion had been sent back to Calcutta and almost all Europeans along with prominent civilians had left the islands by the earlier sailings for some safety places in the mainland, fate of the local people was left at the mercy of the Japanese army. Of course, out of panic, some inhabitants of Port Blair also left their homes on 24 February, 1942 for settling in far off villages but the others stayed back to face the destiny.

A bare half a dozen of Europeans including C.F. Waterfall, the Chief Commissioner, Major A.G. Byrd, M.C. Donald, Dr. Suringler and other subordinate officers including, Atul

Chatterjee, the Treasury Officer, Dr. Diwan Singh, (Whose family has already left the island on 13 March) Rama Krishna, Durga Prasad, etc were left to run the administration. A body of 237 Military Police and a band of 162 Civil Police were kept to look after the law and order. Before the Japanese occupation, total population of the islands including the local-born and convicts was somewhat 34 thousands.

To sum up the whole situation, war historian Woodburn Kirby writes, "As early as the 7th of February, 1942, Imperial General Headquarters (Japan) had issued orders for their capture (A&N Islands). The opportunity to do so occurred when reinforcements were being sent to Burma by sea after the occupation of Rangoon. A battalion of 18th Div. which was enroute to Rangoon from Malaya together with a naval component consisting of detachments from 9th and 12th Special Base Forces sailed from Penang on the 20th March and three days later Port Blair was occupied and an airbase quickly established".

It is interesting to note while Mr. Cripps was negotiating in Delhi for the transfer of powers, Japanese bombers started pounding in Trincomale and Vizagapattanam taking off from these islands and as a result, evacuation began even in Calcutta.

Surprisingly when the 'Quit India' Movement, took its decisive turn against one foreign country Britain, at the same time, another imperialist power, Japan occupied the Andaman & Nicobar Islands and hoisted the flag of Nippon on the Indian soil. Hence, it's a queer coincidence while the people in the mainland were struggling for freedom and 'Do or die' was their war – cry, in these islands, the people were struggling for survival and forced to submit to Japan's tyrannical outcry, 'obey or perish'. So, the history of the Andaman and Nicobar Islands during the Japanese occupation is also the history of a foreign domination which ultimately turned out to be a reign of terror.

Japan' s slogan "Asia for the Asians"

During war, everywhere it is the first and foremost act of the war logistics to provide security and safeguard to the occupying forces. According to the strategy, it is believed that enemies within only multiply the strength of the enemies without, so quislings are to be created to act as touts or agents to frustrate resistance movements and fight out the enemies outside. The victorious armies always float some 'ism' to earn the confidence of the local people and throw money and materials to the touts to provoke the people to betray themselves.

This thing repeated during the Japanese Occupation in the Andaman and Nicobar Islands. Whichever countries the Japanese had occupied, their primary task was to inject a feeling of allegiance to the Emperor of Japan among the people and create a group of quislings among themselves. In these islands, they followed the same policy as they had propagated in Indonesia. It was a unique and scintillating proclamation, "Asia for the Asians". This grand deliberation had two pronged mission, firstly, to incite hatred against the British as imperialist and secondly, to induce a feeling of good wishes for the Japanese as saviour and thereby earn people's support to the Japanese as their Asian brethren.

The Japanese aimed at the total extirpation of western influence and complete submission of the local people forgetting their own cultural identity so that they would welcome the Japanese forces as their own brethren. This sort of emotional manipulation was the spearhead of Japan's war strategy.

The Buddhism was the major religion in the region under Greater East Asia Co-prosperity Sphere. The ideology enunciated by Japan played a crucial role in the power – politics in the Far East and South East countries. To the Buddhist countries, Japan posed as a champion of Buddhism and made propaganda in her favour to subdue the people but to other countries, she presented herself as "saviour" whose moral commitment was to protect their brethren from the western servitude.

In Indonesia, Japan for the first time floated a high sounding grandiloquence – "Three 'A' movement" with three proponents, *'Japan, the Leader of Asia', 'Japan, the Protector of Asia,' and 'Japan, the Light of Asia.'* Whatever may be the grandeur of these slogans, the ideology did not hold good in Indonesia as the people looked down upon the Japanese as alien as the French had been to them. Moreover, the religion of the majority in Indonesia being Islam did not harbour the Japan's proclamation as the champion of Buddhism.

In Malaya, though the Japanese failed to sow the seeds of malice against the British, some success to infuriate the Malayans against China was sighted.

In Burma, as it happened in the Andaman and Nicobar Islands, almost all the British officials along with their Indian counterparts left the country safely before the trumpet of the Japanese victorious forces was heard there.

After occupation, to play the same game of winning the hearts of the local people, the Japanese allowed them to enjoy a share to run the civil administration. Usually, in all these countries the Japanese followed the prevalent system of administration with certain changes in collaboration with the local people under the high handedness of Japanese military overlords. Their intention was to fulfil their mission without affecting the sentiments of the people. But in those areas where the European influence was strongest, the Japanese tried to eradicate them with a view to convincing the people that they were against the injurious western tradition but in favour of Asian culture. At the same time, they tried to encourage the quislings to array the field as their faithful agents. Sometimes they inspired the people to set up puppet government as Germany had done in France.

After the fall of France in June 1940, Japan tried to exercise her command over the new naval base of Thailand at Singora. To fulfil her desire, Thai-Japan Treaty was signed in December, 1940 with P'ibun Songgran's government in Thailand. After sudden attack on Pearl Harbour on 7 December, 1941, Japan's troops landed on Thailand where P' ibun government capitulated and agreed to co-operate with Japan in wars against America and Britain. Now being assured of local support, Japan plunged into a two pronged attack, the main army devastated down the Malaya peninsula and the other moved towards Burma. Japan attacked with air and ground supremacy Sumatra, Bali, Java and the Phillippines simultaneously. After occupying Cambodia and Laos, Japan occupied the whole of French Indo-China.

Ultimately, on 15 February, 1942, the fall of Singapore became evident. Rangoon was attacked on 7 March 1942 that led to its fall on 13 March. By the end of April, the whole of Irrawady was captured. Thus, five months after the sudden offensive on Pearl Harbour, Japan marched victoriously throughout the South East Asia with breathless speed and fulfilled her design of "Greater East Asia Co-prosperity Sphere". Now, the road to the AndaNico became wide-open to welcome the Japanese army which could easily occupy the Islands on 23 March, 1942, without having least chance to be chased or threatened by the Allied Powers.

6 Japanese Occupation And Aftermath

Advent of Japanese Forces

The author of " History of Second World War", S. Woodburn Kirby remarked, "One of the repercussions of the loss of Rangoon was the evacuation of the Andaman Islands. These islands had considerable strategic importance for they flanked the approaches to Rangoon".

The Japanese knew the strategic importance of these islands and chalked out the plan to occupy them ingeniously. So from Burma, Japan hopped over the AndaNico, which seemed to them an ideal launching ground for invasion to India. According to Woodburn Kirby, Imperial Headquarters Nippon had issued orders for the occupation of the AndaNico Islands. Meanwhile Japanese reconnaissance planes flew over the islands obviously for the lookout of any mobile unit of the Allied Forces.

The British Officials in these Islands had a clear instruction from the authorities to evacuate and the job was perfectly done. While the Japanese submarines were cruising around these islands since 6 January 1942, complete black-out started and air raid-alert-'siren' only made the people more panicky. However, on 2 January, 1942, *S.S. Maharaj* sailed for mainland with full load of passengers. On 9 January, many more left the islands by a naval ship '*Alanga*' and on 1 March, 1942 the Gorkha battalion left the island by the first available ship. On 13 March the last ship with evacuees left the islands for good. Only the islanders were left completely at the mercy of the Japanese forces.

At the beginning of March, 1942 the Japanese Intelligence had information that there was no defence at all. Their warplanes started flying low over Port Blair on 19 and 20 March and made surveillance safely in the islands. So, on 22 March in the evening the Japanese forces comprising of a battalion of 18th Division together with a naval component consisting of detachment from 9th and 12th special Base Forces sailed from Penang and reached Port Blair on 22 March, 1942 at mid night. Though they knew it very well that in the islands there was no army, still for safety's sake, one gun of a battleship fired the first salvo but the echo ended in silence and no return firing was heard. Instead, what surprised the Japanese was the terrific sound of an explosion shortly after the firing. Actually it was the work of Mr.Alexander Ooty, (Lutty), D.A.E.W., the British Wireless Officer In-charge, who was entrusted to blow off the wireless station by the British Government and did the job by blasting the wireless installations. Afterwards it was a complete eerie silence throughtout the night.

Of course Shri Durga Prasad, the Chief Forest Officer had been instructed by the British to destroy the Chatham Saw Mill and marine workshop by bursting before the occupation of the Japanese but he refrained to do so as he had felt that the destruction would cause only untold miseries to the islanders who were solely dependent on them for their livelihood. Later, it was felt that defying the order of the British, he did the right thing and served his own countrymen wisely.

However the explosion done by Ooty, no doubt made the Japanese Forces confused. Having been ensured of no resistance at 6 o'clock in the morning of 23 March, 1942, the troops started landing from all sides in different formations under the command of Lt. Yoshimura of Japanese Navy, Officer Commanding of the landing forces. Their systematic landing in different points proved that they had detailed information about the areas for safe landing and the shortest roads leading to Aberdeen.

The Japanese occupying forces landed at three different points, one at Rangachang, another at Corbyn's Cove and the third one at Aberdeen Jetty in three pronged formations. It was just like a trident attack. The landing forces included the Navy and the Army treading towards Aberdeen in three different routes. The incharge of each column had a detailed map of roads, villages and strategic locations. So within no time the whole island came under the occupation of the Japanese Forces.

Shri Raghuvansh Lal Avasthi, an eyewitness during the Japanese occupation writes in his book, "At the Feet of Mother India," "I cannot forget the memorable scene of 23rd March, 1942 morning. The Japanese warships had surrounded the Island, particularly Port Blair and warplanes flying overhead were in constant communication with ground forces and the Japanese soldiers with fixed bayonets roaming all over the town".

Indeed immediately after arrival, the Japanese forces took control of all important places and posted armed sentries not only within the town but also in far off villages. All the Europeans including the Chief Commissioner, Waterfall and other Anglo-Indians were arrested. All captives were divided into two groups, Indians and Europeans. In the evening on 23 March, the Indian P.O.W. were lectured by Lt.Yoshimura that Japan was a friend of India and Japan treated Indians as friends and brotherly people so all of them were released. They captured all arms of the police, and seized ration goods and treasury. In due course the Naval Command took over charges of marine dockyard, set up new telegraph office at Southpoint, captured the Chatham Saw Mill and seized the central supply depot at Dundus Point where a buffer stock of essential goods including medicines and other provisions was raised by the British in order to be utilized at least for three months at the moment of emergency. The Headquarters of the Army at Haddo and that of the Navy at Aberdeen were quickly established to run the functions of defence, and control laws and order. Soon Aberdeen where at every hundred yards armed soldiers were posted, became the hob-nob of military activities. Japanese occupation strategy was so well-conceived and time-bound that the whole occupying process took hardly twelve hours to establish their command in every nook and corner without receiving a single shot of gun in rebuff.

Saga of an Unsung Hero

Just after occupation C.F. Waterfall, British Chief Commissioner was not only made prisoner of war but also assaulted inhumanly. While he was coming by his car to surrender, in front of present Model School, he was dragged out of the car and forced to trample the Union Jack which was flying on the bonnet of his car.

On the very night of their landing while all the naval ships and seaplanes were either anchored or wagging, at dead of night suddenly the sky dazzled with frightening flashes owing to the bombardment by the Allied Air Force. Though there was no damage, this airraid made the Japanese skeptical and revengeful. How much they were vindictive, reflected ominously next day.

After occupation, all the strategic points at Port Blair were kept under strict surveillance and all Europeans were taken into custody. Having been rest assured of security, the Japanese naval authorities allowed their soldiers on the very next day after their arrival to go care free and enjoy themselves for a couple of hours. Although living under the shadow of death because of the possibility of airraids, the occupying forces would become violent whenever they got a chance. This indulgence often made them desperate and libidinous.

So on 24 March, 1942 when they were allowed to enjoy themselves, they moved out in erratic mood. Some of them resolved to plundering and even molesting women. Soon a rumour spread that the Japanese soldiers were entering in houses, taking away whatever they liked and even insulting the women folk. This was something incredulous in the peaceful life of the islanders. So everybody was stunned and worried.

That day around 1.40 p.m., some madcaps among the Japanese soldiers appeared loitering near the house of Ashique Ali in the Aberdeen Village. Once they began to catch chickens. On chasing the birds, they entered in the nearby houses and some of them misbehaved with the ladies. Actually their expression was obscene and their attitude was vulgar.

Zulfiquer Ali, alias Sunny(Sonny) was observing every movement of those soldiers. When he could not tolerate their filthy behaviour any more he protested vehemently which made the Japanese more arrogant and frolic. They vituperated the youngman and cut nasty jokes at the ladies. Sunny reacted violently. He could not bear with the vulgarity of the strangers towards the womenfolk. He rushed to the house of Muhammed Ali and came back soon with a gun. He was so furious that he could not hesitate to fire at them. Though nobody was hurt, the Japanese being frightened ran way. But in no time they came back with many more to punish the boy.

At the sudden turn of situation, Sunny became confused and apprehending the danger, he fled away. Soon the Japanese cordoned the whole area and surrounded the house of Akbar Ali, father of Sunny. They began to charge hand grenades to destroy everything. They issued ultimatum, 'either produce Sunny or face dire consequences'. Meanwhile they set fire to the house where they thought that Sunny had absconded. When the fire began to spread to nearby houses, it was felt that very soon the whole village would be gutted completely. The villagers were at a loss what to do. The Japanese were adamant but how the kins could push their own son to the jaws of death.

At that crucial moment, Narayan Rao, Chief of Police Force hit upon a plan to save lives and properties of the villagers. He persuaded the Japanese authorities to give some time to produce Sunny and allow the people to extinguish the fire. When they agreed and left threatening the people that next morning Zulfiquer must be handed over to them, Shri Rao tried to convince the people that the calamity could be averted only if Sunny would surrender himself. He told the people that he knew, it was a very shocking and inhuman proposal but there was no other way to save themselves.

Though he had dubiety in convincing the villagers and the family members of Sunny, he tried his level best to make them aware of the cruelty of the Japanese. He met everybody and at last talked to the young man. Though he was too young to realize the gravity of situation and guess what was awaiting on his surrender as he was then only twenty years old, he however felt that everything depended on him. He was very bold and philanthropic. In order to save lives and properties of his own people, he decided to surrender and took heart to face the destiny.

But nobody imagined how pathetic and barbaric the sequel could be. On 26 March 1942 at 9.45 a.m. being summoned by the Japanese, the villagers assembled at the ground in front of the then Browning Club (now Netaji Club) to witness the extent of punishment, the Japanese designed for treason they called it. The people did not have any idea about the sort of punishment to be bestowed. Everybody was terrified. Sunny was tied to a post. He looked intrepid, not broke at all. Zulfiquer looked really 'Sunny' on that sunny day.

No sooner had the Japanese Officer passed the order, than bestial torture started showering on Sunny. To quench their thirst of vengeance, the Japanese soldiers applied all sorts of martial arts of blowing, kicking, battering and hooking. They even exercised all the tricks of 'Yu yutsu' on Sunny crashing and smashing his flesh and bones. Lynching was so terrible that every body burst into tears and sobbed mutely. Though their hearts bled, nobody dared cry. And Sunny was so miserably trampled, bludgeoned and beaten black and blue that his whole body was smeared with blood. Everybody along with his parents and relations had to witness this heart-wrenching sight without heaving a sigh. It was terrible and pathetic.

This orgy of blood went on till Sunny was senseless. When he was almost dead, he was made alert and a firing squad comprising of a band of twelve gunmen pounced a volley of bullets at him to ensure death. Thus, a young man set a crowning example of the highest spirit and bravery by sacrificing himself for a noble cause to protect prestige and chastity of womenfolk and save the property of the people.

In the history of these islands, Zulfquer Ali is the solitary example who preferred death to clemency. He was the only son of this soil who laid down his life to protest against the Japanese tyranny and preferred self-sacrifice to ignominious submission. His sacrifice was so great and glorious that he cannot be compared to anybody else whosoever faced death during the Japanese occupation.

No doubt the forty five souls of *Homfreygunj Murder*, seven hundreds who were forced to death by drowning near Havelock Island, three hundreds who were killed in Termugli Island and others who were killed in Dugnabad or elsewhere were all innocent but being accused of spying, they succumbed to the Japanese bestiality. Surely they were not spies but their contradictory statements may be under threat of death, inspired the Japanese to collect proofs of their involvement in the espionage against the Japanese authorities. Actually at the point of death they accused one another of spying and died a miserable death of no noble cause.

Hence, this act of blasphemy and cowardice cannot be glorified as an act of martyrdom. Simply they were the victims of their own follies and circumstances, not for resistance or remonstrance. Naturally the cause of their death was no doubt pathetic but not so great as that of Zulfiquer's. He was indomitable, undaunted and chivalrous. Really he is a martyr in the true sense of the term.Of course, his dead body was allowed to be buried in front of the Browning Club and a humble mausoleum under the canopy of the sky still speaks mutely the glorious sacrifice of Sunny.

After the horrific killing of Sunny Zulfiquer Ali, the islanders though deeply anguished at the harrowing sight, had to throttle their heart-rending afflictions and agonies. Their impulsiveness in sensing the impending dangers led them to appeal to Major Hira Kawa to assuage their anxiety and fright.The Japanese authorities being convinced of their submission, however, assured the people of no further deterioration of the situation until and unless there was any defiance of the Japanese rule or dishonour to His Excellency, the Emperor of Japan.

Thus, the saga of an unsung hero ended in the surrender and resignation of the whole population. Of course, this was natural for a vanquished populace but their helplessness or absence of virility cannot be a source of consolation or a cause of exculpation for the generations to come. Even after more than fifty four years of independence, only due to inanity and unawareness of the people, it is a pity that Sunny Zulfiquer Ali still remains unsung and neglected otherwise no other date than the 26 March should have been honoured as a martyr's day for these islands.

On the stone plaque of his grave, a memorabilia was written in a very touching expression in Urdu,

"Fool to do din bahare janfizan dikhla gaye,
Hasrat uun guchon pe hai jo bin khile murjha gaye."

It is really a golden tribute to a divine soul.

Gesture of Goodwill

Just after their occupation, the Japanese endeavoured to exploit the sentiment of the local people by propagating the view that they were the Asians and the Indians were their brethren so the British were their common enemy. They would help the Indians achieve freedom from the yoke of the British. To exhibit the gesture of their goodwill, the Japanese authorities arrested the British Chief Commissioner, Waterfall and other Europeans but released all Indians.

Their next step led to the release of all convicts including hardcore criminals incarcerated in the Cellular Jail by the British. The motive behind these activities was to prove that they were friendly to the Indians and the British were their common enemy. On the third day after the occupation, a public meeting was held where Colonel Bucho, the Civil Governor, spoke first that the Japanese came to these islands as saviour. To fan up the sentiment 'Asia for the Asians' he further said that they were all Asians and it was a bounden duty of all to help one another. He even reiterated that they had deep regard for Subhash Chandra Bose, not only for him being the Supreme Command as Head of Azad Hind Government but also for his undaunted spirit and Himalayan personality. In his speech, Colonel Bucho emphasized on their good wishes to run the civil administration in collaboration with the local people. In Malaya, Burma, Phillippines, East Indies, everywhere they had introduced 'Home Rule' to run the administration. In these islands also they would introduce the same pattern of administration.

Among the islanders, Dr. Diwan Singh spoke on that occasion, "The Japanese, like us are the Asians. The British were *Firungees.* We fought many a battle of freedom against the British but we never succeeded because they believed in dividing us. The Japanese now assure us that they will help us attain freedom from the British. They give us that pledge and therefore, they want us to co-operate with them everyway. In the light of what they say, they deserve our co-operation. But I want to warn you that freedom is not something, which anyone can give us on a platter. To achieve freedom we have to fight..."

Initially the islanders were moved and welcomed the Japanese as a better substitute for the British. Some of them even believed that the Japanese had come as 'God-sent blessing'.

To assess the stance of the Japanese, Compton Mackenzie remarks, "the Nips issued pompous proclamations about the mighty Nippon Empire after they landed, in which they promised to give the inhabitants an example of its beneficent rule."[1]

Actually, the islanders were completely moved by the Japanese verbosity and submitted to them. To bring back normalcy, the Japanese authorities proposed to form a Peace Committee.

Indeed, peace was utterly needed because soon after the evacuation, owing to lack of supervision, the convicts took the liberty to escape from their barracks and fled to the villages. They resorted to all sorts of nuisance. Money and Women happened to be their targets. The villagers also took up arms and challenged the miscreants that resulted into massacre. The first thing the Japanese army did, was the deployment of sentries everywhere to ensure law and order, and instantly all the marauders as well as run-away convicts were arrested. In the middle Andaman, the situation had been worsened rapidly but the Japanese Army controlled the state forthwith. Hence, to install peace was the prime necessity pro-bono publico.

According to a secret report sent by the Japanese authorities at Port Blair and tapped by the British Naval Intelligence, it states, "two weeks after landing of the Japanese on South Andaman Island... the Peace Committee was established and it was organized by a Chairman and ten members for the purpose to settle land problems, supply goods, arbitrate disputes and also judge all civil affairs. This committee lasted for nearly eight months, until the time of the completion of *Gunseisho* (Military Administration) on December 2 of 1942."

There were special Cells, 'Kikans' to deal with and mobilize the Indians in favour of Japan. Major Fujiwara of the Fujiwara Kakan in Singapore expressed his view. "Japan must capture the heart of the Indians, a thing she had singularly failed to do with the Chinese. Japan must help them obtain their freedom.[2]

The actual intention behind the formation of the Peace Committee was apparently to ensure law and order, but deliberately to make the public aware of the supremacy and magnanimity of Japan towards the islanders. It would work as an instrument in the hands of the Japanese authorities who had dossiers of each and all. They had already singled out the English knowing prominent persons and fixed them with certain assignments as members of the Peace Committee so that they could keep a constant watch at them.

Formation of Peace Committee

The Peace Committee was formed in the first week of April, 1942 under the Chairmanship of Dr. Diwan Singh and other members were Narayan Rao, Ramakrishna, Thanzin, Durga Prasad, Haji Subhan Ali, Bhagwan Singh, Khan Saheb Nawab Ali, Moti Ram, Het Ram, Amrit Lall, Ratnam, Brij Lall, Abdus Subhan and Kesar Dass.

As to some other source, Haji Subhan Ali was the President, Dr. Diwan Singh, Vice-President and Het Ram, General Secretary. The members were Shiv Ratnam, Ramakrishna, Master Abdus Subhan, M.Bagsoobhoy, Brij Lall, Venkat Ratnam, Maung Maung (Burmese) and M.Mohammad (Moplah).

In their report, the Japanese acknowledged the work of the Peace Committee. It states, "Peace and order of this (Andaman) island was maintained mostly by the activity of the Peace Committee until the establishment of *Gunseisho* on May 1942".

The main function of the Peace Committee was to dispose of the local disputes in the same way as the 'Panchayat' does now-a-days. The Japanese were also happy as the islanders were quiet and co-operative.

Thus, the first round to win over the people was complete. Now the Japanese decided to go for a second round by establishing *Gunseisho* (military administration) in collaboration with the local officers and they planned for a walk-over in the final by introducing *'Miniseibu'* (civil administration) to be run totally by the Japanese civil officers.

Narayan Rao, originally a sub-inspector of Police, was promoted to the rank of Superintendent of Police by the British on the eve of their departure. He, being the head of the Police Department surrendered to the Japanese at the time of arrival but quickly earned their confidence after the heart-wrenching incident of the gruesome killing of Zulfiquer Ali. His rank in the Police Department remained intact and was co-opted in the Peace Committee as a responsible member.

Establishment of Gunseisho

One day in May, 1942, Narayan Rao informed the public that the Japanese Government desired to establish an Administration in the form of Home Rule under Colonel Bucho being the Governor of the Administration. He selected thirty men mostly of his confidence and asked them to be present at the Commander's Headquarters at Aberdeen.

When they turned up there, the Commander explained the structure and duties of the Administration. Though it was civil in nature, it would be headed by a Military Governor to be nominated from the Japanese Navy and all other posts would be filled up by the thirty prominent local persons through election. They would exercise their franchise to elect their men for the posts.

Gunseisho would be constituted with the following dignitaries:

- Governor from the Japanese Navy
- One Assistant Commissioner to assist the Governor
- Two Tahsildars, one for Aberdeen and the other for Wimberlygunj. They would work under the Assistant Commissioner.

- One Executive Engineer for the whole territory. He would be the Head of Public Works Department and responsible for the maintenance of roads, buildings, bridges, electricity and water supply. Dilthaman Tank was then the main source of water supply. There were also many well-maintained wells to meet the needs of the people residing around them.
- One Engineer cum Harbour Master – He would look after the repairs and maintenance of sea-vessels as well as road transports. He would be the Head both of Transport and Marine Departments. Inter island ferry services and Island-mainland voyages would be controlled by him.
- One Superintendent of Police to look after the law and order in the whole territory.
- One Assistant Superintendent of Police to assist the S.P.
- One Senior Medical Officer for the whole territory. He would be assisted by one Assistant Senior Medical Officer, one lady Medical Officer and a few Indian doctors. There were hospitals at Ross Island, Bamboo Flat, Dundaspoint, Haddo, Atlanta Point and Mayabunder.
- One Intelligence Officer under direct communication with the Japanese authorities.

For all these posts except that of Governor, nomination forms were submitted but after the appointments of Assistant Commissioner and two Tahasildars, the Japanese felt that all the thirty men were very close to Narayan Rao and the administration run by one group might pose a threat for the Japanese so the election for the remaining posts was suspended and within a few days, all these posts were filled up as to the desire of the Commander.

Thus, *Gunseisho* was formed with Colonel Bucho as Governor and other posts were filled up from the islanders.

They were as written by B.B. Lal[3] in his 'Regime of Fears and Tears' :

Gopala Krishna	—	Assistant Commissioner.
Ramakrishna	—	Deputy Commissioner.
Narayan Rao	—	Superintendent of Police.
Durga Prasad	—	Chief Forest Officer.
Dr. Diwan Singh	—	Chief Medical Officer.
Govind Rao	—	Executive Engineer.
Moti Ram	—	Head, Education Department.
Saheb Nawab Ali	—	Supply Officer.
Thanzin	—	Engineer cum Harbour Master.

It is interesting to note that the Japanese authorities kept the same local officers who had already been holding the similar responsibilities since the evacuation by the British. Moreover, if we compare both the lists, it is found that those who constituted the Peace Committee were inducted in *Gunseisho* and it may easily be concluded that these people were in the good books of the Japanese authorities. So long they served the purpose of the Japanese, they were the favourites to them but when they were found unwanted, they were exterminated.

Function of Miniseibu

Gunseisho was established in May 1942 and lasted for nearly eight months till 2 December, 1942 when *Miniseibu* was put into operation. Of course *Miniseibu's* civil officers arrived from Japan only in February, 1943.

The administrative set-up as well as the functions of the Andaman *Miniseibu* were almost same as those of *Gunseisho*. Its objective was to protect the local population and also promote the public welfare. *Miniseibu* made every effort to maintain law and order; took interest in development of industries, repairing of roads and prevention of epidemics in the islands but its main work was to increase the production of food staff by introducing self-sufficiency system. On the other hand, recognizing religious freedom, much attention was paid to education and also attempts were made to make the local people happy by encouraging wholesale amusements. (*Source*: *History of Japanese Administration in the Andamans*, Defence Ministry, Govt of India.)

At the beginning of the new year, senior Naval Officer Eguchi took over the charge as Governor of the Civil Administration, *Minisiebu* which was to be under direct control of the Admiral. He was assisted by a senior Intelligence Officer, Ckamoti along with a staff of the Intelligence Bureau, Auzuma, a Warrant Officer of the Navy who was assigned to prepare a detailed survey report of the land and people of the island in the perspective of war. Thus, the Japanese exercised overall control over the civil administrations through *Miniseibu*, of course, in the plea of doing welfare to the people. *Miniseibu* though termed Civil, was actually manned only by the defence personnels in white military uniform. *Miniseibu* was constituted of the following staff:

(a) Chief of Police with two Assistants
(b) One Agriculture Expert
(c) One Agriculture Officer
(d) One Finance Officer
(e) One Education Officer
(f) One Head of the Indian Independence League

Execution of Byrd

Meanwhile on 1 May, 1942, there was an interesting news published in the "Andaman Shimbun"[4] that on the occasion of the birthday of His Excellency, the Emperor of Japan, Pushkar Bagchi, formerly a convicts' Officer, but promoted to the rank of Chief Naval Intelligence Officer during the Japanese regime, was specially decorated with a medal for his excellent service to the Japan Government in the Andamans.

Pushkar Bagchi was a crooked and felonious type of man. He was sentenced to rigorous punishment for six months for taking bribe but released by the Japanese after their arrival. He was very cunning and vindictive. Taking advantage of the changing situation, he hit upon a plan to take revenge against Byrd who had awarded him the punishment. Bagchi took into his confidence a lifer, named Ram Swaroop and surreptitiously managed to plant some broken parts of a wireless set with the help of a co-prisoner in the premises where Byrd was kept under house arrest. The plot was hatched up properly and Ram Swaroop was briefed accordingly to give witness against Byrd, the Personal Secretary to the British Chief Commissioner, Waterfall who had already been sent to Burma as prisoner of war.

One day the drumbeaters moved round the Aberdeen Village announcing that there would be a public trial of Byrd on 5 May 1942 and all were asked to witness the punishment. Byrd was brought in handcuffs at the centre of the ground. Bagchi read out solemnly all the charges levelled against Byrd. Ram Swaroop confessed that he was an accomplice of Byrd and admitted all the crimes. Bagchi declared that the most serious charges being considered as treason were the conspiracy against the Emperor of Japan and the espionage against His Excellency by sending messages to his enemy, the British. He continued addressing Byrd, "You are guilty of all the crimes and according to laws, your punishment is death".

No sooner had the death sentence been pronounced than the most barbaric torture started on Byrd. By applying all the tricks of *'Yu Yutsu'*, his ankles were broken, his arms toisted and his shoulders crushed. He crumbled and crawled but he was not spared. Some one showered kicks at his back and the others punched blows on his stomach. His body was turned into a life-less lump of flesh and blood.

Witnessing the gruesome sight the people were shivering in terror and agony. An eerie silence prevailed there as if everybody present had stopped breathing but the old Byrd endured the ordeal calmly. When his plight was ineffable, convulsion started, the old men yearned for water but all in vain. To the contrary his head was severed in one stroke to quench the thirst of the earth. Earlier Mr. Ooty, the Officer-in-charge of Wireless and Telegraph Office faced the same trial and met with a brutal end after enduring bestial torture.

At last, Bagchi cited the magnanimity of the Japanese Government in granting clemency to Ram Swaroop who was repented and showed courage to become an approver. On granting pardon, the Japanese Government emphasized that though he was a co-accused, he was given a pardon because he was an Indian, their friend. Through this incident, the Japanese tried, to popularize the slogan 'Asia for the Asians' and at the same time demonstrated the extent of their vengeance if anyone dared defy the authority of the Japanese.

After reoccupation of these islands, Compton Mackenzie visited the AndaNico to assess the extent of atrocities inflicted by the Japanese to the islanders. He has mentioned the incident of gruesome murder of Major Byrd. When the British and Indian officials were evacuating in March, 1942, the Government asked for volunteers to look after the local administration. Among those volunteers was Major A.J. Byrd. A convict called Pushkar Bagchi who was the manager of a cinema hall in the mainland, murdered a man and received a life sentence on transportation. Later, he had been employed by Byrd but sacked for malingering. Hence to take revenge himself after the Japanese appointed him the Chief of Naval Intelligence, he forged a letter of Byrd which purported to give instruction about the establishment of an espionage service. Ultimately this concocted story of espionage led to the killing of Byrd.

Mode of Japanese Administration

What was reported about the atrocities of the Japanese Administration in the Andamans, was very much true. At the beginning, they were somewhat friendly and looked after the welfare of the people, of course, after giving priority to the defence and security of their own. They built the airstrip at Lambaline which had been left undone by the British. All the convicts who had been released from the Cellular Jail by the Japanese soon after their occupation, were rounded up and deployed in the construction work of the airstrip. Hundreds of the Nicobarese were engaged in this strenuous job on scanty food and no money. In a record time of three months, the runway was made serviceably and a regular air-service was undertaken to conduct flights to Rangoon and Singapore. They planned for construction of a new airport between Mithakhari and Hathi Tapu. It was rainy season,but the local farmers were not allowed to cultivate. The Japanese forced them to work as they did during construction of the Burma–Siam Railway. There the tomb stones only tell the gruesome facts of Japanese atrocities. Later the work to build an airstrip was dropped owing to sudden change of war scenario.

Almost one year after the Japanese occupation was so far the best period, the islanders ever experienced. Every week, two shiploads of cargo carrying rice, wheat, oil, ghee, potatoes, onions and all condiments reached Port Blair regularly. Besides food stuff and clothing, arms and ammunition were also imported in huge quantities. Hence, during this period there was no shortage of food or any essential goods. Moreover, on arrival of the cargo ships the local people were enagaged in unloading the goods and paid for it so they were happy.

The Japanese gave top priority to the agriculture and tried in all possible ways to make the islands self-sufficient in food production. Not only the soldiers but also the common people were directed to utilize their nightsoil in the agricultural fields as manure.

The Japanese started a dairy farm at a place earlier known as 'Cha Bagicha'. The Civil administration, *Minisiebu* where with the Japanese, the local male and female labourers worked in the cultivation works to produce vegetables, cloves, elachi etc. The Japanese never allowed the field lay without plantation. Sakarkand, Topioka, lobia, Vindi, Kumra, Sugarcane etc. were produced. Seeds and saplings were supplied free and for manure, nightsoil was used. The agriculture farm was kept under the supervision of Osaka, known as *'bachha masta'* (Sir).

The Japanese inspired 'Grow more campaign' and the propaganda officer was M.A.Gafoor of Aberdeen village. During the supervision of the Loganathan Commission of the Azad Hind Government, this programme was followed with all earnest and Maj. Alvi of I.N.A.was in-charge of it.

For improvement of road transport, they built a new road connecting Junglighat, Dairy Farm leading to Vijay Bagh. They even built footpaths inside the jungle to carry arms and materials for fortification.

Role of Indian Independence League

Meanwhile considering the war scenario of the South-East Asia being changed rapidly in favour of Japan, the Indian Independence League (I.I.L.) was formed in Tokyo on March 28, 1942 with Rash Behari Bose being its de-facto President and the Indian National Army was constituted on 11th December, 1941. The Japanese took initiatives in all the activities patronized by I.I.L. and helped establish branches of the Indian Independence League in all the countries in South –East Asia under their occupation. In these islands also they took necessary steps to open a branch of I.I.L.

The Japanese brought to Port Blair Baba Hari Singh alias Hari Usman who was a freedom fighter and attempted to kill Lord Hardings, the Viceroy of India. Once he was on board of a famous ship, *Koma Gata Maru* carrying a huge quantity of arms and ammunitions for the revolutionaries of Bengal but the mission failed and members of Gadar Party who were travelling by the ship, were either killed or arrested by the British. However, Baba Hari Singh managed to flee in disguise and settled in Sumatra. Due to his inspiration and the Japanese patronage, a branch of the Indian Independence League was formed at Port Blair with Dr. Diwan Singh as its Chairman.

Ramakrishna has written in his memoirs, "The Andaman branch was also affiliated to the mother organization with the difference that this branch remained completely under the sphere of influence of the Japanese" [5] He further said that the local branch of I.I.L.did not have any activities other than holding meetings and raising fund while the local branch of Indian National Army conducted a few drill-classes under R.L.Avasthi[6] who was one of the first members of I.N.A.from this island. Later, he became a victim of the Japanese displeasure and was sentenced to death but he was pardoned and sent to Penang along with Dr. Rama Nand[7] in 1942.

All these activities were reported in the two page Government news bulletin, 'Andaman Shimbun'. One such report goes, "A public meeting of the I.I.L. was held on Sunday, the 7th june 1943 at 4 pm. Naval Commander Major Hirakawa, Mr Koyama were present. The meeting was called to hear from Mr. Osman... open speech by Dr. Diwan Singh.....people agreed to form a national army and a sum of more than Rs. 4000 was collected on the spot".

In due course, at Port Blair, some more voluntary organizations were formed. They were, *Sat Sangat, Seva Samity, Bhajan Mandali*, etc. Kesar Dass, popularly known as Master Kesar Dass had inborn talent of a singer. Under his guidance, young boys and girls congregated under the banner of *Sat Sangat* and through their *Bhajan Mandali* spread the message of love and integrity among the islanders. His troupe sang patriotic songs in the historic meeting in Gymkhana ground where Netaji Subhash Chandra Bose delivered the sensational speech on 30 December, 1943.

Dr. Diwan Singh was a physician working under the British Government but elevated to the post of Chief Medical Officer by the Japanese Government. He was the Chairman of both the Peace Committee and the Indian Independence League. He maintained a close contact with one and all. He started Seva Samiti and school in New Gurudwara for the welfare of the people.

During those days of uncertainties, the roles of Master Kesar Dass and Dr. Diwan Singh were highly praiseworthy. *Bhajan Mandali* under the guidance of Kesar Dass and *Seva Samity* at the influence of Diwan Singh played glorious role by creating awareness and augmenting morale of the half-hearted people to cope with the changing situation. So long these philanthropic activities undertaken by the stalwarts like Diwan Singh, Rama Krishna, Kesar Dass etc. were confined among themselves and in no ways hamper the interests of the Japanese, they remained sympathetic to some extent towards the islanders. Indeed the Indian Independence League existed in name only and ceased to exit when the Japanese turned down the proposal to supply guns to drill with. But when the situation changed and the Japanese became suspicious of espionage, the members of I.I.L. became easy victims as they were all English knowing people.

Opening of Japanese Schools

In order to earn goodwill and co-operation of the islanders and with a view to exercising contact and command over the population, the Japanese took interest into the social service. The only Government school at Port Blair had been closed on the eve of evacuation and most of the teaching staff went back to the mainland. Now the Japanese opened a school at Ross Island to teach Japanese to the islanders so that they could run the administration. The Japanese language was completely Greek to the islanders and to the Japanese, Hindi was similarly Latin. So verbal communication had become a great problem. After his arrival at Port Blair, Lt. Commander,

Hira-Kawa, took over the administration and a person whose surname was Saha, was brought from Japan as interpreter. Preliminary things were done by him but the Japanese were eager to communicate themselves with the islanders in their own language.

For the use in general, a hand book, 'Nippon – Go-Annai' (guide book to learn Japanese) was compiled by *Minseibu Somuka* and printed at *Andaman Simbun* Press.

A few paragraphs from the book are quoted here in Roman scripts to ascertain the importance of '*Deabacha*'.

"Jab se hukumat aaliya Japan in jazzair men aai hai yahan ke awaam ki yeh khawahish thi ke woh Japani zuban men kuchh rusuukh hasil Karen. Barkhilaf Angrezon ke aadat ke Japani afsaran aur sipahi yahan ke logon se aazadi se ke saath dostana suluk kar rahe hain. Baaza uqat ghalat fahmiyaan bhi zahur men aati hain jiski wajah sirf yeh hai ki hum ek dusre ko apna matlab nahin samjha sakte yanni hum Japani zabaan aur Japani log hamariza baan nahin jante.

Is taklif ko rafa karne ke liye yeh kittab shaaya ki gai hai iske mukammal hone ka daawa to nahin kiya ja sakta lekin is se yeh sahuuliyat zurur ho jaegi ke kisi had tak hum ek dusre ko apna matlab ba asaani samjjhange.

Is baat ko madde nazar rakhte hue is kittab ki saiiz choti rakhi gai hai ta ke yeh jeb men aasake aur bawakte zururat istemal kiya jaa sake". (From a Regime of Fears and Tears; p39)

In Ross Island, KHAIHO SHIONEN JUKU, a Japanese school was set up to teach Japanese language to some hundred local students from almost all walks of life. In the first batch there were B.R. Sharma, Richardson, Mustaq Ali, Hari Narayan, Sadique Ali, Jagan Singh, Daryao Singh, Hari Kishen, Master Sukh Singh, Inayat Ali etc. After being taught the working knowledge in spoken Japanese, and primary course in written Japanese, they were attached to the Japanese officers in different places as interpreters. They were given food and a good salary which naturally inspired others to learn Japanese in order to have favour of the Japanese authorities. Later Shyamnath Babu became a teacher of the Japanese school at Ross Island.

In due course the Japanese school at Ross Island was shifted to Bamboo Flat to enable the villagers to learn the language so that the Japanese could have direct link with a greater section of people.

This way, the Japanese fulfilled two purposes, first to have interpreters for easy communications and second to create a faction among the islanders by favouring a section of people who would do the job to spy upon the public.

For general education, a government school was run at Quarry Hill by the Japanese. All subjects except English were taught there. Moti Ram was the Headmaster and the teachers were Brojendra Lall Saha, Abdul Gafoor, Kesar Dass, Paras Ram, Imdad Ali, Abdul Jalil, Ramnarayan etc.

On 28 Sept. 1942, Master Abdul Gafoor was ordered by the Japanese to attend and inspect schools. Children were taught the national song of Japan. They started to learn Japanese, play Japanese games and count Japani digits – 'Ichi (one), Ni, Shan, Sho, Go, Ruko, Sichi, Hachi, Kyn-ju, Harnai-jo'. Due to the lucidity the old people still remember Japanese and even the children due to its melodious rhythm, recited abusive words of Japanese such as 'Wagoiri Khunoiri'.

But with the increase of spying and bombing, all English knowing teachers and educated persons were arrested, tortured and even killed. Among them Pratapnath, an English teacher of the high school and Abdul Jalil were killed.

Notes

1. Compton Mackenzie : 'All over The Places', p132
2. Peter Ward Fay : 'The Forgotten Army', p75
3. B.B.Lall : He was 12 years old when the Japanese Forces occupaied the islands in March, 1942. An active member of the Local Born Association, retired as Deputy Education Officer in 1988.
4. *Andaman Shimbun* : A news bulletin, published by the Japanese authorities from Port Blair since their occupation.
5. Deputy Commissioner under The Japanese Administration, Editor, Andaman Shimbun. He welcomed Netaji Subhash at the then Browing Club as he was then the President of Indian Independence League. But after Netaji's departure, he was arrested and subjected to sever tortures by the Japanese. After reoccupation, he was tried by the British for collaborating with the Japanese but acquitted.
6. R.L.Avasthi, I.N.A., joined the British Govt. as Wireless Operator.
7. Dr. Ramanand – Senior Medical Officer, Ross Hospital.

7 Nicobar Under the Japanese Occupation

Prior to Japanese Rule

'Car Nicobar' is by far a modern name for the island which was earlier known by many a name as 'Carecusaga', 'Carenicubar', 'Cornalcabar', 'Car Nicubar' etc.besides its ancient names like 'Nagabalus' or 'Naccavarum'.

After the exploits of the Nicobars done by the Portuguese in the 16th Century, a Danish East India Company ventured to settle in these islands in 1660 A.D. from its base in Tranquebar at the Malabar Coast of India in order to plunder the forest and marine products of these islands. After the futile attempts of the Danes, the Austrians and other Europeans made occasional attempts but failed to settle. Of all attempts to colonize the Nicobars, the Portuguese were the pioneer whereas only the British became successful to exercise their power commercially and politically.

On 16 April, 1869, Car Nicobar along with other islands was brought under the British control with its Headquarters at Port Blair by a formal proclamation.[1] During the British regime, there was no untoward incident and the Nicobarese being simple and peace-loving, were never involved into any conflict with the British. At the outbreak of the Second World War, the picture changed completely. During 1941-42, after the capitulation of the British forces in Malaya and Burma, the Japanese easily occupied Port Blair on 23 March 1942.

The Japanese Occupation Forces took only three months to set right the civil administration and enforce military rule all over the Andaman islands. They did not spare even the aborigines. For the sake of their safe movements in the jungle and to undertake the construction work of bunkers and pillboxes around the coast without impediments, the Japanese even dropped bombs in the Jarawas infested areas causing severe damage to their inhabitations. After exercising their rule all over the Andamans, the Japanese cast their onerous attention towards the tribal areas in the Nicobars.

Encounter with the Japanese

Prior to evacuation, the British made the Nicobarese aware of the evil nature of the Japanese and entrusted Richardson with the duties of the Assistant Commissioner. On the morning of 4 July 1942, a strange cruiser with a Japanese flag on it was seen approaching the coast between Arong and Mus villages. The cruiser anchored off Mus village. The first landing party consisting of fully armed contingent of Japanese soldiers along with a few officers with swords drawn in their hands came ashore in two boats. The occupation forces went round Car Nicobar Island and took into custody most of the headmen of the villages along with Richardson who was the most revered personality among the Nicobarese. He has left behind important notes in his diary which is considered as an authentic source of information about the Japanese reign of terror in these islands.

The Commanding Officer of the Japanese forces first enquired of Mr. Scott[2] and other Officers. He further queried of any British documents left by them before evacuation. On being ensured of no trace of Scott or any other British and absence of any documents, the Japanese erected a post with some scribblings in Japanese on it to declare their occupation of the islands. Then in a short speech, he informed that the Andaman and Nicobar Islands were now under their occupation and the former British Chief Commissioner, Waterfall was arrested and remanded as a prisoner of war. Major Byrd was put to death and others were arrested. The islanders were now free from the British yoke. The Nicobarese would be awarded with the same freedom if they co-operated.

Afterwards on being summoned, Richardson informed them that there was no Radio set in the islands and the gun owned only by him had already been seized.

Though the Japanese had landed on Car Nicobar first on 4 July 1942 and went back after a brief sojourn, they started their activities only after 2 August, 1942, when they came back for the second time with men and materials. Again on 24 December, 1942, two large launches, each towing a lighter boat brought in huge supplies of military goods, trucks, tanks, guns and food items to start preliminaries for the defence.

What really made the Japanese worried, was the absence of an airstrip at Port Blair. So soon after landing, the Japanese chalked out their strategy for the defence of their establishments and to accelerate their offensive manoeuvre. On priority basis they took up the construction work of an airstrip at Lambaline which was left undone by the British. At Car Nicobar they pressed their demand for the supply of the Nicobari labourers. Richardson discussed the matter with all other headmen. As they had no other go but to meet the Japanese demand to escape their vengeance, on 4 January, 1943, five hundred Nicobarese along with 300 pigs, cattle etc. were sent to Port Blair to appease the Japanese. Within three months, another batch of 500 men was brought to Port Blair where they were forced to work day and night to construct the airstrip in exchange of a bowl of rice. Eventually many of them died of bestial torture and starvation.

On 4 August, 1943, Captain Ueda arrived at Malacca with a naval party of two hundred strong to undertake the construction work of an airstrip at Car Nicobar on war footing. Richardson, then Chief Captain was instructed to extend all sorts of help and almost 1000 Nicobarese were engaged in the construction of a jetty at Malacca which was completed at a record time of four weeks only. Now, it was possible for the Japanese to disembark and store a huge quantity of military equipments for elaborate defence excellence. In due course, a strength of 1000 Japanese soldiers, almost equal to the total population of the Island was stationed in the coastal barracks and the area was declared prohibited for the islanders, so they had to move into the interior parts of the Island.

Era of Reign of Terror

From the very beginning the Nicobarese were submissive and never disobeyed the orders of the Japanese authorities but the saddest part of the episode was that inspite of their submission, they were subjected to inhuman torture and exploitation. While there was severe scarcity of food and other commodities, for their hard labour, they were paid only with paper money printed by the Japanese, which really had no exchange value.

The situation was worsened when on 3 September, 1943, two Allied planes pounded a Japanese ship, anchored off Malacca and sank it. Richardson described this incident in his memoirs as the beginning of Japanese reign of terror at Car Nicobar.

As the frequency of raids increased, the Japanese became more and more hostile and vindictive. They assumed what had happened at Port Blair concerning espionage, presently repeated at Car Nicobar.

At the beginning, they tried to brainwash the people by infusing hatred against the British in order to arouse fellow feeling for the Japanese as the saviour and thence systematic process of indoctrination began. All the local people were directed to assemble at the playground of Mus and take oath of allegiance to the Emperor of Nippon. Lieutenant Sumi being the Civil Administrator for the Nicobars would address the people every Sunday to motivate them in favour of the Japanese.

Besides brainwashing, the Japanese took measures to intimidate the people. Earlier they recruited the Nicobarese for all sorts of construction works and thus deprived the island of her able-bodied men. All the English-knowing prominent Nicobarese including Dr. Jones were arrested. All the headmen were asked to surrender the Union Jacks. Every one obeyed the order except the captain of Arong who failed to show the place where he had hidden the flag so he was mercilessly killed. Thus, he became the first victim of the Japanese vengeance. The muslim traders, who were very much enthusiastic to welcome the Japanese as their saviours too, could not escape the torture of the saviours. Most of them were marauded and many of them were put to expulsion or execution.

The more the air raids increased, the more the Japanese became furious and hostile for the spying. As Malacca was found more secured, it was decided to shift the Headquarters of Captain Ueda from Mus to Malacca. Forcibly the Nicobarese were engaged to construction works of roads, barracks, hut, trenches and bunkers. Even the sick were not spared. A serious patient of pneumonia was beaten mercilessly and forced to work and eventually he expired. But this had no impact on the heinous attitude of the Japanese and brought no change in their behaviour.

On 2 October, 1944, there was another incident of bombardment by the Allied Air Force and twenty six people, mostly civilians were killed. Of course, one of the bombers was hit by the Japanese anti-aircraft guns and wreckage of the plane with the body of the dead pilot was found strewn near Perka village.

Next day before dawn, there was a massive air-attack by the Allies over Mus and Lapati. The people of far off villages were terrified to hear the thunders of the bombing and dumbfounded to see the sky overcast with the volleys of fire and coils of smoke. It was so tumultuous that every one became terror-stricken. The attack caused immense damage. Arms-depot at Lapati was totally blasted. Most of the buildings including the Mus Hospital were badly ruined. What made the thing worst was that the Japanese became more revengeful and bestial.

All the headmen and other influential persons including the Chief Headman, Richardson were rounded up and dumped in a concentration camp at Tamaloo under strict vigilance of armed guards. All the detenues were forced to build air-raid shelters and trenches. With the increase of air raids, a new concentration camp was built in the deep forest at the centre of the Island. Wells were also dug to supply drinking water.

During July 1945, the Allied air–raids were more frequent and made the Japanese more ferocious. Liquidation started and people were dragged out of the concentration camp in batches after short intervals to meet the end. Among the dead, there were most of the family members of Richardson i.e. his son, son-in-law, brother-in-law, his nephew and others. It is suspected that more than a hundred Nicobarese, mostly Christians were killed by the Japanese on mere suspicion. As to the information, they were twelve from Port Blair, two from Teressa, one from Nancowry and ninety from Car Nicobar. Dr. Jones who came from Malabar and settled at Car Nicobar, also met with the same fate while he was called in to translate some leaf-lets dropped by the Allied planes but he was never seen alive.

Time and again Richardson was summoned to the Japanese Headquarters and interrogated round the clock either to confess his involvement in the spying activities or to disclose the whereabouts of the British rockets or important documents etc. Though he was innocent, his name was at the top of the hit list. Among others in the list, there were Abednego, Harry Lawrence and Edward Kuchat.

Life at Car Nicobar, was very much uncertain and nobody knew when his turn would come. Finally, the death knell rang for Richardson. He along with a few others was brought to the Headquarters. Every body felt for them as it seemed their last journey. But by the grace of God, the end was different. Instead of facing the firing squad, they were asked to sit down, offered cigarettes and informed that His Excellency, the Emperor of Japan had become very kind to declare the end of war and as a sign of magnanimity of His Highness, Richardson and others were pardoned.

Reoccupation

After the surrender of Japan, the British Forces reoccupied Car Nicobar on 22 October, 1945 at 11am. On that day, everybody on the shore was overjoyed to find Mr. R.W. Scott, the former Assistant Commissioner of the Nicobars coming out of the British naval ship to greet them. In his memoirs, Richardson writes, "To our great surprise Mr. R.W. Scott, our former Asst. Commissioner stepped out. For a few seconds both of us could not utter a single word. Instead tears were rolling down from our eyes. There was joy at being liberated mingled with sorrow for those no longer with us."

After reoccupation, Compton Mackenzie, distinguished writer of war history visited Car Nicobar and observed, "At first the invaders (Japanese) behaved fairly well but when we (the Allied) started bombing the airstrips, they indulged in the same spy scare as on the Andamans. In all seventy five Nicobarese were tortured to death."

Among others who survived of the reign of terror, besides Richardson, there were Abednego, Ledie, Peter, Hussen, Moosa Ali and Hachia of Car Nicobar; Wlias, Mongo, Koiny and Moitrat of Nancowry. They were sent to Singapore to give evidences in the War Prisoner Trials against the sixteen Japanese Officers for their crime. As to their evidences six of the officers were sentenced to death and Capt. Ueda, Lt. Sumi and Miniyuki were pronounced imprisonment for various terms.

Consequences

Though the diabolical era of the Japanese rule ended with the surrender of Japan, it had some indirect impact on the social and economic system of the Nicobarese.

The Japanese first introduced bicycles as the premier conveyance, best suited to the natural set-up of Car Nicobar. Now-a-days, bicycle is an essential household item in all Nicobari families.

During the Japanese rule, what affected miserably was the economy of the Nicobars. Earlier barter was the only mode of transaction. Copra and betel nuts being the only source of income, could mitigate the demands of daily life through exchange of commodities. But the Japanese introduced the paper currency against the payment of labour or goods they seized so for the first time the people got used to currency system and learnt to spend money to procure goods whatever available. Thus, in due course the money economy has been in vogue among the Nicobarese

Earlier they were exploited by the dishonest traders who taking advantage of barter system used to deprive the Nicobarese of the real value of copra and betel nut. During the Japanese regime, all these traders were treated with expulsion or execution. Even during the British rule, they were not allowed to settle again in the Nicobars. Thus, the Nicobarese got rid of these dishonest traders and became conscious of the value of their products in terms of money. After independence, *Penam Henang* or village co-operatives were formed to boost up economy and protect the interest of the Nicobarese from the credit-based exploitation of the old traders.

Another incident occurred during the Japanese days proved a boon in disguise in the life of the Nicobarese. To face the Japanese tyranny, all the village-headmen formed into an informal group and accepted the Headman of Big Lapati village as the Chief Headman of entire Car Nicobar with a view to bearing with the Japanese atrocities in a body. Thus, the Japanese unknowingly generated a feeling of unity and oneness among the Nicobarese.

Notes

1. Selection from 'Records of the Government of India', Vol. LXVII papers relating to the Nicobar Islands, Calcutta 1858
2. Mr. R.W.Scott, Assistant Commissioner of Car Nicobar, left the Island on the eve of evacuation.

8 Visit of Netaji and its Impact

Subhash, the Springing Tiger

To recall the magnanimity and majestic personality of Subhash Chandra Bose, it is better to quote a few lines uttered by Col. Shah Nawaj Khan standing on the dock on 5 November, 1945 at the trial against the officers of I.N.A. at Red Fort. Shah Nawaz Khan very boldly expressed his belief, "It will not be wrong to say that I was hypnotized by his (Subhash's) personality and his speeches. He placed the true picture of India before us and for the first time in my life, I saw India through the eyes of an Indian. I was most impressed by his selflessness, his absolute devotion to our country, his frankness and his refusal to bow before the Japanese wishes".[1]

Subhash Chandra Bose was indeed a great personality and in all distinctiveness, he was a class by himself. He was a unique phenomenon of twentieth century India. To win freedom was only and ultimate aim of his life. Studying the history, he realized that salvation of motherland would be achieved only through the freedom struggle, not merely from within but valiantly from without so that the very basis of British imperialism would be shaken and uprooted. All-through his life, he dreamt for freedom, struggled for freedom and laid down his life for freedom.

He was really a seer by spirit and gallant fighter in action. He was a dreamer in practice and philanthrope in vision. He was committed to an ideal task of thoughts and deeds. He met General Tojo, Premier of Japan on 10 June, 1943 and explained his intentions and expectations. Tojo was so moved and convinced that on 16 June, Netaji was invited to pay a visit to the Diet. Premier General Tojo asserted in the Diet, "Japan is firmly resolved to extend all means in order to help, to expel and eliminate from India the Aglo-Saxon influences which are the enemy of the Indian people... to enable India to achieve full independence in the true sense of the term."[2]

Only after the assurance of help from Japan in the war of independence and two days after his return from Tokyo, on 4 July, 1943 Subhash formally received the Presidency of the Indian Independence League. Later, on 21 October 1943, he became the Head of the State, Prime Minister and Supreme Commander of the Army of the Provisional Government of Free India at Singapore. He was the first to take the Oath, " In the name of God, I take this sacred oath that to liberate India and the thirty eight crores of my countrymen, I, Subhash Chandra Bose, will continue the sacred war of freedom till the last breath of my life."[3]

At the installation ceremony of the Provisional Government and Indian National Army in Singapore, Subhash addressed his fellow armymen, "Let your battle cry be, 'to Delhi, to Delhi', How many of us will survive this war of freedom, I do not know. But I do know this that we shall ultimately win and our task will not end until our surviving heroes hold with the victory parade on another grave yard of British empire— the Lal Kila or Red Fortress of ancient Delhi"[4].

Long back in November, 1943, a Greater East Asia Conference was convened in Tokyo. The representatives of different Governments installed by Japanese authorities in their occupied territories—Burma, Malaya, East Indies, Philippines and Manchuria were to attend the conference. In November 1943 Subhash Chandra Bose was invited to attend as Head of Azad Hind Government which had been formed on 29 October, 1943 at Singapore, but he was bold enough to refuse as he was not the Head of any free state or territory.

In *"The War of the Springing Tiger"*, Gerrarred H.Carr observes, "Netaji met Prime Minister Tojo and pleaded about the transfer of Andaman & Nicobar Islands but he (Tojo) did not like the idea. At that time Tojo had enough problems and was not willing to invite trouble with the Admirals."

Subhash was a great statesman and dominating personality. He met with Hitler, Mussolini and Premier General Hideki Tojo at par the equal status enjoying the highest protocol maintained by his counterparts. When he refused to attend the conference, Tojo realized the consequences of his refusal and immediately on 6 November, 1943, he had to announce in the Greater East Asia Conference that the Imperial Government of Japan would shortly be ready to place the islands under the jurisdiction of the Azad Hind Government as the initial evidence of her readiness to help in India's struggle for independence. Situation was so delicate that Japan had to take decision to hand over the islands in order to give Subhas the status of the Head of a Free Indian Province so that he could be treated at par with the other Heads of Governments in South East Asia.[5]

In Greater East Asia Conference, Tojo concluded,"………I would like to announce here and now that Japan is ready to transfer the Andaman Islands to the Provisional Govt. of Free India,"[6].

Netaji expressed his happiness over the Japan Government's decision to transfer the islands to Azad Hind Government as "these islands stood as a symbolic hell of British tyranny, where hundreds of freedom fighters had been treated with inhuman tortures." He further said "The return to the Provisional Government of Free India of the Andaman and Nicobar Islands which are the first part of India to be liberated by Japanese Army from British rule, has infused a new hope and great confidence into our fight for freedom".[7]

Philip Mason has rightly remarked in his book, *A Matter of Honour*, "Subhash Bose… was a man of burning enthusiasm".

Really he was and naturally he became jubilant when the Andaman and Nicobar Islands were handed over to the Provisional Government of Free India. It was not merely a handing over of an Indian state but a clear assertion of the existence of a true government having its own territory.

Itinerary of Netaji on 29 December 1943

As soon as the transfer of Indian Territory to Azad Hind Government was announced in the Diet, Netaji decided to visit these islands, the only territory his government could possess. On 29 December, 1943, accompanied by Ananda Mohon Sahay, Major Abid Hasan and other two officers of his government, Netaji arrived at the Lambaline Airport at 11.00 a.m. by a Japan's special bomber. He was accorded a ceremonial welcome and received by Admiral Ishikawa, the Commander-in-Chief of the Japanese Forces, Vice Admiral Teizo Hara, Civil Governor Jyochi Renusakai and other dignitaries. As to the protocol befitting to a Head of Government, he inspected a Guard of Honour given by the naval contingent. A selected group of local people and Indian officials stood in two rows to greet Netaji.[8] Then Admiral Ishikawa accompanied him to the residence of former British Chief Commissioner at Ross Island. The road from the airport to Aberdeen jetty where a launch was kept ready to carry Netaji and his staff to Ross Island, was lined up by men, women and children to welcome him.

Prior to the war, Ross Island was the seat of British Administration but after evacuation, it was deserted apprehending naval bombardment by the Japanese. Since Japanese invasion, Ross Island has been remaining uninhabited. Netaji spent three nights there in the official residence of former British Chief Commissioner and by the turn of the wheels of history, the residence of the imperialist British had become the official residence of the Head of Azad Hind Government.

Later describing his visit to the Islands, Subhash expressed his feeling, "During this visit, I and the members of my party had the unique experiences of our lives when we stood on the soil of Free India for the first time. It was an unforgettable event for us to see our National Tricolour Flag fluttering in the air over the former British Chief Commissioner's residence on Ross Island".[9]

Afterwards, he himself explained the emotion, "For Indians, the return of the Andamans represents the first territory to be liberated from British yoke. By the acquisition of this territory, the Provisional Government has now become a national entity in fact as well as in name".[10]

"The liberation of these islands has a symbolic significance because the Andaman Islands were used by the British as a prison for political prisoners. Most of the political prisoners sentenced to penal servitude for conspiracies to overthrow the British Government and there have been hundreds of them, were locked up in this island." He further said, "Like the Bastille in Paris, which was the first to be stormed in the French Revolution, setting free political prisoners, the Andamans where our patriots suffered are the first to be liberated in India's fight for independence but it is always the first piece of territory that has the most significance".[11]

The objective of Netaji's life was somewhat emotional as he all through dreamt for a 'Free India' but he was staunchly practical as he raised a firebrand army, Azad Hind Fauj to strike at the very root of the British imperialism in order to achieve independence. His primary aim to visit Andaman was obviously sentimental. It was a pilgrimage for Netaji but the official objective was different.

It was to settle the formalities of handing over the territory. Japan Premier, Gen. Tojo said that for the duration of war, mutual agreements would have to be arrived at with regard to the defence and administration of these islands. So the official objective of Subhash's visit was to settle the process of transfer of administration of the islands from the Japanese authorities to the Azad Hind Government. On 29 December, 1943, at his official residence in Ross Island, the matter was formally discussed with Admiral Ishikawa, the Head of Japanese Administration in these islands. Both of them had an official meeting to settle the process of handing over the charges of local Administration.

In "*The Springing Tiger*", Major Hugh Toye writes, " the Admiral in agreeing the appointment of an Indian Chief Commissioner, told Bose that for cogent strategic reasons there would be no complete handover during the war, but that if the Commissioner was prepared to co-operate, some departments of civil administration could be transferred."

Subhash was wise enough to accept the deal to avoid confrontation with Japan on the eve of a long march to invade India. He knew it very well that the handing over of the islands to his government was just a beginning, not an end. To win freedom of whole India, not a part of it, was only the ultimate mission of his life. To cross the Stygian ferry, he only wanted to exploit the situation and not to disparage it. Col. G.S. Dhillon[12] has rightly remarked, "Netaji had a characteristic foresight of planning for the future".(Memoirs) This was the reason why Lt. Col. Loganathan, the designated Chief Commissioner for the AndaNico to work on behalf of the Azad Hind Government, could not take complete control of the Administration. Naturally, he tried to concentrate mainly towards Education, Production of food, Handicraft, Propaganda and Publicity, Civil Judicial works and Women's Welfare.

However, we should not forget that all these happened when the war was in full swing. Lt Col. Loganathan, later promoted to the rank of Major General was too prudent to mistake what could have been the consequences if he had insisted for more power or total control over the islands whose defence was completely in the grip of Japan's military authorities for obvious reasons. Moreover, the I.N.A. was absolutely on war path as the Provisional Government had already declared war against Britain and America and the invasion to India seemed imminent. So Col. Loganathan knew it well that to be impetuous and wayward would only spoil the whole thing and the main intention of Ajad Hind Government would be foiled. Shri Avasthi has rightly observed, "An ordinary soldier of a conquering nation has more power and authority than a big officer of a conquered nation. My country should keep this point in mind when they criticize my boss and leader Netaji Subhash Chandra Bose for any commission or omission on his part.....".[13]

Obviously for security reasons, to follow protocol and to maintain decorum, the itinerary of Subhash was challked out by the Japanese Intelligence and his movement was always under strict vigil of the Japanese officers. Five young men who knew both English and Japanese, were engaged as interpreters cum attendants but they were strictly instructed not to talk to Subhash until and unless he himself talked to them. Hardly any of the local people particularly the English knowing ones dared approach Subhash as they were terribly frightened of being tortured at any time by the Japanese because the spy cases had already started and on the plea of interrogation, apprehension or execution was a common affair.

It is, therefore, doubtful whether Mushtaq Ali,[14] or any one of the attendants had any scope to whisper to Subhash that Diwan Singh was under terrible tortures being confined in the Cellular Jail. Iqbal Singh has mentioned such hearsays elaborately in his "The Andaman Story" without putting a question mark to why Mushtaq Ali had singled out the case of Diwan Singh alone while several hundreds of innocent islanders had been undergoing the same orgy of bloody persecution in the Cellular Jail. Suba Singh who accompanied Col. Loganathan rightly cast doubts on the authenticity of the statement made in the name of Mustaq Ali. Moreover, Ramakrishna who was the Deputy Commissioner in the Civil Administration under the Japanese authorities and the Chairman of the Indian Independence League of Andaman Branch at the time of Netaji's visit had never mentioned in his memories the name of Mustaq Ali or any one else for any inconspicuous dialogue with Netaji. As to the opinion of Smt. Shakuntala Sivram, "Mustaq Ali of Southpoint whose father and brother were in the Cellular Jail, was scared to say anything to Netaji"[15].

In his memoirs, Ramakrishna further writes, "It must be recorded here that Netaji, being a casual visitor who saw the Islands for the first time and who was quite unaware of the fact of torture and maltreatment meted out to the Indians on ground of espionage, took everything here as normal and never suspected that the Japan Officials could deliberately hoodwink him. Of good nature and of a lofty character himself he had no suspicion of Japan's behaviour".

In his "A Regime of Fears and Tears", B.B. Lall has never apprised of any person who ever met or muttered anything to Netaji. Hence accountability and credibility of such hearsays as mentioned by Iqbal Singh is always illusive and misleading and can never be granted as authentic fact.

However, on 29 December, 1943, a dinner was hosted by the Admiral in the guest house at Ross Island itself considering the safety and strain after his daylong weariness. Some of the Japan military personnels and Japan civil officers, along with a few Indians as the Heads of Departments attended the dinner party. Netaji was always surrounded by the Japanese, so no Indians could get a chance to whisper and Netaji in his magnanimity had never suspected any intrigue.

Itinerary on 30 December 1943

Next day on 30 December, Netaji had a hectic schedule. From Ramakrishna's memoirs, "A public meeting was arranged on the only *maidan of* Port Blair (Gymkhana on the seashore opposite to Ross Island) in which a large number of people were ordered to attend. Netaji came from Ross and reached the *maidan* in a ceremonial procession made up of Japan officers in a number of cars. On arrival, he went up the rostrum and unfurled the Indian National flag, the first ever hoisted on Indian Territory. The author (Ramakrishna) was the Chairman of the Andaman Branch of Indian Independence League, gave a welcome address and presented a purse of Rs. 10,000/-for the I.N.A. After which Netaji addressed the gathering".

A few lines more from *"A Regime of Fears and Tears"* of B.B. Lall, "He (Subhash) hoisted the Indian Tri-colour to the accompaniment of the Indian National Anthem *(Subh Sukh Chain Ki Barkha barse/ Bharat bhag hai ja ga,/ Punjab, Sindh, Gujarat, Maratha, Dravida/ Utkal, Banga Suraj Ban Kar jag par cham ke/ Bharat nam subha ga jaiya ho"*-sung in the tune of *'Jana Gana Mana'* without any alteration) by Kesar Dass[16] and party. He inspected the Guard of Honour presented by the Azad Hind Dal, the students of the Japanese School and the Japanese Armed Forces. He addressed the gathering and announced that the Imperial Government of Japan had ceded the Andaman and Nicobar Islands to the Azad Hind Government and also made a mention of his desire that arose in his heart to visit the Andaman Islands and to reside in the Chief Commissioner's bungalow and fly the Tri-Colour there and his desire had now cherished.[17]

Netaji addressed the people in Hindustani[18] which was adopted as the national language for Azad Hind Government. His towering personality and his heart–wrenching speech made the people overwhelmed and enlivened. He briefed them with a short account of his future plan and activities. He cleared his stand that the Japanese government was helping us with men, materials and military support to win India's freedom and it was a bounden duty of one and all Indians to work hard and be determined to sacrifice even their lives for the sake of motherland. Here, at Port Blair on the Gymkhana

Ground, Subhash uttered the historical oracle, 'Give me blood, I will give you independence', standing on the soil of 'Free India' with a Tri-Colour National Flag fluttering overhead. Like a springing tiger, looking at the Cellular Jail, the symbol of British tyranny, he being charged with emotions renamed Andaman as *'Shaheed'* and Nicobar as *'Swaraj'* amidst clamour and exaltation.

Hugh Toye writes in his book, *"The Springing Tiger"*, that it was at this meeting that Subhash received the freedom of Port Blair from the Japanese authorities.[19]

During the trial at the Red Fort, Delhi against the Indian National Army on 5 November, 1945, being cross-examined by the counsel for prosecution:

Lt. Col. Loganathan said : My authority for the statement that the Andaman and Nicobar Islands were ceded to the Provisional Government of Azad Hind is a broadcast from Tokyo. I cannot remember the exact wording of the broadcast.

Question: I put it to you that the Andamans and Nicobars were never ceded by the Japanese to the Provisional Government of Free India.

Loganathan: I would not have gone there if they had not been ceded.

Question: I put it to you that all they did was to promise to give them after the war was over.

Loganathan: No.

Subhash was sincerely eager to pay a visit to the Cellular Jail where numerous freedom fighters were incarcerated, mercilessly tortured and savagely treated. So to visit the jail seemed to him a journey to a divine place of pilgrimage. Being escorted by Japanese officers he visited the Cellular Jail and found there the actual convicts busy with their daily works such as cleaning, sweeping, planting and cooking. Though he was taken to one or two wings to have a look into the cells etc., he was intentionally kept away from the wing no. 6

where hundreds of innocent islanders, being accused of espionage were put to severe tortures.

To quote from Ramakrishna's memoirs-, "Alas! if he had seen persons whose skins were missing from thigh, scrotum, abdomen and chest, and could not wear any apparel, a few who had no flesh on their breeches, a few who had no skin on parts of their bodies, the result of burns by petrol, a few who could not walk straight, the result of constant kneeling on sticks, a few who had deep knife cuts all over the body sprinkled. Alas! If he had seen these with his own eyes!"

As to his itinerary arranged by the Japanese, he also visited nearby villages along with a number of Army and Naval officers who were shadowing him all the way. "At places he was made to meet some villagers in a crowd. Things were so arranged that he heard no one from the crowd but spoke himself to the crowd" (Ramakrishna).

On 30th evening, a dinner party was arranged on behalf of Subhash at his official residence, (the former British Chief Commissioner's Bungalow) in Ross Island. A number of Japanese Army and Navy Officers, Indian Officers as Heads of the Departments, the Executive members of the local Indian Independence League and the members of the Peace Committee were invited. After the dinner, all came to the sitting room and Netaji was at the centre of discussion.

Though the Japanese Intelligence was out and out vigilant, Ramakrishna being the Chairman of the local Indian Independence League dared take a chance to request Subhash to visit the Headquarters of local branch of I.I.L and meet the members of the working committee. Ramakrishna writes, " Netaji readily accepted the invitation. He had a big heart and an open mind. He could not refuse the invitation of his own Independence League." He further writes, "The Japanese were visibly perturbed at the turn of the event. They never wished any one of the Indian community to speak to him in a rendezvous not dominated by them. They were perplexed momentarily but their ingenuity gave birth to a novel procedure to frustrate the disclosure of the actual facts."

Itinerary on December 31,1943

Next morning when Subhash arrived at Browning Club (later known as Netaji Club) at 8 am. escorted by Japanese officers to meet the members of working committee, the hall was found filled to its capacity by men, women, children obviously collected by the Japanese overnight. There was utter confusion. So the plan of Ramakrishna to get a chance to talk to Netaji privately was cunningly foiled by the Japanese. Even the members of the working committee could not enter into the hall and went astray. Amidst hue and cry, Ramakrishna, the Chairman of the local branch of Indian Independence League welcomed Netaji who addressed as usual but nothing was heard because of confusion. However, Ramakrishna somewhat managed to hand over a sum of Rs.5000/-on behalf of the citizens of Port Blair to Subhash as a token of integrity to the Azad Hind Government. To bid him farewell, Ramakrishna requested him to take over the charge of the islands as early as possible and Netaji conceded to. Netaji was really moved on listenting to the national anthem sung by Kesar Das and honoured him with two ten rupee notes as a gesture of good will for the islands. He still preserves the two notes as the most precious gift in his life.

As to the programme, Netaji was to leave Port Blair on 31 December, 1943 but apprehending Allied air attack, his journey was postponed. He had to spend altogether three nights in Andaman and left for Singapore at dawn of the New Year's Day of 1944. During his sojourn in Andaman, the Japanese did not take any risk to let the people talk to him and tried their best so that Netaji might not get any hint of the real state of affairs prevailing in these Islands. In the name of security, he was always surrounded by the Japan military personnels and men of their Intelligence Department were so vigilant that no one was able to whisper to Netaji alone or report their grievances secretly.

But Subhash was a superman of superb intuition to apprehend everything. Though the Japanese were successful to forestall every means to prevent Netaji of getting a clue of the paradigm of atrocities inflicted to the innocents by the Japanese authorities, yet their unusual eagerness and meddlesome alertness made Netaji suspicious. Last day after witnessing the chaotic situation inside the hall of the Browning Club, it might have induced Subhash to conceive of something wrong going on there. Probably it was the reason of his quick consent to the request of Ramakrishna to make arrangement for early taking over the charge of administration of the islands from the Japanese.

Role of Loganathan Commission

By the close of 1943, the war scenario took a sudden turn and the Allied Forces went on for total mobilization in the South East Asia after their tremendous success in the Pacific Operation. Though Subhash was awfully busy in his manoeuvre strategy, he did not forget his commitment. He appointed Col. A.D. Loganathan, the Chief Commissioner of the Bay Islands. He was briefed by Netaji and directed to submit reports regularly. On 22 February, 1944 Col. Loganathan along with four INA officers—Major Mansoor Ali Alvi, Sub-Lieutenant Mohd. Iqbal, Lieutenant Suba Singh and stenographer Srinivasan arrived at Lambaline airport, where they were accorded a ceremonial welcome by the Japanese authorities.

During his trial at the Red Fort, Lt. Col. Loganatham said, "When I was sent by Subhash Chandra Bose to the Andaman and Nicobar Islands, a letter of authority was given to me. The original letter given by the Japanese Foreign Office to the Head of the State, Subhash Chandra Bose, was handed over to me to be taken with me to the Andamans and kept in my file in the Andamans. I was the Chief Commissioner of the Andamans. The Governor was to be appointed after taking over all the departments. .....

He further said,

"Verbal instructions were given to me before I went to the Andamans by Subhash Chandra Bose as to what I was to do there. The instructions were, consistent with the local difficulties, I should as soon as possible, take over the whole of the Islands. That was all. I made reports to Subhash Chandra Bose once a month.

Refreshing my memory from my diary which I kept at the time, I can state that the date of the taking over ceremony in the Andamans was the 21st. March, 1944"

Considering the war situation, total control of the administration was not handed over to Col. Loganathan. In reality, the Japanese military authorities were not ready to give away the full charge of administration to him. In an article, a correspondent of the *Hindusthan Times,* who visited Port Blair just after the reoccupation, writes on 17 October, 1945, " He (Loganathan) was told by the Japan authorities to learn the work during the first year and study the local conditions before he was given full powers of his office."

Hence, before assuming effective powers of his office, during the first year, his fellow officers dedicated themselves to deal with the following sectors.

(a) Education (b) Production of food– agriculture.
(c) Civil Supplies (d) Propaganda and publicity
(e) Civil Judicial works, (f) Women's welfare

During his trial at the Red Fort, Delhi, Loganathan was further asked by the Counsel for prosecution –

Question: 'I put it to you that they (Japanese) said that for the duration of the war they would only transfer such deptts. as did not interfere with the defence of the islands.'

Loganathan answered: That is true

Question: I put it to you that the only department which was completely handed over to you was the Education Department.

Loganathan: The only department I took over, was the Education Department.

Question: Did you refuse to take over the other departments?

Loganathan: If the Police Department was not handed over to me, I was not prepared to take over the other departments.

Question: The Police Department was not infact handed over.

Loganathan: Up to the time I left, the Police Department was not handed over.

Question: I put it to you that the other departments were also not handed over.

Loganathan: I refused to take over the other departments."

Afterwards they were allowed to comment or suggest on the activities of Jail and Police Department.

On 21 March, 1944, the Headquarters of the Civil Administration of the Azad Hind Government was established in the house of Pratap Nath Nag near the Gurudwara, presently known as Dr. Diwan Singh Gurudwara at Aberdeen Bazar. Notwithstanding Japanese aversion, Loganathan and his staff devoted themselves to do whatever they could for the welfare of the people. Major Alvi was In-charge of Education Department and tried to give military training to the youngsters under the banner of the Indian National Army. Lt. Suba Singh was to look after the general administration and Sub-Lt. Iqbal was entrusted with the duties to look into the matters pertaining to Jail, Police and Judiciary. Srinivasan was to attend the Chief Commissioner as Secretary. Before assuming their duties, the formality of handing and taking over charge was performed.

B.B. Lall writes in his *"A Reign of Fears and Tears"*, " An announcement to this effect was made by Colonel Loganathan that the Civil Administration stood transferred in the hands of the Azad Hind Government but the defence and means of communication will continue with the Japanese Military Authorities". (p61). Since their arrival, Loganathan and others were busy to set right their positions through negotiation with the Japanese authorities so they had to spend more time with Japanese personnels than on their intercourse with the local people. Naturally, at the beginning they were misunderstood by them and mistaken as the agents of the Japanese but within no time the people realized their faults and forshook their erroneous notion. They started coming to them to express their grievances and seek their advice. The staff of the Commission always tried to console them and inspire them to tolerate all hazards with the spirit of sacrifice and dedication to achieve the salvation of Mother India.

Social Services of the Commission

The Staff-members of the Commission took sincere interest in social service. *'Balak Sena'* was formed in the local schools with a view to imparting physical training and discipline. The volunteer corps of Indian National Army was raised in order to give military training to the local youths. In due course, the Commission could earn the confidence of the people. Whenever there was any sort of misrule and torture, the Commission tried to intervene and do whatever possible for the redress of the people. But the benevolent gesture of the members of the Commission and their intimacy with the people annoyed the Japanese authorities. It is said that the activities and movements of the members of the Commission were closely watched by the Thokuman, or Thokomohan housed in the Secretariat of the Chief Commissioner, used as a combined Headquarters for the Japanese Intelligence and Police. Even the people were marked whenever any of them would come to the office of the Commission or meet the members.

Hence, interference of the Japanese authorities even in the trifling matters marred the relation. In every case it was either turned down or denied until and unless it was pursued persistently. Naturally Col. Loganathan became disgusted and the relation with Japanese authorities deteriorated day by day.

Of course, the members of the Commission did not shun their duties. So long they were in the islands, they became the source of inspiration and consolation to the people. From the very beginning, Maj. Alvi being the In-charge of Education Deptt. tried to impart the ideology of nationalism and patriotism, and framed the syllabus accordingly, Besides the Boys school, a naval school was founded in Ross Island. Apart from formal education, rudimentary knowledge of Japanese was also taught. In the final examination of class tenth, held in April, 1944, and conducted by the Commission, eight students passed. On behalf of Azad Hind Government, a Certificate of Merit was given to each of them and they were absorbed in the public services as clerk, compounder and teacher.

The anniversary of the foundation day of Azad Hind Government was celebrated on 21 October, 1944, in the ground in front of the then Browning Club at Aberdeen and the occasion is still a scintillating memory of the islanders. As on 2 October, 1944, Chief Commissioner Col. Loganathan had already left for Singapore, Maj. Alvi hoisted the Tricolour National Flag and inspected a ceremonial Guard of Honour performed by the local contingent of the I.N.A. In the public meeting arranged in the club hall, Major Alvi reminded the people of the pledge of dedication and sacrifice, and asked them to bear with all sorts of sufferings and miseries until India, their motherland was free of British yoke. For the recreation, a cultural programme of folksongs and folk dances was held. On that day, the people had had the taste of freedom and enjoyed the fervour of entertainment.

Another social function was organized at the aegis of Lt. Suba Singh in February, 1945 to observe the harvesting ceremony. On that occasion, a farmers' meet was convened in which the Indian and the Burmese farmers got scopes to interact with the Japanese officers of *Miniseibu*. As a result of this convention, 'Grow more food' campaign got impetus with a view to making the island self–sufficient in food production. That day on behalf of the Azad Hind Government, a mid-day meal was offered to each and all participants. These are the simple instances to show how the islanders were involved into welfare activities and consoled through entertainments even during the reign of terror under Japanese overlordship.

When Subhash paid a three-day visit to Andaman, many innocent people including Diwan Singh were subjected to terrible torture in the dungeon cells of the Cellular Jail. Before the arrival of Loganathan, owing to inhuman treatment, Diwan Singh expired at the mid-night of 14 January, 1944 and other thirty three persons were shot dead and many were awarded long term of imprisonment.This was the second spy case.

How many succumbed to bestial tortures, are still unknown because their dead bodies were not handed over to their relatives.

Ramakrishna writes, "Netaji Subhash Chandra Bose's visit to the islands gave people certain amount of consolation. They considered that there was someone who would extend his protective hand in the hour of adversity. Soon after his departure came the Chief Commissioner and his staff from Singapore. People were now doubly assured by the progress of events and felt certain that the administration having come to the hands of Indians, conditions would improve and the reign of cruelty and terror would cease".

Tussels with the Japanese

However, in reality, the factors decried the expectation as during war, the combatant's policy is only to kill or be killed and in-between there is no way to contemplate. So the Japanese followed the natural rule of the battle and their every action was guided by the policy of defence or offence. They pursued the policy of extermination in order to survive themselves without caring a fig for humanity. To them ruthless elimination was the guiding principle for survival. Indeed, they paid least attention to the advice or suggestions of the Commission if it went against their principle.

To cite an example, it happened in the case of a few fishermen who used to go daily to catch fish by motor boat under guard of a Japanese sentry. One day suddenly an Allied submarine appeared and forced the motor boat to stop. The Japanese guard tried to escape by swimming but he was shot dead. Coming across another motor boat, the submarine disappeared and the fishermen were rescued. But they were arrested on suspicion that they had sent signal to the Allied submarine. Though Col. Loganathan intervened, all four or five fishermen were hanged inside the Jail but Sarang and his mate were released. This was the third spy case.

Indeed, since the Japanese ruled over the islands hardly for a year and with the beginning of the second year of their rule, espionage started and put the Japanese in despair and made them vindictive.

As the frequency of Allied air-raid increased, it had become a daily happening that the islands were bombed from the sky and shelled from the warships, so the movements of Japanese ships practically stopped. Naturally, they were infuriated and resorted to indiscriminate arrests and execution. In June, 1944, another group of islanders was arrested on charge of espionage. Detention, interrogation and inhuman tortures went on for two months. Col. Loganathan reacted and vehemently protested against such arrest without trial. This time the Japanese military authorities yielded to the demand and all were released. For the time being, the agonies of the Islanders were pacified and they heaved a sigh of relief. This was the fourth spy case.

Compton Mackenzie after scrutinising the whole situation opined, "I am glad to set on record that Col. Loganathan of the I.N.A.did his best to help the people in South Andaman".

But the war situation deteriorated speedily and took a serious turn in favour of the Allied Forçes throughout the littoral states. The sky came under the command of the Allied Air Force and the sea was possessively cruised by the Allied Navy. The Allied bombers pounced havoc by terrific bombardment and the Japanese Navy proved unmatched to combat with the Allied flotilla. Apprehending the landing of the enemy imminent and their further reinforcement or regular supply of food and war materials seemed impossible, the Japanese plunged in to take vengeance against the innocents. With the random arrests started the last spy case in September, 1944. The Japanese became desperate to squeeze out the information about the espionage so all the English knowing people were arrested and put into the torture chamber in the Cellular Jail. Horrible tales of bestiality leaked out stealthily from the jail and made the whole population terror stricken.

This pathetic incident created agony and tension, and the members of the Commission became very much worried. Indeed, they were on the horns of a dilemma. If the charges of espionage were genuine and based on facts, it really posed to be a threat to the security of the Japanese as well as the I.N.A. and at the same time, spying in favour of the British by their own countrymen was an ignominy for them. Moreover, just after assuming the office of the Chief Commissioner at Port Blair, a proclamation was issued by Subhash Chandra Bose as Supreme Commander of I.N.A. in March, 1944 to state, ".....if any of acts poses to undermine the intentions of the Provisional Government of Azad Hind and I.N.A. or of our Ally, the Nippon Army and any one dares to commit such acts......rebellious acts, acts of damaging or destroying, acts of spying etc. he shall be executed or severely punished......"

Hence, the officers of I.N.A. at Port Blair were very much perturbed and worried. On the contrary if the charge was found false and numerous innocent people were subjected to tortures for no fault of them, it must be stopped. Very soon they came to know that the whole matter was concocted and baseless. Col. Loganathan talked to the Japanese military authorities but all in vain. The innocent people still believed that the Commission would find out ways for their redress through Netaji Subhash who was to them an arch angel, the protector. But how to communicate with him?

During his trial at Red Fort, Delhi, Col.Loganathan said, "With regard to the investigation of spying, the Japanese had their own investigation. They did not object to our association but they would not completely hand over the investigation to us. We were not satisfied with the investigation which they were carrying out. ..... With regard to the statement that 'a few of them are said to have died of injuries developed while under trial', it means that they died under tortures while in custody. That was what I meant to convey. I could not put that in such clear terms because I said, my letters were being scrutinized. I wanted the report to reach the other end so I had to couch the terms and convey the meaning at the same time.... When I was in the Andamans, gross atrocities were committed by the Japanese in spy cases. I was aware of that but I was unable to remedy the matter. I wanted the Head of the State to know that every report was being scrutinized by the Japanese authorities. I came to know of it unofficially, not in writing. By the term, "Japanese methods" in my report I mean, gross atrocities......"

Ramakrishna writes, "The intervention of Netaji whose Headquarters were at Singapore, was practically impossible. The only means of communication were the occasional air service or the telegraph. Both these means of communication were in the hands of the Japanese. What reached Netaji and what reached here from him were known only to the Japanese. Complete black-out of the news of local suffering existed."

Withdrawal of Commission

So to overcome all these barriers, Col. Loganathan hit upon a plan and feigned acute illness. Treatment in the local hospital seemed undone and on 2 October, 1944 he was sent to Penang. In November, 1944, he submitted a report of his administration to Subhash who was very much shocked at the miserable plight of the people. Soon he met the Japanese Premier, General Tojo who agreed under duress to send a judge to try the undertrial prisoners in Andaman. This time the Japanese instead of aggrevating the situation chose to conciliate subtly and sent under pretention of a judge, a Lieutinent in the Japanese Navy from Singapore to try the case of espionage. In those trials the innocent people whose offence could not be proved, were set free in batches though the brutish tortures and savagery made them moribund and deadened. Some six hundred ill-fated victims including some women all except thirty three were released and rescued from the jaws of death.

The following write-up shows how much honour and regard the people of Andamans and Nicobars owe to Netaji:

Old Settlers of Andamans Owe A lot to Netaji

It was the most crucial period of the Japanese Occupation period —the months of September-Nov. 1944 when the third fabricated case of espionage was being tried by the Japanese Armed Forces—under the Japanese Lt. Governor known as Shriakan.

Thousands of persons almost all English knowing were intentionally involved —in order to get rid of all of them. As the Japanese could assert that those English knowing persons are loyal to the Britishers and will not come round to acknowledge the Japanese Govt.—besides they will get others even their own children biased opinion about the Japanese. So a plot was engineered known as 3rd case of espionage under the leadership of a very honest, sincere popular local Forest Officer, the then incharge of Forest Dept. during the Japanese period of occupation.

The trial process began in early September 1944—more than a thousand persons were involved. As a result there of 600-700 persons were sorted out to cause inhuman & unbearable tortures to make all of them admit the guilt to complete the enquiries conducted by the Japanese Armed Force.

That area of Cellular Jail having seven wings was packed up with under-trials a different world where cries a lamentations of the sufferers rented the air. It was dreaded as a Hell created in that period of Japanese regime. A lot of people succumbed to the inhuman tortures & died in Jail. My brother who was taken alongwith me for trial on the 25th Sept, 1944 could not bear the torture and died inside the Jail on the 29th Nov. 1944 when the undertrials were being set free. His dead body was not given to the parents—that was the most horrible memorable day of my life that my mother, a paralytic patient & other relatives could not make cries, weep and lament had managed to fly over to Bangkok to divulge the horrible news of preparation of the mass killing of 600-700 victims.

The chivalrous Netaji was moved in a very serious manner to exert at personal level for the safety of the lives of such a large number of innocent undertrials having admitted to the navy services, charges of espionage on account of inhuman tortures, and bodily pains. Even the family members were tortured to compel the victims to admit the guilt.

He had a trunk call with the then premier of Japan Gtn Togo—to convince him for retrial without inflicting inhuman tortures and bodily pains & other acts of atrocities.

The Japanese Premier was so very convinced, ordered for retrial, in fact deputed 4 persons from Tokyo to conduct retrial without inflicting tortures and bodily pains. All the undertrials denied the charges and were set free.

The Japanese Forces however kept 35 persons, who were all released at the announcement of peace in Sept 1945.

But for the timely intervention of the legendary patriot Netaji Subhash Chandra Bose, lot of permanent residents of Andamans, the generation of convicted patriots would have been certainly lost.

The ever grateful people of Andamans of older generation (a few of whom are still living) & their descendants & their offshoots who are now Doctors, Engineers, Advocates, Teachers, Lecturers, Forest Officers, Vety Officers, Clerks & Secretaries, for the loss of the dear relative to all the members of the family of the fear that the Japanese will cause harassment, difficulties & hardships as to how the news had reached us.

That the kind hearted Col. Lokanath, Chief Commissioner designate of I.N.A had tried his best along with other I.N.A. officers as not to inflict inhuman torture and bodily pains to extract confusion, was not heard. He etc. etc. feel so grateful to the real philanthropic action of the national Hero Netaji whose name is tagged with the history of geneological trace of descendants of old settlers, whose ancestors were deported to Andamans, just after the cessation of 1857, the first batch of the convicted patriots had arrived on 10th March, 1857.

The ever chivalrous and gallant Netaji had saved the lives of those worthy descendants of deported convicts of the participants of the national upheavals of 1857 had done really the most memorable act to remember Netaji as "A Living God" among the genuine Local population".

(The above write-up by Shri RC Biswas, Social Worker and A Senior Citizen aged 80 years, a resident of school line was published in *Daily Telegram*, Port Blair dated 23 January 2000).

The old people who were saved from the inevitable death, still carry the horrible memory of those abysmal days. One of them, Shri R.C. Biswas, an eyewitness expressed his feelings in a local newspaper on 14 February, 1981, "The islanders especially the intelligentsia of the local born community owe a special regard, love and respect for their best friend and saviour, the dynamic Netaji who was instrumental in saving them all from the intended mass massacre".

In the absence of Col. Loganathan, Major Alvi was In-charge of the Commission on behalf of the Azad Hind Government. Major Alvi was a dedicated I.N.A. officer. He tried to infuse in the hearts of the people the spirit of patriotism and wanted to redress their sufferings as far as possible but the Japanese military authorities were not allowing him to do anything of his own. Due to unwarranted intervention by the Japanese officers, the relations of bad blood between them developed. Moreover the war situation terribly deteriorated and the threat of impending landing of the Allied Forces compelled the Japanese to become more interested for their own defence. Meanwhile, in January 1945, the Allied blockade of the islands made their condition worst. Practically the movement of the Japanese ships was completely stopped and the acute shortage of food grains and other essential commodities pushed the islanders to the extent of starvation. The Japanese currency lost all its value and cloth, rice, wheat, sugar etc. were not available. The people had to subsist on roots, leaves, wild corns and pulses. Even to have a piece of sweet potato was a delicacy.

Heaping of sorrow upon sorrow, the disaster of Japan on the Burma front and misfortune of the Azad Hind Government forced to withdraw the Commission from Andaman on 22 July 1945. The members of the Commission left the islands only a few days before the atom bombs were dropped on Japan and bound her to surrender. Thus the islanders lost their only source of consolation with the departure of the officers of the Azad Hind Government. Their condition was now from the frying pan to fire.

Notes

1. "Famous and Historical Trials" by K.L.Gauba, Orient Paperback, New Delhi, p152
2. *'The Indian National Army' by Dr. Tilak Raj Sareen pub in* 'We Fought Together for Freedom', *edited by Ravi Dayal, Oxford, p 194*
3. "Netaji Subhash Chandra Bose and Indian War of Independence," by Dr. Satish Ch. Maikap, published by Punashcha, Kolkata, p 185.
4. Toye, H, "The Springing Tiger", p 92.
5. 'India's Struggle for Freedom' by Maj.Gen. A.C.Chatterjee, Chakraborty & Co., Kolkata.
6. Dr. Satish Ch. Maikap, "Netaji Subhash Chandra Bose and Indian War of Independence," Pub: Punashcha, p 209.
7. 'Netaji – A Pictorial Biography', Edited by S.K.Bose & B.N.Sinha, Ananda Publishers, Kolkata, 1979
8. Eye witness by senior citizens like Chandrabhan Singh even mentioned in his interview at A.I.R., Port Blair that at the airport people shouted in jubilation 'Netaji Ke Jai', 'Nippon, Nippon Jai' etc.
9. Bose, S.C. "The Indian Struggle,"p 401.
10. Ibid.
11. Ibid.
12. "From My Bones", Memoirs of Col. Gurbaksh Singh Dhillon of I.N.A., Aryan Books International, New Delhi, 1998
13. Raghuvansh Lal Avasthi, "At the Feet of Mother India", 1995, Varanasi, pp20.
14. Mustaq Ali learnt Japanese, served as an interpreter to Netaji. He was also put to jail and tortured along with Diwan Singh, Farzand Ali was his brother – Regarding Mustaq Ali's so called version, there is no written document or no mention in any of the memoirs of his contemporaries.

15. "Andaman Ke Itihas Ka Safar," Shakuntala Sivram, 2003, Confluence International, New Delhi, pp139.
16. Interview of Master Kesar Dass, broadcast in All India Radio, Port Blair. He mentioned the names who accompanied him in the chorus. They were Moti Ram, GovindRam, Abdul Aziz, Ram Ratan, Krishna Kumari, John Lobo etc.
17. "A Regime of Fears and Tears", by B.B.Lall, a retired Deputy Education Officer, born and brought up in these islands, an eye witness of the period of the Japanese Rule, Pub. Farsight, New Delhi, p54
18. "History of Freedom Movement in India," by Tara Chand, Vol – IV, p419 'Hindustani was adopted as the national language, Jai Hind as the form of greeting, the Congress tricolour as the national flag and Tagore's poem as the national anthem.
19. 'Famous and Historical Trials', by K.L.Gauba, Orient Paperback, New Delhi.

9 Reign of Terror and Torment

Sequel of Spy Cases

At the beginning, the Japanese were somewhat cordial to the islanders. They started schools to teach Japanese so that mutual understanding and communication could be made possible for the interest of all. The islanders were always dependent on the supply of food stuff from the mainland. The Japanese endeavoured to maintain the supply of rice, wheat, oil, ghee, potatoes, onions and all condiments, and made them available to the islanders, of course, in meager quantity. Every week, two shiploads of cargo were brought to Port Blair. People were engaged to all sorts of manual labour even loading and unloading of cargoes in exchange of money, which could be spent to procure food, cloth and other commodities from the government store. Japanese authorities seized all British currency and introduced paper currency in wide scale and circulation of the same was unrestricted. The "*Andaman Shimbun*" the only news bulletin was brought out under strict control by the Japanese to ventilate only the local news and Government circulars.

To express their friendly gesture and sympathy for the islanders, a Peace Committee was formed and the civil administration started functioning in co-operation with the local people. Even they would allow the islanders to hold public meetings to express their feelings of indignation against the British. One such meeting held on 16 August 1942, was presided over by the Japanese Governor H. Eguchi. The meeting ended by a closing song, '*Bande Matram*' sung by Kesar Dass (*Andaman Shimbun*, 18th August, 1942).

Paper Currency introduced by the Japanese military authorities in the Andaman & Nicobar Islands.

However, in all intents and purposes, the atmosphere was not adverse, if not, congenial and the islanders were getting accustomed to the changing phases. But the situation took a sudden turn vis-à-vis the interest of Japan when the Allies began offensive manoeuvre in these islands. Towards the close of 1942 bombardment of cargo ships was exercised extensively by the Allied Air Force and the Navy. The regular bombing by the Allied Forces carried out from 10 USAAF base in N.E.India by B–14 flying fortress and B-24 bombers and drastic shelling from cruising submarines stationed at Cylone on locations of strategic importance were so certain and shooting the targets was so accurate that Japanese military authorities became confused. How could the air or sea offensive be done perfectly at the right moment on specific targets until and unless the prior information was communicated to the Allied Forces? The Japanese became suspicious of the alterior motives of the islanders and were sure of the secret spy activities being conducted from this island. Further, they were able to intercept some radio signals being dispatched from this island but failed to locate the spot.

Hence, like Gestapo, Thokomohon, the Japanese Intelligence Department having hard-headed guys with bulldog tenacity, was pressed into action. They had already detailed dossiers of each and everyone so they could easily identify the English knowing persons who forthwith were arrested on the slightest pretext. Even the members of Peace Committee were not spared. The more the Japanese were hard-pressed and cargo movement seemed impossible, the more they became diabolic and vindictive.

Auzuma, a naval Warrant Officer under the Senior Intelligence Officer acted in the same manner as Eichmann did under the Command of Himmler. While H.Eguchi became the Governor of the territory, Auzuma was given free hand to work out 'the final solution' of the problem. Hence, with the accession of the new Governor, came the doomsday for the islanders. Like Geheime Staatspolizei (Gestapo) Auzuma hatched a plan to allure the people to work as his agents and supply information whatsoever needed by the Japanese. By "total solution of the Jewish question" what Goering had instructed Heydrich, was exercised in word and spirit by Auzuma in the islands by random arrests, inhuman torture and finally by liquidation.

In due course the Japanese started arrests even on the plea of signaling by torch lights or spot firing to guide the British agents or bombers. People under suspicion of sending signals or passing on messages to the British, were subjected to severe torture. By January 1943, some three hundred local people and Indian officials were arrested and kept behind the bar in the 6th wing of the Cellular Jail. The Japanese were very innovative in designing the novelty of torture considering the severity in savagery. They resorted to many varieties of tortures such as flogging, beating, kicking, blowing, water treatment, electric shocks, burning, piercing pins in the nails and many more horrendous ones.

Hashida, the Japanese officer was a beast in nature and the chief architect of bestial tortures. One of such inhuman tortures has been described by Smt. Shakuntala Sivram in her book, "*Andaman Ke Itihas Ka Safar*", p137 that Laxman Das Sankhwa, Tahasildar, was arrested on the charge of spying and tortured to death. All his skin was taken off. In spite of severe torture , he did not accept the charge of spying and while his wife was being stripped in front of him, he was compelled to agree to the charges and was beaten beastially to death. Motilal, the then Jail warder, was the witness.

No one knew what was going on inside the jail and due to persuasion of the Chief Commisioner, Loganathan all except seven persons were released on serious warning of dire consequences if they talked to any of the treatment they had undergone in the Jail.

First spy case

But on 30 March, 1943 those seven unfortunate souls including Gopal Krishna, Narayan Rao, Itter Singh, Khaliq, Dr. Surinder Nag, Suba Singh were taken to the sea-shore at Dugnabad behind the Jail and shot dead on the charge of spying. This is known as the first spy case.

Second spy case

This was the beginning of the process to eliminate the educated ones, particularly those who had worked under the British and could easily be detected as the British spies. Again in August, 1943, Ratan Chand and Faizal Hussain were arrested and tortured to confess. This way six hundred souls were subjected to bestial torture at the presence of their wives and children to squeeze out confession of their involvement in the espionage. On 23 October, 1943 Diwan Singh was arrested and tortured for three months and succumbed to injuries on 14 January, 1944. Similarly, Moti Ram, the first graduate of this territory and popular teacher died of inhuman torture in the jail. All these terrible incidents evinced to the sequence of the second spy case.

The situation became worst when the Allied Forces clamped blockade and made the movements of Japanese Cargo vessels carrying consumer goods and other war materials virtually impossible. Naturally, the Japanese realizing the impending danger causing serious scarcity of food stuff and deficiency in supply of arms and ammunition, became very furious and revengeful so they started the indiscriminate arrest of common people and inflicted brutal torture to make them confess of their involvement in spying. In reality the whole population was terror-stricken. No body knew when his turn would come. Life was so uncertain that during daytime very few dared stay back home. Usually to escape arrest and torture, they would flee the jungle.

This was the period while the civil administration was run by a civilian, Governor Renusakai and an incarnation of Devil. The Police Department was run by another civilian, Mitsubashi who himself was the *'Satan'*. Both of them served in Nanking under the Japanese Occupation and earned name to mastermind mayhem and perdition. All these circumstances led to the beginning of an unprecedented era— era of reign of terror and torment, which made the pages of the history of the Anda-Nico tarnished and ignominious.

Operation Baldhead, the Secret Mission

Though all the intentions behind the inhuman tortures to the innocent people were not easily perceptible, it was primarily the dreadful espionage of a few under the guidance of a daredevil, Denis McCarthy who was an officer of Indian Police and had served in these islands as the Commandant of Military Police before the Japanese invasion. He was so prescient and prudent that prior to evacuation, he took to his confidence the headman of Ferrargunj village and briefed him of the impending dangers that would befall upon them during the Japanese occupation. He further cleared what their role should be and made some secret arrangements for future communication. Fortunately, he was assigned with the secret service of going to Andaman with a view to collect tidings of great strategic importance for the Allied Forces.

In October 1942, Denis McCarthy was summoned by, R.W.Scott, Ex. Assistant Commissioner of Car Nicobar and asked his readiness of "going back to the Andaman Islands to make an appreciation of conditions there under the Japanese occupation." On his willingness, Mr. Scott took him to the Headquarters of Military Organizations where he was able to convince them that McCarthy was the right person to be selected as he had the necessary knowledge of local conditions and locations in details of the island. Moreover, he had contact with the local people who were in confidence of him.

Ultimately, Denis McCarthy was entrusted with the secret mission of espionage coded as "Operation Baldhead," in the Andamans. To do the job, he selected a party of five persons to accompany him in Andaman. They were Sergeant Dickens, a British wireless and telegraph operator, two ex-military policemen, Jamadar Habib Shah and Havildar Gyan Singh and two Ranchi forest workers, Havildar Joseph Bakla and his cousin Peter. The last four persons had already served in the Andamans prior to Japanese invasion. After selection, they had to undergo an intensive training first at Khadakvasla and later in Colombo for several weeks. Then they set out on a very dangerous but thrilling mission.

The whole operation was chalked out by Colonel Christopher Hudson who was responsible to complete all preparations for arming and equipping the party. It was arranged as such that they would travel from Colombo on board a Dutch submarine, the 0.24 whose Commander was De Vries to reach Andaman very secretly.

McCarthy writes, in his unpublished diary "The submarine journey was quiet and uneventful. From the third day, we stayed submerged in daylight. The fourth evening we made landfall and soon picked up out beach. After dark we made our landing, every thing going smoothly, thanks to the efficient handling by the Dutch crew and within half an hour all our equipments were ashore. By midnight the camp had been set up well back in the jungle, near but not on a stream."

On 18 January, 1943, the party for 'Operation Baldhead' was planted incognito to a place on the west coast of Middle Andaman, four miles south of Flat Island and seventy miles from Port Blair.

For transport, they had foot boats and for uniform, they had very dark green outfits. They were armed with stenguns and supplied with vegetarian rations. They were of course, carrying a net to catch fish and a 0.22 rifle with a silencer for pigeon catch. The vegetarian ration consisted mainly of dehydrated pumpkin. There were some good ghee, and excellent dehydrated potatoes but only enough for eight meals and a little rice. Some chocolates also per head, was a very welcome addition.

After a week's preparation, McCarthy along with Habib Shah and Joseph Bakla began the perilous and hazardous journey towards Port Blair. Travelling by night in two foot boats, McCarthy and Habib in the first one towing Joseph in the second with a fishing line, they were going down the west coast against the current and on the first night got down only five miles from Homfrey Strait. The second night they camped at the south of Spike Island on the site of an old Jarawa hut and later entered into Middle Strait. In this way they spent more than a week traversing the long trip through dense forest, fraught with dangers of being traced out by the Japanese patrol or spotted by the hostile *'Jarawas'*. Even the thorny bushes, intricate network of eerie creepers, plagued by leaches and centipedes, could not refrain them from trekking and treading.

McCarthy writes, "We hid the footboats half way up a hillside and camped for 24 hours. Then followed some days of rather dreary walking through the jungle, across step ridges. To avoid leaving traces, we did not cut a way through the thorns, which can be very exasperating. But worst were the leeches".

At last they reached near Ferrargunj village and at midnight, McCarthy and Habib entered the house of *Pradhan*. After a brief dialogue the headman informed them of "a great deal of conditions in the Andamans, but chiefly of the terrible brutality of the Japanese" and further said that Byrd was brutally killed, Ooty met the same fate and Waterfall was deported to face the trial of death. "They (Japanese) had continued with a string of summary execution, brutal assaults and rape." So the rule under the Japanese was no less than a reign of terror.

However, McCarthy could establish a spy network taking into confidence a few Burmese and also *Loka*, the Chief of the Great Andamanese tribe. He collected a lot of information and arranged a post-box, which was in a hole in the ground under a particular tree for secret communication.

McCarthy was optimistic about the rendezvous and went to a hill top (presently known as "single pahar" possibly 'signal pahar' near Port Mout village with his devices to send secret signals to the Allied Forces. McCarthy writes, "we sent a wireless/ telegraph signal back to Headquarters and were much cheered to see three Flying Fortresses came one day and bomb what we assumed were targets indicated by us and then return intact without any fighters in pursuit".

Thus the 'Operation Baldhead–I' was successful and the party except Habib Shah who died of a misfire from his own stengun, was brought back to Colombo on 29 March, 1943 by a submarine.

What McCarthy initiated, was pursued by another ex-policeman, Bakhshish Singh and other British Officers in successive operations, Baldhead II, III, IV, and V. Till the middle of 1944, all these operations went on successfully enabling the Allies to have information about the movements of Japanese fleet and the locations of their defence installations at Port Blair which were damaged or destroyed decisively by bombardment.

The Japanese were very worried of incessant bombing by the Allied Air Force on targets for certainty. They were sure that the local people were instrumental in sending out news of their establishments. They often intercepted messages sent out from the island but could not locate the place where the secret signals were being sent from. Naturally their wrath knew no bounds. Numerous military outposts were set up and hundreds of innocent people were tortured brutally to secure hints of spying.

The Japanese Intelligence went into all out hunts. A search party under Hayashi San, Head of the Intelligence, was sent to Shoalbay. Daryao Singh who studied in the Japanese School at Ross Island and worked as interpreter in the Intelligence Department, accompanied the search party which was though successful to spot an Allied submarine yet could neither catch the spies nor locate the exact place of transmissions. The search party even visited Havelock and found footprints and other articles that carried the proofs of the presence of strangers but the venture was just like a wild goose chase.

Indeed the work-outs of 'Operation Baldhead' were so perfect and astounding that the Allied Headquarters could get all information quickly and plunge into action instantly. Some examples can be cited here to show how speedily the Allied Headquarters reacted on time-bound messages of the team of 'Operation Baldhead'.

Through secret message and by aerial photographs, the Allied Headquarters came to know that the Japanese soldiers had taken shelter in the nearby villages and they happened to be easy targets of the Allied bombardment. More surprising was the attack of an Allied submarine on the Japanese soldiers while a large number of them were enjoying sea-baths at the Rangachung beach. In response to a message, all of a sudden the submarine surfaced and opened fire at close proximity killing hundreds of them.

The Japanese military authorities were shocked at the incident and surprised at the ready action of the submarine obviously in response to a secret message. The incident also exposed the miserable failure of the Japanese Intelligence. The Admiral of the defence however, accepted his responsibility and committed suicide. This incident made the Japanese more aggressive and vindictive.

In this atmosphere of distrust and dismay, most of the educated crawled, trade and business cringed, even the justice denied but the opportunists strutted. They grew new claws and blatantly exploited the situation to fulfil their lust and desire by coaxing and flattering, and became sycophants. Hence, the general public remained helpless and became victims of adverse situations. They never dared defy the Japanese. So to save their skin, they blasphemed and accused one another. This sinister situation led to indiscriminate arrests and culminated to the stigma of 'Operation Round – Ups'.

Operation Round–Ups

Indiscriminate arrest of innocent people was commonly known as 'round-up'. Because of the vicious circle of suspicion and denunciation, and with the help of the network engineered by Azuma, a Warrant Officer and Mitsubashi, the Chief of the Police a unique scheme for liquidation was conceived and set into action. The stooges who in order to get favour of the Japanese, were turned into tail wagging canines, took advantage to settle their old scores. One of such felons was Puskar Bagchi who was made the Chief of Intelligence by the Japanese as a reward for his dedication to the cause of the Emperor of Nippon. He left no mean ways to serve the Japanese. He hatched the whole plot against Byrd who was brutally tortured and killed.

Like Bagchi, there was Dr. Rama Nand who poisoned the mind of the Japanese against Dr. Diwan Singh who was the Chairman of Peace Committee and protested against all nefarious activities of Bagchi and others. He even refused to hand over all stocks of medicine for the exclusive use of the Japanese. When the Japanese became desperate to catch spies, the enemies of Diwan Singh tried to implicate him in spy cases so his movements were restricted.

Though indiscriminate arrest and torture were going on, death sentence was pronounced first on 30 March, 1943 against seven persons on charges of espionage. Among them Narayan Rao and Gopala Krishna who were the members of Civil Administration, were shot dead at Dugnabad. They were entangled with the first spy case.

List of persons sentenced to death in the 2nd Spy Case executed on 30.1.1944 submitted to the War Crimes Court at Singapore

1. Prem Shankar
2. Hira Singh
3. Bachan Singh
4. Ghulam Sarwar
5. Farzand Ali
6. Balwant Singh
7. Nur Hussain Malik
8. Rahalkar
9. Ratan Chand
10. Sher Singh
11. Raj Ratan Das
12. Nur Ahmed
13. Dalpat Ram
14. Abdul Jalil
15. Kauri Singh
16. Gujan Singh
17. Radha Kishan
18. Bakshis Singh
19. Mohar Singh
20. Sattyam Das
21. Gopal Singh
22. Mulk Raj
23. Mehma Singh
24. Harnam Singh
25. Jaswant Singh
26. Nur Inahi
27. Pokhar Singh
28. Karnail Singh
29. Anant Lal
30. Uttam Singh
31. Jai Ram
32. Sangara Singh
33. Lachman Das
34. Sahib Singh
35. Mir Alam
36. Basant Lal
37. Partab Nath
38. Daulat Ram
39. Gurdiyal Singh
40. Gobinda
41. Santok Singh
42. Paras Ram
43. Teja Singh

Now came the turn of Diwan Singh who was allegedly charged in connection with the second spy case. He along with some members of Indian Independence League as well as those of the Peace Committee was arrested and kept inside the Cellular Jail. At least six hundred people were there who underwent a long session of severe torture. Diwan Singh was taken to be the main culprit and made a pawn to bestial torture. His hair and beard were forcibly plucked still he did not confess and succumbed to the tortures on the night of 14 January, 1944.

He was tortured to death so brutally as it was only compared to the death of the great Danish Pastor – poet – playwright, Kaj Munk, the most beloved man in Scandinavia. After inhuman torture inflicted on him, his dead body was thrown on the road with a sign pinned to it, "Swine, you worked for Germany just the same". This was the sequel of Hitler's express order as reprisal for the Killing of Germans in Denmark.

But the events of torture did not cease and like Diwan Singh many a hundred innocent souls met with the same miserable end on different occasions.

On 30 January, 1944, forty four suspects of so called spy cases after prolonged torture inflicted on them were taken to a lonely place called Homfreygunj, 18 km. away from Port Blair, and gunned down. Their dead bodies were all dumped in a 'L' shaped trench dug by themselves. Presently this place has been sanctified with a martyrs column and glorified as '*Balidan Vedi*'. This incident reminds the same cruel treatment as applied to the Jews by the Germans, the accomplice *'de superior'* of the Axis nexus.

Alas! there were many more innocents who died a blood-curdling death inside the Cellular Jail being accused of espionage. And those 700 hungry people, who were allured with a bright dream of a new life having food and prosperity, were taken by boats near Havelock and awarded death by drowning on 4 August 1945. The harrowing fact of tortures and executions are described in the following pages.

Genocide leading to Mayhem

As to Ramakrishna, "... the occupation forces were fighting against an underground intelligence and espionage force. In a revengeful mood, the Japanese Military authorities, without the knowledge of the Japanese Government or the people there, resorted to cruelty and transgressed all canons of human behaviour".

The Japanese became diabolic with the inopportune condition of war. The more the debacle was imminent, the more they became violent. Even when the fall of the Nippon Empire appeared to be a reality and her supremacy dwindled to collapse, her fang still went on spitting venom over the wretched islanders.

To overcome the acute shortage of food grains, cloths, medicines, and even fish, fowl and goats, the Japanese raided the villages to collect food grains as much as they could in exchange of Japanese paper currency which had already lost its value. The Japanese issued ration cards only in the city to the adults but not in the villages, on the contrary, the villagers had to give 10% of their produce. What was left with the cursed people was either to live on the morsel of food or to die in starvation. As a result of malnutrition what followed next was the spread of diseases causing senility, infertility increase in mortality rate. The scarcity in medicine, mainly the live saving drugs, made the condition worst. For want of anaesthetic drugs, even the amputation was carried out without anaesthesia and it seemed a butcherly deed.

It is said that a man with his wife and a child was put to death for stealing a little of sugar. In another case, for possessing a little more rice, a man was burnt to death forcefully. The food crisis was so severe that even the members of the occupation forces suffered terribly and did not get minimal for their sustenance. To cope with the appalling shortage of food, the Japanese soldiers began to kill any four-footed animals that they happened to find moving on the ground. In no time, bulls and buffaloes were slaughtered and the cultivation suffered awfully due to the want of plough-animals. Even the milching cows were not spared.

All the able-bodied persons were forcibly put to hard labour to complete the construction work of the new airfield even during the threshing season affecting the cultivation severely.

In exchange of their labour, they were paid in war time currency which had no real exchange value. The situation was so miserable that a seer of rice was sold at rupees one hundred which was beyond the purchasing capacity even of the upper class. Ramakrishna writes, ".....the inflationary spiral caused by the occupation will be clear from the following prices-

One egg from Rs. 1/-to 2/-, one lb. of mutton from Rs.40/-to Rs.50/-, one lb. of fish from Rs.40/-to Rs.50/-, one lb. of vegetables from Rs.10/-to Rs.15/-, one half worn sari from 100/-to Rs.150/-, one shirt from Rs.200/-to Rs.400/-, one lb.of Gur from Rs. 50/-to Rs.100/-, one cigarette from Rs.5/-to Rs.10/"

The sea-shore being the prohibited area for the public, fish and salt were not easily available. Almost all the fair price shops were closed. Contemplating the battle at the threshold, no portion from the emergency food reserve was issued to the public. So, the people had to live on whatever the wild leaves and roots, fruits and throw–away grains available. At these moments of untold miseries, a very few persons like Harkishen Lall, in-charge of the Japanese grinding mill and Rammurthy of a government shop secretly helped their brethren of course, meagerly even at the risk of their lives.

To solve the acute food problem and to ensure the emergency reserve to be kept intact for their soldiers, the Japanese military authorities hit upon a very inhuman and heinous plan to eliminate the hungry souls to lesson the burden upon food supply, leaving only those who might be of any use for them. As a result of this cruel policy, hundreds of innocent people were shot dead and many of them including women and children were drowned in the sea.

The Japanese followed the same horrible policy of liquidation earlier incubated by the Gestapoes in Poland but that was more horrendous and terrible. However, the whole population of the islands was put under the thrashing thumb of Thokomohan, Japanese Intelligence Department under Hayashi San. The activities of Thokomohan can only be compared to those of Gestapoes. All men, women and children were enumerated and marked as educated or illiterate, able bodied or invalid. They were brought to the Headquarters in batches for interrogation or detention. Strict instruction was circulated that everybody must gather in a moment's notice whenever the Japanese authorities ordered.

'Nantai' another vicious wing under the cover of Naval Industries Department set up to produce household goods i.e., toothpaste, soap, etc., became active to keep a strict vigilance over the women folk by allotting some tailoring, needle and crochet works to them and the men were given some technical training in soap-making, candle making etc. in order to bring them in good book. They were issued identity cards and given salaries along with some favours of cigarettes, rice, sugar so that they would not have any suspicion over the Japanese cruel plan. Thus, the entire population were brought under the sinister control of Thokomohan. *'Nantai'* with its office at Biggiline in a barrack was manned by Japanese civil officers, but the Police and Jail departments were kept at the vigil of Thokuman. Earlier it was working underground but with the intensity of Allied attack and eventuality of terrible scarcity of food, it began to work openly with two nefarious motives, one to sustain a spell of terror and the other to work out the policy of elimination.

In order to eliminate, one day 60 to 70 old and invalid persons were rounded up and kept in isolation to try out their heinous plan. Loganathan came to know of the Japanese intention and somehow intimated Subhash who was terribly shocked and brought the matter immediately to the notice of the Japanese Government. As a result Admiral Ishikawa was withdrawn and new Commandant was posted. For the time being, the Japanese military authorities remained indolent but availed the first opportunity to work out their plan.

In June, 1945, when the concerted aerial bombing had become frequent and the landing of the Allied Forces posed a constant threat, some islanders dared escape stealthily in small boats or dingis. One day a boat carrying 30 men, women and children was caught and brought back. On the shore they were tied to trees and killed instantly in front of other people.

Actually the Japanese military authorities had become very much infuriated as their Intelligence failed to detect the location of espionage. Frequently, they intercepted the secret wireless messages but could not identify the persons who were involved in the spying job or locate the site where the radio messages were being dispatched secretly from. The consequences were terrible as the Allied bombers hit the targets very perfectly. So they spent no more time to implement the policy of elimination.

Final solution

What became known to high Nazi Circles as the *"Fuehrer Order on the Final Solution"* of the Jewish question apparently was never mentioned in paper and most probably it was given verbally to Goering, Himmler and Heydrich who passed it down to be executed. Ultimately, about eleven million Jews were exterminated. The *'Final Solution'* of the Jewish question actually meant the complete extermination of all Jews in Europe and the "final solution"went on till the very end of the war.

In the Andamans, the dictum of the *"Final Solution"* was so crookedly planned and cunningly executed that it can only be compared to the ingenious policy of elimination of the Jews superbly hatched by General Eichmann. The Jews were enticed by the allurement of their professed land and entertained in a make-shift city where several hundreds and thousands volunteered to settle there. They were brought to the city where they expired meticulously in the gas chambers while taking bath in the bathrooms which were nothing but lethal gas chambers.

In the same manner with same dexterity, the distressed islanders were imbued with the prospect of a desired land of 'no starvation' by bringing the virgin land under cultivation. By then the people were so famished with hunger that they were ready to do anything and everything for a piece of bread. The situation was so pathetic that even the little boys learnt the tricks to please the Japanese and were even turned to informers for 'roti', rice or sugar.

At the close of July, 1945 several hundreds of villagers were collected by the local police under a Japanese military officer with a vague assurance to take them to a virgin land as their new home and put in the Cellular Jail. On 4 August, 1945, they were huddled up in a number of covered trucks and carried to Aberdeen Jetty where a steamship '*Akbar*' and two L.C.T's were waiting to carry the human cargo to the destination, only known to the Japanese. The lone hope that was flickering in their mind, was, perhaps they were being taken to a new island for cultivation and for the prospect of food, they were a little jubilant and the proposal seemed to them hortative.

That day the sea was very rough and the weather was inclement and stormy. The silence of the Japanese guards, thunders from the pitch black sky and the bellowing of the turbulent sea perhaps all were singing the swang song for the ill-fated islanders. No sooner had the boats neared Havelock

Island, than to their utter surprise, they were ordered to jump in the roaring seas. They were terribly shocked and frightened as they were dreaming of a new life of no starvation. Naturally, they were hesitant and not prompt to obey the dreadened order. The Japanese guards started pushing, throwing, kicking, bullying them. Those who were trying to escape by swimming, were located with the help of search lights and either mercilessly shot at or slaughtered by the propellers of the LCT's on being cruised three or four circles over them. By the grace of God, only a few could reach the shore and were forced to live a life of beasts to escape death. Among them Saudagar Singh and Govardhan lived long to tell the horrendous tales of their struggle to survive.

After the surrender of Japan, on landing of man of war *'Dilawara"* at Port Blair, carrying the reoccupation forces under the command of Brigadier Solomons, M.S. Balasubramanyam, P.F.S. II and R. Joseph, B.E.M. were immediately detailed to carry out a search for survivors of the cast-aways on the Havelock sea, the sequel of one of the major Japanese atrocities[1].

The report of the enquiry conducted by the Allied forces in HaveLock Island and published in *The Statesman*, dated 27 October, 1945 is as follows-

"Brig. J.A. Solomons, Commander of the Allied occupation forces, has ordered a thorough investigation into the finding by Allied reoccupying troops of over 100 bleaching skeletons on the sands of Havelock Island in the Andaman group.

"It is alleged after the Japanese Civil Governor had declared that the Japanese would be unable to feed the civilian population of Port Blair, about 700 natives, including women and children, were told that they were to form a new colony on Havelock Island and that they would embark at night. They set out but a few hundred yards from the island they were attacked with lathis and flung into the sea. Many were drowned and those who managed to swim ashore were attacked by hostile Burmans.

"A search party from H.M.I.S., Narbada, under the command of Lieut. W.B.M. Tealor, found two survivors and 114 skeletons on Havelock Island. One of the survivors told him that but for the Burmans, about 300 to 400 people might have survived.

"Indeed just six weeks after this incident, the Japanese sent a search party to find out if any one still survived to become a witness of the demoniacal act. The party could capture ailing Mohammed Hussain and brought back to hide him along with 10 others already kept there at Bambooflat. So that no body could know of the crime. Later, Hussain appeared at the war crimes court to give evidence along with others but he did not mention the act of cannibalism in Havelock Islands during their days of terrible distress in exilement.

"Commenting on these accusations, the Japanese Admiral formerly in command of the islands explained that as it was necessary to ease the acute food situation at Port Blair, a party of 236 'evil-minded looters and lawless men' were deported but there was some difficulty in disembarking from the landing craft owing to rough weather. On hearing of the attacks by the Burmans, he sent a party of Japanese to rescue the survivors, and 11 Indians were brought back."

On 26 February, 1947, Compton Mackenzie, an eminent writer visited Havelock Island and writes, " The island was the scene of a Japan outrage only a fortnight before surrender. Vice Admiral Hara, the Japan Commander at Port Blair, became apprehensive about the food situation and a round-up was made of six to seven hundred men, women, and children who were locked up in the Cellular Jail. About two hundreds of these five hundreds were herded into boats and thrown into the sea off Havelock Island. Most of them drowned or eaten by sharks, those who managed to get ashore perished of starvation".

Ramakrishna who was the Deputy Comissioner under the Japanese regime, writes, "Those who reached the shore found themselves marooned. They were face to face with starvation and caught snails and shells from the shore, and ate them raw to satisfy the hunger. Some of them grew worse than beasts of prey and started killing one another for food. Afraid of each other, they spread out in batches. Dead bodies of many of those, thrown overboard or mutilated by the propeller were washed ashore. Some of them started eating the dead bodies. Hunger drove them to be cannibals".

But with this barbaric disposition of the human cargo at the sea, the satanic and sadistic perversion of the Japanese did not cease. Quickly on 10 August 1945, five days before their surrender started another 'round-up'. Some five hundred souls—men, women and children collected from the nearby villages were kept in the Garacharma village under strict watch, day and night with no regard to human necessities of life. On 13 August, just two days before their surrender, the Japanese took the wretched people to a small island called Tarmugli via Tytlerghat 20 kms. from Garacharma. There they were all lined up and shot dead. Their only crime was that they were human beings having hunger and thirst and out of despair they perhaps mumbled for it.

After reoccupation, a British search party visited the Island and found only heaps of bones of innocent people. Their sacrifice was no less glorious than that of those murdered in Homfreygunj. At least the Japanese had the satisfaction that they had murdered 44 people in Homfreygunj on the charge of espionage but for the mass murder of about 700 people in the sea near Havelock Island and 300 people in Tarmugli Island, the Japanese had no reasons to cite. In the history of the Andaman and Nicobar Islands, the sacrifice of these thousand unnamed and unsung people shall be written in golden letters to glorify their saddest death, even if the present generation ignores their sacrifices and disregards their helplessness.

Of course, there is a significant difference between the incidence of the massacre in Homfreygunj and watery grave in the sea near Havelock Island as well as carnage in Tarmugli Island. For the 44 souls of Homfreygunj tragedy, at least there are people to demand the official sanction for their glorious martyrdom and the State Martyrs' Memorial, *Balidan Vedi* already has been erected in honour of them but for those unfortunate thousand innocent people, wretched men, women and children, there was none, not even their own kins to shed a few drops of tears in silence at least on those ominous dates, 4 August and 13 August. They died unsung but their souls still remain unhonoured due to our indifferent gesture. It's the most pathetic sight, while the people are led to pay homage to the 44 souls on 30 January at Homfreygunj every year, those thousand bereaved souls remain ignored and neglected to languish and lament on 4 August and 13 August which pass by unnoticed.

But with these episodes the odious acts of Japanese barbarism did not end. Again on 14 August 1945, they started collecting people from the neighbouring villages and kept them at Port Mout village. They were destined to be killed but miraculously on 16 August, the round-up stopped and the people were set free to go back home. Subsequently, all other persons arrested or detained by Thokomohan and Nantai were released. From 16 August, the Japanese authorities began to distribute paddy, rice, cloth and other commodities to the public but the secret of Japanese graciousness was not disclosed to the people. Rumours spread and wild guesses were afloat but the news that Japan had surrendered and accepted the terms of dictated peace unconditionally, was not known to the people.

Notes

1. Annual Report – Andaman and Nicobar Administration, 1945 – 1946 p. 4, SL. 16.

10 Resistance or Submission

General Condition of Islanders

In the history of these islands never the people had reacted or revolted. It is the irony of fate that they lived in a tyrannical atmosphere of the Penal Settlement where justice had no say and punishment was the rule of the day. Due to savagery and bestial treatment, they were morally indolent and physically wreck. No doubt they were pious, honest and God-fearing but they lost their vivacity and fortitude to react or protest. For everything gone against, they would only blame themselves for their ill fate. It is however, astonishing to note when the whole India had plunged into the movement of 'Quit India', and every one was ready to sacrifice everything in the frenzy of 'do or die', the people of these islands remained inert, ignorant and unconcerned.

According to B.B. Lall, a prominent person of Port Blair, born and brought up in these islands, writes in his book, *"A Regime of Fears and Tears"*, "When the Second World War was in full swing, the islanders, unaware of the happening going on all over the world, were leading a carefree life. There were a few radio sets available with middle and upper class people as in those days Radio set was considered as a luxury item. The "*Press Telegram*" was the only Government paper which was read by a few and in other words it would be appropriate to say that except a few citizens others were quite ignorant of the day to day happening going all over the Globe".

But in other places under the Japanese occupation, the scenario was quite different. Everywhere, in Indonesia, Burma, Malaya, Phillippines where the military dominated administration under the Japanese rule was instituted, the general condition of the people was miserable because the military officers had no idea of civil administration nor did they care for the welfare of the locality, so discontentment and hatred terribly shattered the limit of endurance of the people. But when we talk about the excess of Japanese torture and brutality inflicted upon the people of these islands, we never compare with the extent of atrocities carried on in other South East Asian Countries during the same period and never feel how they vivaciously survived those hellish days and counteracted courageously.

D.G.E. Hall's remarks in his famous article 'The Challenge to European Domination' are enough to get a pen picture of the horror and terror prevailed in those countries under the Japanese occupation. He writes, "The Police came under the direction of the Kempeitai and probably no one will ever know the full extent of the terrorism carried on against the native population. Thousands of Chinese were massacred soon after the surrender of Singapore, especially those who had anything to do with the China Relief Fund. Rape was a real scourge in occupied Malaya. The requisitions for forced labour were perhaps the worst form of tyranny. The European and Eurasian prisoners of war were treated with unparalleled harshness..."[1]

Resistance Movements

The saying goes, 'Tolerance has no limit but intolerance knows the limit.' In those countries, the excess of atrocities made people mad for liberation and out of intolerance they started resistance movements. At times, the Europeans helped them build up a revolutionary force and in other cases, mercenaries from the neighbouring countries joined them to fight against the Japanese armies. In all these countries, the communists formed the leading force in the anti-Japanese resistance. In these countries where the Japanese replaced the British, the Dutch or the French rule, the anti-colonial nationalist movements, which emerged earlier, now organized armed resistance against the Japanese rule. Her atrocities in these countries were also responsible for the growing intensity of the armed resistance against the Japanese.

In Malaya, the Chinese Communists were the main spring of the guerrilla warfare. Even the role of Kuomintang Chinese helped the local people organize the movement. The tooth and nail struggle by nearly seven thousand men and women together with three hundred British has been vividly described by Lieutenant Colonel Spencer Chapman in the book *'The Jungle is Neutral'*. This dare devil people resorted to all sorts of underground activities leading to complete collapse of Japanese system of communication and thereby keeping them totally unaware of the Allied force's attack.

In French Indo-China, Ho chi Minh, the *vis-vitae* of the Vietnamese Communists, formed the Viet Minh League in 1941 and started guerilla warfare against the Japanese troops. The Viet Minh League was the spearhead of the resistance movement after the failure of a number of nationalist risings. Indeed, Ho chi Minh's guerrillas made the task of liberation easier. By the turn of fate when Japanese surrendered on 2 September, 1945, Vietnam was liberated and proclaimed the Democratic Republic of Vietnam.

In Burma, the people as a whole gave no support to the Japanese rather the Anti-Fascist People's Freedom League under the leadership of Aung San was formed to fight against Japan. The resistance movement was initially started by the British in connivance with the Karen people but was nipped into the bud brutally by the Japanese. Earlier students, nationalists of the Burmese Thakin Party being trained in Japan, helped them with guides and supported them with topographical intelligence but later on utter frustration and dismayal reality they organized an anti Japanese resistance movement and acted as a boomerang against Japan.

In Indonesia, the Japanese occupying forces had declared the country to be independent of the Dutch rule and expected their cooperation in return. But the Indonesians had no desire to exchange Dutch for Japanese rule. Even the left-wing Gerinda Group of the old Partai Indonesia proclaimed that the *Greater East Asia* idea had one aim of depriving other peoples of their freedom through the same process of domination as the Japanese had exercised in Manchuria, China and Indo-China. This national feeling infused in them a spirit of sacrifice so when the Dutch asked for 18,000 volunteers for resistance, one lac enrolled themselves to fight against Japan.

The Japanese tried to make the people divided and two groups were formed. One group under the leadership of Sukarno and Hatta submitted to the desires of the Japanese authorities and the other headed by Sjahrir and Sjarifuddin in opposition of the Japanese rule organized a resistance movement. Here also, the Communists were the leading spirit.

In Thailand, Pridi having been failed to establish an independent government in the north, was made regent by Japan. Taking advantage of his privileged position, he organized an underground movement and maintained secret touch with Free Thai Movement getting strong and powerful support from America and Britain. So Japanese policy of domination got stuck there.

In all these countries the distress of the people was multiplied not only by the Japanese atrocities but also by the Japanese currency system particularly the uncontrolled issue of paper money that led to uncontrollable inflation, scarcity of food, appalling unemployment, suspension of industrial production. Due to deliberate neglect of medical treatment and health measures, epidemics of malaria, small pox, cholera and plague caused a heavy toll on the people and that of renderpest brought in severe scarcity of cattle.

No where in Malaya, there was any fifth column traitors or the Japanese army was assisted by nationalist elements nor there was any incident of firing on the British by the Malayans. Before her invasion, in South East Asia, Japan tried to stimulate nationalist rising against the Western powers but failed. On the contrary the terrible consequence of her invasion led to the rise of resistance movements which ultimately played a crucial role in the final collapse of Japanese imperialism in Asia.

Even in Philippines, whole area was infested with spies and guerillas who were playing hide and seek and giving much trouble to the Japanese forces.

Above all, Burma was the worst sufferer in consequence of the Japanese invasion. Many of her towns had been the targets of Japanese bombers. On the eve of Japanese attack, also the retreating British army destroyed her oil wells, mines and river bridges. Her railways were completely defunct due to Allied airraids. The victorious forces captured her machineries, scientific apparatus and all valuably articles. Her trade and commerce turned out nil. Being a major rice producing country, her agriculture suffered a lot and complete stoppage of rice export led to mere subsistance farming.

During occupation by the victorious forces as well as retreat by the vanquished army while almost all the countries in South East Asia had suffered an immense loss of men and materials, the Andaman and Nicobar Islands were occupied by the Japanese forces without firing a single bullet, causing no damage to the islanders and the British on evacuation incurred no harm to the people.

During the British retreat in 1941-42 in Malaya, the great dredges in the European run tin mines had been ruined. Buildings and machineries on the rubber estates were destroyed. Also in Burma, the retreating British army devastated not only the mines and oil wells but also railways and river transport.

The occupation of Burma and Malaya led to the flight of Indians and Europeans through Burma to India. The British Government followed discriminatory policy and only the Indian evacuees had to face indescribable miseries for want of any help from the British. Thus the sufferings of the Indians aggravated the anti-British feeling. So there the Japanese army faced no betrayal rather enjoyed retrieval at least at the beginning whereas in the AndaNico, loss of property and wealth during the Japanese occupation or the British retreat were almost nil or negligible in comparison to the havoc done in other South East Asian countries.

Sex Tortures and Molestation

What was quite common but very pathetic and calamitous for a country, usually perpetrated by the invading army was sex-tortures. In Malaya, Burma, Singapore, Indonesia, Phillippines, China and Korea not only rape was rampant, but also the girls were forcibly made sex-slaves. They were even exported to other countries as comfort-girls. The requisitions of girls for 'Comfort–Centres' to entertain the Japanese soldiers were the worst form of tyranny. What happened in recent past in Vietnam owing to sex-tortures by the American soldiers, was very much conspicuous in South East Asia due to sex exploitation by the Japanese troops.

Victor Purcell observed, "...The Japanese conducted rape in a grand scale and it was a real scourge in all these countries. Sex–tortures created an immense social hazards and inevitable decadence of morality which have reflected upon a whole lot of illegitimate children. It has posed a great social and moral crisis for the generations to come."

Fortunately enough, this calamity did never befall on the Andaman and Nicobar Islands. Of course some wild rumours had spread that Pushkar Bagchi, an ambitious man, would abduct widows and young women in order to appease the lust of the Japanese Officers. But this rumour seemed slanderous because no evidence whatsoever was available to bear the proof of the mischief. It cannot be denied that in every society, some concubines or whores are always available and for arguments sake, it may be accepted that they might have been sent for entertainment to the Japanese by the touts.

Moreover, the testimony of B.B. Lall which is the most authentic version, defies the validity of the rumour, He writes in his book, "Since the Japanese soldiers were prohibited to enter into any civilian houses so the Japanese officers had to think about the comforts of their soldiers to satisfy their hunger for sex. The Japanese officers with the help of some notorious people tried to solve this problem locally but they were disappointed. Therefore, they brought Korean girls for this purpose. They were kept in the barrack of South Point where the Government school was run prior to the Japanese occupation. Some of them were also kept in other villages where Japanese soldiers were stationed". (page 40, *A Regime of Fears and Tears*)

One of thousands of Korean sex-slaves, Kim-Hak-Sun gave a very pathetic evidence, "How can I forgive them! We were no more than sex animals. We felt like a public lavatory and nothing more than a tool for soldiers".[2] Indeed, Japan's conscription of Korean women to entertain Japanese troops, was so inhuman that it created widespread commotion among the Koreans and Japanese Premier, Kitchi Miyazawa had to apologize publicly for admitting all the crimes and expressing deep sympathy for them "I express a deep sympathy for the victims, I express a deep sense of remorse, a deep sense of reflection and regrets".[3]

It is, however, a great solace what had happened to the Korean girls, never happened in these Islands.

Formation of Puppet Governments

It has been proved that the main aim behind the propagation of the philosophy, "Asia for the Asians" was to fulfil their objective of winning co-operation of the local people and securing total submission rather allegiance to the Imperial Japan. They however, decided that everything must be done to win over the local people and instigate them to resist Allied attack. Besides, to create a privileged class of people who would work in their favour, the Japanese authorities moved to form a puppet government with the semblance of independence or Home Rule.

In Burma, besides formation of the Thakin Party, on 10 August, 1943, a ministry was formed under the Presidency of Dr. Ba – Maw who declared himself as 'Adipaoi' in Pali meaning 'Supremo to the Burmese Government'.

After landing on Indo-China, 1940, a Thai-Japanese pact was signed in December, 1940, P'ibun capitulated to Japan. He and his high officials adopted a policy of full cooperation with Japan. France was forced to hand over Laos frontier and Japan enjoyed a privilege and command over the Thai Government.

In Indonesia, in September 1943, a Central Advisory Council was formed to provide share to the people to run administration at the aegis of Japan.

In the Philippines, a puppet government was formed on 15 October, 1943 under Jose P.Laurel to act as to the dictations of the Japanese authorities to resist the Allied attack.

In Singapore, a Malayan Consultative Council was established with the same intention.

The same method to set up a puppet council with the semblance of independence was pursued in the Andaman and Nicobar Islands. They proclaimed their 'brotherhood' and fellow feelings what they had propagated in the Phillippines, Burma, Malaya, and Indonesia. In these Islands, they expressed their eagerness to set up 'Peace Committee' and in order to provide a share in the administration they inducted prominent islanders in 'Gunseisho' which lasted till the arrival of the Japanese civil officers in February, 1943 to form 'Miniseibu' in place of Gunseisho.

Consequences

At the beginning, the Japanese authorities in these islands were cordial and sympathetic. The islanders were so moved that they even assured co-operation. They took oath of allegiance to the Emperor of Japan. The Japanese also enlivened hopes and aspirations of the people by uttering promises. Compton Mackenzie writes, "..The Nips issued pompous proclamations about the mighty Nippon Empire after they landed, in which they promised to give the inhabitants an example of its beneficent rule".

But soon the islanders realized the hollowness of the Japanese promises which were mere wartime propaganda to serve their own purposes. The so-called Committees or Councils in the name of Home Rule were nothing but hoax.

This sort of hypocrisy and treachery resulted in disillusionment and apathy led to the outbreak of resistance movements. While in all South East Asian Countries, anti-Japanese activities became vigorous and violent, the people of these islands withstanding tortures and atrocities, remained physically morbid and mentally crippled.

As regards tortures and atrocities, the curse befell on the wretched islanders only after the divulgence of the spy cases, of course, intrigued by very few. So long there was no trace of anti-Japanese activities, the Japanese authorities were quite friendly. But when they could intercept wireless messages and witness helplessly the accuracy of Allied bombardments, they turned violent and vindictive. On mere suspicion, several hundreds of innocent people were cruelly killed.

Even then the quantum of atrocities carried on in these islands cannot be compared with the magnitude of cruelty and persecution executed in other South East Asian countries. It was so catastrophic that it was not possible to know the full extent of the terrorism and impossible to assess the loss of lives and property. In Singapore alone, several thousands of Chinese were massacred soon after the Japanese Occupation. Thousands of Burmese people were forced to work in the construction of the infamous 'death railway' connecting Southern Burma with Bangkok through Kanburia. Thousands of Indonesians were transported for forced labour in New Guinea and Northern Malaccas. Most of these ill-fated forced labourers either perished in the gutters or breathed last in the dungeons. The innumerable cemeteries situated near the Burma–Thailand 'death railway' even today bear grim remainders of ineffable brutality which caused to be perished in duress or starved to death. Due to utter neglect of health measures and owing to forceful seizure of hospitals, looting medical stores and modern equipments by the Japanese, the epidemics broke out. Famine and malnutrition made the thing worst. All these factors contributed to the manmade calamity that led to catastrophy in "Greater East Asia Co-prosperity sphere" designed by the Japanese.

Hence, without going into comparison, we can conclude that loss of one life or thousands worths the same woes and agonies but the absence of resistance and lack of awareness among the islanders or their total submission to the tyrant cannot be justified. Leaving aside the glorious sacrifice of Zulfiquer Ali, not a solitary example can be cited where one happened to be desperate enough to shun the veil of cowardliness in the person and spirit to murmur even a mildest protest. Such callousness or absence of virility among the moribund islanders is nothing but ignominy that remains ever as an unoblivious scorn and burning wounds for the generations to come.

Dr. Van Mook has rightly summed up the effects of Japanese misrule in South East Asia during and after the Japanese occupation. In a statement, he commented that during the period under Japanese occupation, those who suffered most, were the common people. Japanese economy was frightful and Japanese administration was a farce. Food and other commodities became scare. Even the traffic was prohibited in order to facilitate pillaging by the military. The system of finance consisted of printing presses, turning out crude government notes so inflation acquired disastrous proportions.

To assess the precarious condition of the islands, Ramakrishna writes, "... Convict stations were all deserted, villages depleted on account of mass murder, men, women and children were practically naked, the saw mill was crippled, roads were all broken up and all places unusable, all elephants were at large and cattle, goats and fowls were not at all seen any where." Agriculture suffered awfully because of the policy of the Japanese seizing all cattles, fowls, goats, milch animals, even plough animals affecting the cultivation miserably. The Japanese even killed elephants for its meat.

No food, no medicine, no means to earn bread, no way to escape persecution led to a life of no security, no peace, no prospect. People lived like animals, awaited when the regent of death would beat the death-knell.

This was the horrendous and disdainful condition of the islands while the British reoccupied.

Notes

1. *'A History of South East Asia'* by D.G.E.Hall, Macmillan, 1968,p 821
2. Seoul, 18 January, 1992(AP), courtesy *The Telegraph*
3. Ibid, 5 June, 1992(AFP), courtesy, *The Telegraph.*

11 The Anda-Nico in War Scenario

War in Progress

The Japanese forces easily occupied the Anda-Nico Islands on 23 March, 1942. Since then, they were busy in fortifications and reinforcements. So long they had the command over the sky and the sea, they faced no problem but within one year, the war scenario got a sudden turn. Naturally it affected the defence strategy of the islands. Though Japan was busy in the Burma front it was to protect the Bay Islands because of their strategic importance.

The 18th Division Commander of the Nippon Imperial Forces reported to H.Q. on 18 February, 1943, "Enemy's (British) strength not less than 3000 – 4000. They are proceeding southward in two or three files. It is presumed that the main line shall reach Taetcong. The enemy has connection with their airforce planes and avoiding encounter with our forces. Information regarding enemy's situation has been clarified by our forces at Katha area. The collected information states, it is found that the enemy is British Indian Army 97 Garrison led by Colonel Wingate, who is leading the main force southward near Taonman. The group near Pinleb is one part of the Garrison. The 33 Company marching through Compal suddenly encountered with the Gorkhas of the British Army. The Commander of our division was killed during this encounter".[1]

The Allied Forces, however, planned to capture Rangoon and reinforce their strength in collaboration with the Air Force and the Navy to compel the Japanese forces either to surrender or to retreat. Apprehending the imminent turn in war situation, there were certain changes made in the British Royal Force too. On 18 June, 1943 Major General Auchinleck was appointed the Supreme Commander of British Indian Army and for South East Asia, Major General Mountbatten was appointed the Supreme Commander. He was a Naval officer and expertised in landing operations. He argued that landing operation by sea route was more effective than land operation itself.

As to his suggestions, the British Army and Navy was given vigorous training in landing operation in Bombay and its suburb. They were being trained for landing on the Andaman and Nicobar Islands.

However, in the first week of October, 1943, Japanese Air Force Division reconnaissance (scout) plane informed that at Chittagong mouth of the river, at Chittagong harbour, at Coxbazar, the total number of ships was 61. The number of enemy planes air-raided was 457 and number of raids was 72 times. Compared to the invasions of September 1943, its number tremendously increased.

From this report, the Japanese Forces concluded that the confrontation with the enemy was very near.

It was also decided that Burma and Andaman area were decisively the main battle fronts. The enemy against the Japanese Area Forces was mainly the British Indian Army whose main object was to snatch Singapore which was the nucleus base on the southern sphere both politically and militarily. The British Army desired to connect the East nucleus base with that of the West base that is Andaman Islands. They would make Andamans their base and proceed to Sumatra, then advance towards east to Malaya Peninsula. The last step-stone would be Penang to make their stronghold to attack Singapore.

Considering the situation, the 7th Area Force had formed a manoeuvre scheme founded on the war strategy.

The Policy of the Japanese Forces: The 7th Area Force would unite and cooperate with the Navy and the Air Force to destroy the enemy and to maintain peace and security in Andaman, Nicobar, Sumatra, Java and Borneo Islands.

General points of Japan's Manoeuvre Scheme

a) Main Defence Line — Lines connecting Andaman & Nicobar, Sumatra and Java.

b) The 29th Force should defend the Andaman and Nicobar Islands with the help of the Navy and the Army. Port Blair and Nancowry should be well-protected. The enemy should in no case, be allowed to land nor to utilize any part of the whole area.

c) The 16th Force should destroy the enemy on the ocean only with the help of the Navy and Air Force units.

In the first week of April, 1943, the 7th Area Force had issued an order as the Supreme Command action for the Bay Islands.

The Deployment of the Strength of the Area Force

The Commander of the 29th Force was Major General Ishikuro Teizo and its H.Q. was Taiping. Under his command, Independent Mixed 35th Garrison would be responsible for Andaman area, 36th Garrison for Car Nicobar and 37th Garrison for Nicobar areas.

During the beginning of 1944, the Allied Forces enhanced its frequency of attacks on the Japanese fleet moving towards the Andamans or out of Port Blair carrying foods, ammunition and soldiers. The spies in Andaman were very active and as to the signals the British planes and American submarines could target the Japanese transport fleet easily. To protect the fleet and to baffle attacks, many Japanese officers died a hero's death.

On 3rd June, 1944, The Division Commander awarded double ranks and a citation posthumously to the departed martyr, Sergeant Major Ishikawa.

The citation was-" Sergeant Major Ishikawa Seio, on 14th April 1944, spotted an enemy submarine at 11:20 at the left side of the fleet while patrolling the transport fleet at the offing of Port Blair. He found 3 streaks of torpedo lines and quickly reported to the base. He bombarded the supposed point of the submarine's path. He waved the wing over the fleet's upper portion. The fleet could not trace the enemy submarine, nor the torpedo. The Sergeant threw bomb on the torpedo but it was in vain. So, he plunged himself with his plane into the torpedo and prevented the advance. The sergeant gave his life to save the transport ship. He displayed the soldier's heroic spirit by his pure and patriotic deed. The sergeant was the ideal soldier of Imperial Forces, Nippon".

Despite the British attacks, the Japan authorities took all the steps to strengthen their position in the islands.

In the beginning of 1944, the 28th Air force H.Q. had issued an order as follows:

The Repair of Car Nicobar Airbase No.1:

A simple paving was done once for the runway of 2000 meters x 15 meters but there was a technical fault so the landing and departure of a plane became a problem. The construction unit No. 231 was engaged to do the job in Car Nicobar Airbase No.1. On 10th March, 1944, runway of No.1 airport of Car Nicobar was complete. On the same day, underwater detector setting was over and electrification also was done. (Source: *World History Chronicle*, Japan)

Major Incidents owing to Spying

From the beginning of February, 1944, the appearance of the British submarines was quite often. "*Hokujo*" was on duty for transportation of the armymen at Port Blair. It was blasted at the mid sea near the Malacca Strait and sunk.The amount of loss in 1943 by December was 1,80,000 tons. In January

1944 the loss was 3,00,000. The loss in February 1944 on the whole was about 2,60,000 tons. If other miscellaneous things were added, it would rise up to 5,20,000 tons. If compared to first week of February's expenses that was 5,00,00,000 tons, it is just 1% of loss. However, this account was really a headache for the war leaders. As March set in, the titlaps of the British submarines became noisier and war scenario took incongruous changes.

Considering the destruction of the strength and frequent airraids by the British, Commander of the Japanese Forces stationed at these islands, requested for reinforcement of the Army fighters as well as heavy bombers for the Andaman and Nicobar Islands. The Commander-in-Chief, Takasu, requested the Army to take over the reconnaissance of Andaman and Nicobar Area.

On 29 March, 1944, British Mobile Unit had appeared. On 30 March and thereafter the airraids were doubled and tripled. The South West Area Fleet Force H.Q. was compelled to request the Southern Force to take up the patrolling duty of West Front. For this strength transition, Southern Force Command suggested to deploy the 24th Company (ten Fighter planes) to Port Blair.

For the defence of the islands and other territories on the Bay of Bengal, the Chief of Staff, the First South Expeditionary Fleet Force demanded-

1) Continuance of reconnaissance of the area against enemy submarine.
2) To utilize the front line for the patrolling to be continued.
3) Anti-Submarine mopping of the sea and for that, establishment of electric detector set for marine reconnaissance needed.

From the frequent raids of the British Mobile Unit, it was clear to the Japanese that their enemy had a clear knowledge about transmission and electric detection by their counter detection. The Allied Forces were very sure of their targets so due to their attack on 21 June 1944, not only runway of Port Blair was severely damaged but the shipyard and other transmission centres were destroyed.

The increase in casualty was due to attack of enemy submarine and charge of magnetic torpedoes. The enemy had dropped not only the bombs but magnetic torpedoes also to increase suffering. By March, 1944 the command of the sky and sea went totally in the hands of the enemy. Japan had to face all their whims and tantrums but could do nothing.

Main Manoeuvre of the Vigilance Unit

On 23 January, 1944, light cruiser '*Kido*' and '*Hokujo*' were to depart Singapore and arrive at Port Blair. '*Tsugaru*' the lay-out ship of the 3rd South Expeditionary Force departed Shonun under escort of '*Shikiha*' and on 8 March, 1944 it reached Car Nicobar Island via Berawan and sent one division of Army men to Car Nicobar.

On 25 January the British started its activity in the Bay of Bengal and the number of the Allied Fleet also had increased tremendously. So Japan's Army positioned the 29th Force (12th & 18th Independent Defence Unit) at Malaya and A&N Islands.

The Western Defence Commander ordered as there was no change in the situation, Div 2nd Operation Vigilance was called off. On 11 Feb, a special Cannon Carrier and a mine laying-out ship with 25 mp. started from Singapore to Nancowry Island. On the way the ship *Eijuku Maru* got hit by the enemy torpedo on 18th Feb. but the ship somehow reached Nancowry Bay at 15:15 hours. The army incorporated Independent Mixed Garrisons 35th, 36th, 37th in the 29th Force Unit disposition of all the units were fixed at the Andamans, Car Nicobar, Camorta Islands. On 29 Feb. they were brought under the C-in-C Lt General Tamusubi of the first Southern Expeditionary Fleet Force.

Command of sky and the sea had almost been in the hand of the Allied Forces. The Japanese Forces lost the right of movement and even a torpedo carrier ship could not move in the sea. On 18 March, 21st Torpedo fleet and a torpedo carrier ship and one cannon carrier fought against enemy fighters but all ships were sent to the bottom.

The Allied reconnaissance plane's visit had become very frequent and so was the Allied submarines. There were machine guns firing and cannon firing also from the offing of the Andaman Islands specially at Port Blair by the submarines: Enemy's planes and submarine traffic was quite busy specially in Sumatra sea area. The enemy informers were frequent in. The Army could smell the presence of a transmission base for their submarines. So the army carried out the operation against the enemy and faced a heavy damage but the spies' transmitter base could not be found.

Preparation for War

The Japanese Intelligence came to know about the mass scale preparation of the Allied Forces to attack the Japanese Forces and annihilate them completely. Inference regarding Anti-Japanese plan made the Japanese Commander alert to repel the attack and prepare for counter-attack. As to their inference, the Allied Forces were trying to attack and capture Japan's strategic areas in South East Asia, Rabaul as the centre, Rangoon and Andaman-Nicobar Islands as the chief strategic points. The Anglo-American combined war policy was to capture Japan's strongholds and to make them their bases. Japan decided to enhance its areas of dominance in the Indian Ocean and to take steps for defending Andaman & Nicobar and Sumatra area.

The Allied Forces planned to bring complete disruption and to stop the communication between Nippon mainland (Honshu) and the South Sea. Bombardment on Honshu and other captured areas showed the vindictiveness of the Allies who were bent upon crushing the Japanese in every way.

Observing the motive and expecting the future change in the war situation, the Imperial H.Q. took final decision on new strategic policy. The resolution was passed on 15 September, 1944 at the Imperial War Directive Conference which was presided over by Emperor Hirohito who asked to take immediate action. The aim of Imperial war strategy was that the territories should be under 'Absolute Defence and Security Sphere', which included Andaman and Nicobar Islands. The Nippon Forces must repel the coming enemy and destroy them completely before they would start their attack.

The Southern Command founded its own operation scheme and put importance on the west zone defence manoeuvre for Andaman & Nicobar, Sumatra and Burma. Emperor Hirohito personally enquired of the defence manoeuvre and was informed that the South East Protection Corps No.1 and No. 2 had been enlisted in the 25th Force and stationed at the Andaman and Nicobar Islands respectively under the Commander of the Navy 12th Special base corps.

The Formation of both the Protection Corps

The First Protection Corps Stationed at Andaman: Two Infantry Battalion (8 Companies), one Artillery Battalion (field gun rifle Company), one wireless Company, two Organizers (966 persons), 200 persons for reserve.

The Second Protection Corps Stationed at Car Nicobar: Four Infantry Companies, one Field Artillery Force, Organizers (934 persons), Reserve (300 persons). Further for the defence of the Islands, the H.Q. put two Naval Platoons at Car Nicobar and for naval resistance, two Platoons were stationed at Port Blair.

As there was micro-increasing of the confrontation against the Allied Forces, Japan stressed on unifying of the disorderly

Army units as the territories in Burma, Malaya and Andaman & Nicobar were exposed to defence deficiency. So in January 1944 the 29th Force was ordered to be on the combat line. Major General Ishikuro Teizo was appointed the Force Commander.

The Manoeuvre Policy of the 29th Force Formation : The Force would protect AN Islands and Car Nicobar strongly and annihilate the incoming enemy. Japan had the motive to protect P/B, C/N and Nancowry Islands. With the deepening of the aggression motive and scheme of the Allied Forces at the Indian Ocean, the Imperial HQ Army Block had given a statement, "At present, the most venerable positions and the priority of enemy's attacking target is the AN Islands; It is imminently necessary to strengthen the defence of these islands."

The HQ asked the Southern Command for its opinion about the sending of further troop to these islands. To this, the Southern Command sent a telegraphic reply that it was not so acute that they would send a troop, " Enemy shall first try to grip the stepping stone firmly at Burma's west south coastal area. After consolidating the bases there, they shall be attacking the Andaman and Nicobar Islands, so please allow the Southern Command to increase strength at southwest coastal area of Burma."

However, on 2 December, 1943 at the Manila Conference, the Imperial HQ had, as a response to the detailed opinion produced by the Southern Command communicated the following statement to the centre-

1 To set up 3 Independent Mixed Garrisons for Andaman, Nicobar Islands and Nancowry Island—one garrison each at each island.

2 As connection with the Navy all the three garrisons are to be under the Commander of the 1st Expeditionary Fleet Corp.

On 2 January 1944, Lt Gen. Ishikawa Shigeru, the Commander of the 12th Special Base Troop clarified the position of the defence in the Islands, point by point. The following is the list of the units deployment and formation of each garrison:

(a) Independent Mixed 35th Garrison:

- Gn. Commander—Lt. Gen. Inoue.
- Head Quarters—Port Blair (Andaman Isles).
- Infantry 251st & 254th Companies for Andaman Isles Infantry 255th & 256th Companies for Andaman Isles.
- Independent Infantry 247th Company-Andamans Isles.
- Independent Mixed Garrison Artillery Unit–Andaman Isles.
- Independent Mixed Garrison Engineering Corps–Andamans Isles.

(b) Independent Mixed 36th Garrison Commander – Lt Gen. Sai Toshio

- Head Quarters—Car Nicobar Island.
- Infantry 258th,260th –261st Companies-Car Nicobar.
- Independent Mixed 36th Garrison Artillery Unit—Car Nicobar.
- Independent Mixed 36th Garrison Engineering Unit—Car Nicobar.
- Independent Mixed 36th Garrison Wireless Unit— Car Nicobar.

(c) The 37th Garrison Commander—Lt. Gen. Sato Tameoku.

- Head Quarters — Camorta Isles.
- Independent 262nd –263rd Companies— Camorta.
- Independent Infantry 264th Company—Nancowry zone.
- Independent Mixed 37th Garrison Infantry— Terressa Isles.
- Independent Infantry 265th Company —Nancowry zone.
- Independent Mixed Engineering Corps — Nancowry zone.
- Independent Mixed Wireless Unit—Nancowry zone.

The defence of the Andaman and Nicobar Islands was in the charge of the Navy. Since long, in 1944, it became the manoeuvring zone for the 29th Force also. The Army Units of the Independent Mixed Garrisons in every island came under the command of the Navy Commanders.

In April, 1944 it was viewed that though the ultimate aim of the British Indian Army was to take back Shonun, the nuclear power of South Asia, they would be connecting this with the situation in Burma. Then the British would surely consolidate their base by owning the Andaman and Nicobar Islands from the Burma side and would own North Sumatra. The next step would be landing on North Malaya from where they would proceed to Shonun (Singapore).

Japan knew it very well that the Andaman and Nicobar Islands is strategically very important for this territory as the Base connects Burma with North Sumatra. Moreover, this base would make it possible for the Allies to proceed to Malaya Peninsula. If the British could own these islands, it would be a problem for Japan because these islands would come under the enemy's bombardment sphere. So, Japan felt that strong defence of the islands was an urgent necessity for the 7th Area Force which was trying hard to reinforce its strength such as manpower, ammunition, base construction and materials.

The Preparation for the Transition of Man Power: The defence of the Andaman and Nicobar Islands had been the responsibility of the 29th Force. Moreover, there were the 35th,36th,37th Garrisons which had been trained under the 29th Force. In case of enemy's invasion, Japan felt that it would be more advantageous to bring in forces from North Sumatra than from far away Malaya area. So the 7th Area Force issued an order to the 25th Force to keep 3 Infantry battalions alert. Among three battalions, one should be given training at Berawan to be able to sail out in time of emergency. The other two battalions should be kept for the 7th Area Force to use according to the situation. They were also to be trained to marine mobile.

The Transition of Ship Building 10th Unit: On 26 May, 1944 the 7th Area Force issued an order and direction for transition of Marine Engineering 10th Regiment from Sumatra to the Andaman and Nicobar Islands. The 29th Force Commander was enforced with the transportation of 10th Regiment to Andaman and Nicobar Islands.

Materials for Operation Deposit: The 7th Area Force decided to deposit maximum possible material for the operation in the Andaman and Nicobar Area. For this purpose, the South Command delivered materials as follows:

Bullets for 105 encounters and grocery for one and a half year. Then for emergency's sake; allotment of grocery had been increased for one more year. But the difficulty in depositing materials was felt due to lack of planes and ships to escort the tankers and flights. For this, the transport to the Andaman and Nicobar Islands was done under very precarious conditions.

Colonel Inaoka Toyo, the 3rd Senior Staff of the 7th Area Force observed that it became highly difficult to transport by ship by the end of 1944. So the deposited material continued to be used till the war was over in 1945. This deposit was supposed to prevent the malnutrition of the people.

Enforcement of Water Supply: The coastal area of the Andaman and Nicobar Islands was totally sandy but the interior land was clayey, full of rocks and stones inside. So the engineering work was easier at coast but difficult in the interior region. It was easier to get water from the well at the coast but not in the clayey land. It was difficult even to get drinking water from any other source. So the 7th Area Force sent a group of well–duggers to this Island. An order was issued as follows:

(Okagata Regulation Act No. 25, 15 June 1944,)

1) Southern Fuel Dept. Director must put the Sakui Group under the 29th Force Commander. The tenure of this attachment is supposed to be till one year.

2) The 29th Force Commander should enforce the water system of the Andaman and Nicobar islands by the same unit.
3) Akemi Gyo, the Superintendent should arrange the transport of the Corps.

The List of Arrangement and Formation of the Unit Position: It was mentioned that on 10 February 1944, Independent Mixed Garrisons 35th, 36th and 37th were formed and posted at the Andaman and Nicobar Islands. The Garrisons were spread over in their respective places. The necessary materials were also supplied and deposited for the coming operations. Still the preparation did not progress much, due to "Submarines Mischief" and because of keeping back of the manpower meant for Hanarejima at Malaya region, Independent Infantry, Company, Artillery Garrison and Engineering Garrison were still to arrive at the Islands. In May 1944, the Japanese Intelligence made a thorough study on the potentiality of Port Blair and its surroundings. The report highlighted that except South Andaman and Port Blair, whole of Islands was full of dense jungles and the aborigines led their life in their own ways. Port Blair was a good harbour and had the capacity to anchor upto 5000 to 6000 tons of ships.

The Airport had X-shaped runway which enabled the heavy bombers to land and take off very conveniently. Port Blair had very good roads and the South Andaman had good quality wood so was the presence of good shipping yard.

The population was 20,000 including Indians and Burmese. Food and food products were imported. There was no scope of self-reliance.

The List of Unit Formation: 26 May, 1944 war capability of 7th Area Force:

a) *Combined Units:* Independent Mixed 35 Garrison, Independent 251 to 257 Company, 4 Battalion Gun Artillery, Heavy Planes 8, Infantry Cannon 2 (360 members) Independent Mixed 35th Garrison Infantry (member 360) 94 Style Guns, Independent Mixed 35th Garrison Engineering Corps (180 members), Independent Mixed 35th Garrison Wireless Corps (178 members).

b) *Direct Command Unit:* Shipyard Engineering Unit 10th regiment —120 soldiers hospital, the 14th regiment-the third building transport Unit, Field building, the 47th company one platoon

c) *Base Unit:* The 10th landing Unit at Port Blair, the 4th ship wireless Unit, the 3rd ship repair group, the 8th Air Force wireless Unit, the 47th Airport Company.

Unit Already Under Command: Independent Ship Engineering Corps Company arrived on 6 January 1944, 135th military hospital—functioning from 3 August' 1944. One part of 14th Division 3rd Construction and Transportation Unit, telecommunication first regiment was also in action.

Guns Installed: 18 Field gun, 3 Anti-tank guns, four 94mm guns, four Piccas machine guns, 12 Anti-aircraft machine guns, four 127mm Anti-aircraft machine guns, 240 sten guns were in possession.

The Islands being the Launching Ground

Considering the rapid changes in war situation, the 7th Area Force Command had two schemes, to defend the security of the Islands and to launch attacks from Port Blair on the British establishments in India. So the Japan's reconnaissance planes were always trying to detect the enemy's establishment and assess its strength.

On 11 November, 1944, one reconnaissance plane departed Port Blair and reached Trincomali sky. It spotted one British Aircraft Carrier, one Battleships, two Battle Cruisers, two Destroyers, three submarines anchored at the port. At the same time, another plane left Port Blair at night and reached Colombo sky by 3:40 am. But after sending the message, *"Enemy plane detected"*, it lost contact. Japan's South West

Fleet considered it essential to blow up the assembled British ammunition and other military supply commodities in Calcutta area. So the fleet suggested the South Force Command to execute the invasion jointly with Air Force and the Navy.

The SouthWest Area Chief of Staff, Captain Toguchi Taro observed, "Since October, the British cargo fleet in Calcutta area has increased tremendously. This was the time when the British Navy General Mountbatten calling along the slogan of defiance arrived to Asia as Commander-in-Chief of East Asia Force and with much uproar came towards the Indian Ocean. So the South West Area Fleet of Japan admitted the essentiality to give the enemy a painful attack by blowing up the British cargoes and all the accumulated commodities for war at Calcutta, before the enemy sent them to each front and bases. The manoeuvring of this area was the responsibility of the Army but as they were lacking in manpower, Navy's co-operation had been taken".

Of course, the Southern Force agreed to this approach with no different opinion. The secrecy for the manoeuvre planning needed maximum precaution. Even Supreme H.Q, was not informed of this beforehand as was agreed by both the Navy and the Army, the target of attack was fixed as Calcutta Godown area.

The meeting for the manoeuvre was held from 17 to 19 November, 1944. The strength of the Japanese Area Force was 27 planes from 23 Air Combat Units, 27 planes from Army Combat Units, 18 planes from 28 Air Force Unit. The Southwest Area Commander–in–Chief ordered for 'Action' on 25 November. But the manoeuvre was cancelled due to the gravity of the situation in Mid-Pacific Ocean so Air Combat Unit was ordered to send one part of the strength to Mid-Pacific Ocean area. Besides, the top secret plan seemed to be leaked out somehow.

Successful Raids

Though the plan was dropped, the preparation for the attack went on. On 5 December, 1944 at 14:45 p.m. when Japanese Bombers reached the spot 30 mile. from Calcutta, 8 Hurricanes and Spitfire gave them a fierce attack; there was no casualty to the Japanese planes but 6 British planes were shot down by them. Thus, the Japanese Bombers reached Calcutta sky and dropped 250kg. bombs on Chitpur dock and Hatibagan. 4 places in godown area were in flame. Big cargo ship was in flame. The fire spread all over the dock area. At 18 hrs. all planes came back to Tongui. (Source: *World History Chronicle*, Japan).

Air Raids in Andamans

On 14th April, 1944, a group of reconnaissance planes of Japan while flying over the Indian Ocean faced Twelve B – 24 planes of British Mobile Unit which air-raided Port Blair. Out of them 3 planes were shot down by Japanese expeditionary regiment.

According to the speculation of the local Navy unit, the planes were brought by the aircraft carriers of the Allied Forces. The surprise raids gave a considerable damage. The casualty mounted upto 10 persons and a Navy godown was burnt down. The airport was also damaged. General Dohihara and his group were to go for the inspection to Andaman and Nicobar for the first time but they were air-raided while they were ready to fly on 19 April at 9.30 a.m. at Kota Raja Airport. The plane went up in fire and the pilot died in the plane but the General was safe.

Since 17 May, the news was coming about British air raids. On 17 and 18 June, 1944, British double engine reconnaissance plane hovered over the Andaman Islands in spite of bad weather. But Japan's Force could not combat properly because its Air Force Unit had no support either from the Army or the Navy.

State of Air Raid: On the 21 June, 1944, British Mobile Unit attacked Andaman with a squadron of twine bombers. At 09.15 a.m. there was a group of six planes of the squadron infiltrated Port Blair from 3000 meters high and 290 degree direction. They were divided in two groups and bombarded the airport. There were repeated attacks from air. Rotating anti-aircraft firing was done by the Japanese but the British planes came down and obstinately bombarded from all directions. Japanese force also gave fierce firing at 9.43 a.m and finally repelled them (Source '12th Tokyo unit diary', *World History Chronicle*, Vol II, Chapter 7.)

Result of the Air Raid (from Japanese Sources): Of the enemy, six planes were shot down, four planes blasted in the air, three crew members were taken prisoners.

Casualty: Spot death of seven local men and fourteen heavily injured. Shipyard blasted with one ship burning, Telephone cables cut at several places but repaired soon.But the electric detector was unaffected.

The Japanese Intelligence reviewed that the enemy knew about its transmission and electric detection by their counter detection. The enemy attacked this transmission centre first of all because of the well camouflaged station as there were more 'look out' around the camouflage one so the real casualty as such was none.

The British Mobile Force Unit again intensified air-raids. Previously the air raid used to be for a day only but on 17 October, 1944, it air-raided for three full days adamantly. They were sent by the Chief of the 3rd section of Imperial H.Q., Navy Branch, that the British Navy strength centre point had been shifted to eastern sea area and its fleet force could be expedited to the Indian Ocean by the end of 1944.

Air Raids on Car Nicobar

At 09:25 a.m on 17 October, 1944, 20 or more planes air-raided Car Nicobar Island. Following this, a fleet of two Aircraft Carriers, two battleships, eight cruisers and destroyers appeared the sight region from 10:32 to 12:50. They fired at airport, harbour at 13:27 p.m. They went out of sight on 17th forenoon. Ten or more carrier planes air-raided Nancowry also and fired at the island on 18th. On19th British Force attacked Car Nicobar Island three times. Two air craft carriers, two battleships, three destroyers appeared in sight range at 9:40 a.m and from 11:18 to 12:10 they carried on the firing. Ten or more planes also attacked Nancowry Island on 19th afternoon.

However, Japanese Force took all the measures to rebuff the attack. On 19 October, 1944, the 9th Air Division Marukhawa Unit stationed at Sumatra planned to attack the British Mobile Units. So the Model I nine fighter planes led by Captain Maru Khawa Koichi encountered the British Fighters at and near Car Nicobar. Nine or more British planes were shot down. During this encounter, three planes led by Lt. Abe Nobuhiro,Sergeant Terajawa and Sergeant Major Nakayama nosehit the British ship with their own planes as a desperate attempt to foil the attack without bomb and martyred. Due to their sacrifice *S.S.Illinois*, aircraft carrier was heavily damaged and two destroyers sank. Defence Unit Commander Ikki Sei Choku dived with his plane and the British battleship was on in great fire. Other two were missing, perhaps drowned. This was witnessed by Lt. General Ichiki Seijiki, the Director, Andaman Defence Corps.

Subsequently, 'Letter of Thanks and Gratitude was served to Marukhawa Combat Unit, mentioning, "They are really the sacred and pious flowers of Air Force of Nippon. Really the confidence to destroy one plane for one ship is unparalleled valour of these fighters of the National Decisive War". (Source: *World History Chronicle*, Vol.IV, Chapter 2, "The 9th AirForce Corps Operation Against Enemy Mobile Force".)

British Strategy

Since April, 1944 the British Mobile Unit air-raided on every territory only after having intensive contact and collaboration with their Submarine Unit, regarding pre-manoeuvre, anti-plane disaster measure and rescuing of the crews of planes and ships. But any such collaboration between the two could not be seen. During this time the British East Fleet Unit Commander–in–Chief General Somaveer was succeeded by Gen. Frazer on 23 August, 1944. In middle of November, the Commander of aircraft carrier, Lt General Moody was replaced by Lt. Gen. Bigau. In the *British Historical Journal*, the details of these 'Great Operation Policy' and 'Operation at Sea' had been mentioned.

During last a few months, the Allied Forces were active in reinforcement. Japan assumed that the enemy fleets in the Indian Ocean were doubled of what it was in September, 1944. So their strength was – 4-6 Battle Ships, 3-5 Aircraft Carriers, 6-11 Special Aircraft Carriers.

Though the Allied Force History materials do not make clear of the casualty, British Mobile Force had to bear considerable loss. Though British Aircraft carrier flight deck was made harder than the American one, it was so made that a few bombs would not wreck it any how, yet on that day one Aircraft carrier and one Destroyer were sunk due to force landing of two Japanese planes. The counter attack was so violent that British Mobile Unit stopped its firing at 13:24 hour and went out of sight. But considering all these happenings, on 23 October, 1944 Central Army and Navy agreement regarding Andaman and Nicobar, South Borneo and Celebes was amended.

Regarding Andaman & Nicobar Islands on 8 November, 1944, local agreement at base was made between the Commander, the 7th Area Force General Dohihara Kenji and the 1st South Expeditionary Fleet Force Commander-in-Chief, Major General Tamusubi Kwan. On 10 November at zero hour, the 29th Force Commander Major General Shiguro Teigo had acceded to the duty of the Area Defence which he succeeded from Commander-in-Chief, 1st South Expeditionary Fleet. By the agreement, the permanent Army strength was increased. The deployment of the strength was as follows:

Andaman Islands: Infantry 6 Battalion Mixed Garrisons.

Nicobar Island (Except Car Nicobar): The Navy Unit of the area was 10 base Units under Commander Lt. Gen. Hara Chozo.

Defence of Andaman and Nicobar Islands

Considering the war situation and war strategy followed by the Allied Forces, Japan gave a great importance to the defence of the Islands. Indeed, Japan realized that the most venerable position and the priority of enemy's attacking target was the Andaman and Nicobar Islands. It is imminently necessary to strengthen the defence of the Islands so they chalked out a detailed plan and did everything on war footing measure.

The 7th Area Force had taken steps to keep reserve forces in Malaya for Area Force's emergency use. These Units were Infantry Units 257th, 261st, 265th Battalions which were to be enrolled into the 35th and 36th Garrisons at Andaman and Nicobar Islands. Taking in view, of the experience in the Pacific Ocean Islands Defence, it was felt essential to the Japanese forces to collect all forces at the base and utilize them with resilience to strengthen the defence power.

The first Southern Fleet Corp joined hand with the 7th Area Force and changed the disposition. The 253rd and 256th Battalions, which were stationed at Coco Islands, were transferred to Andaman and Nicobar respectively and came under the 36th Garrison. Thus, the infantry strength was increased. Even in Nancowry area, the 37th Garrison's three battalions were positioned.

The artillery, engineering, communication corps were organized in Manchuria and transportation started in March from Kamayama, Manila and somehow reached Car Nicobar in November, 1944. It took months to reach the Island.

The 7th Area Force Unit planned to assemble and supply ammunition bullets and grocery for one year to Andaman and Nicobar. So 5000 tons of grains were needed but the transport was delayed because of the increase in danger of bombardment and mines. Only 4000 tons of grainery reached so the joint military agreement was mended. The joint agreement to defend these Islands together with South West Area Naval Corps was signed on 1 September, 1944.

Regulations

1. The treaty was made by the Southern Command and South West Area Navy Command on 27 October 1944 for the defence of Andaman and Nicobar Islands.

   Important matters would be decided by the 7th Area Force Commander-in-Chief, Dohihara Kenji and Commander Tamusubi Yuzuru of the First South Fleet Corps.
2. Besides referring to the treaty regarding defence of Andaman and Nicobar Islands, it was to be referred to the revised treaty.
3. The land defence would be totally in the charge of the Army and the seas defence would be totally in the charge of the Navy.
4. December 10, zero hour onward, the 29th Force Commander-in-Chief would take over the duty of direct defence of the land of Andaman and Nicobar from the First Southern Fleet Commander-in-Chief. He would command the 12th Special Base Area Command and all the army and navy groups would be under him.

5. The senior-most Commander would combine and command each base of Andaman and Nicobar for the defence.

Strength Deployment

Criteria of strength of all forces in Andaman and Nicobar—

a) Andaman Island: Army Garrison (infantry six battalions), Navy Special Base Troop specially for Port Blair's defence.

b) Car Nicobar Island:

Army – Combined Garrison (infantry three battalions)
Navy – Vigil corps.

c) Nicobar Islands:

Army – Combined Garrison (Infantry three battalions)
Navy – Vigil corps specially for Nancowry defence.

TRANSPORT: As a rule every troop should be the in-charge of their respective supply transport. But the Navy was expected to cooperate the Army for their increasing supply, transport, boarding and welfare allowances.

The 1st Southern Fleet Corps Commander-in-Chief, Vice Admiral Tanusui Yuzuru had given an order to the Commander Lt. Gen. Hara Kozan to transfer the charge of the land direct defence of Andaman and Nicobar to the 29th Troop Commander. Thus, the common system of defence had finally established and hitherto illogical ways had been eliminated. The 29th Force Commander came up direct in command of the 12th Special Base Force of Andaman, Independent combined 36th Garrison of Car Nicobar and the 37th Garrison of Nancowry area.

Anti-chemical War Preparation

The Area Forces Command was informed that the Allied Forces had used chemicals in bombardment. So, Japanese military authority warned that it was essential that Japanese Forces should start anti-chemical measure at once. So, 7th Area Forces issued an ordinance highlighting the main principle of the preparation for Anti-Chemical war.

1) There should be no regret in defending our people from the enemy's absurd chemical war execution. The most revengeful preparation for chemical war shall be executed by the U.S. Army and Air force in near future.
2) Our Anti-Chemical war preparation must have full execution specially in maintenance of secrecy and endeavour to annihilate the enemy's vindictive plan at any cost.

Inspite of this warning, no such incident happened in the Andaman or Nicobar Islands and the people of these islands had never faced the destiny owing to chemical warfare.

NIGO Operation

However, due to the worsening of war situation, it became difficult for all the forces and their units to have mutual co-operation. Thus, every unit had to have their defensive action by their independent discretion and self reliance.

Failure of Andaman and Nicobar Strength Transit

Japan's 7th Area Force inferring at the British in May 1945, observed, "The enemy is taking advantage of our Navy and Air Force's weak points, not invading the Andaman & Nicobar but straightly landing on Sonun (Singapore) and Malay Peninsula. This is what we calculate about their intention. There is the fear that the Forces who rose to the occasion and strengthened the defence of these islands at main defensive line wavering. So the 7th Area Force has decided to transit the strength to Malay and Shonun as possible as one can".

On 6 May, 1945, the Imperial H.Q. issued an order as follows:

1) To strengthen the war preparation by sending Infantry two battalions from Port Blair and Nancowry Island to be sent to Malay Peninsula.
2) Surface transition will be carried out by the 10th Area Fleet Force. The protection will be done by the 3rd Air Force Unit.
3) The secrecy should be maintained about the plan for transportation. One must endeavour in every possible way. This strength transition will be called 'NIGO' Exercise.
4) After 10 May, the transportation will be done with full caution.

As planned, the exercise 'NIGO' enhanced on 10 May. As both sea and sky were already in the command of the Allies, the patrolling by their aeroplanes and submarines in the Andaman Seas was quite rigid.

On 15 May, the "*Haguro*" and "*KamiKhaze*" which joined the NIGO exercise, got hit by B-24 fighter planes of the Allied Forces at 13:30 p.m. The same night both the fleets had fierce encounter with two U.S. Cruisers and three Destroyers. Both the ships fought vigorously but at last '*Haguro*' had to go to the bottom when three torpedoes hit its body. It was at 02:30 a.m on 16 May, "*Kamikhaze*" also was hit with a bit of damage but she was able somehow to commute upto Singapore.

Again on 16 June, 1945, the 10th Area Force under Force Commander Lt. Col. Hurudome Shigeru had sent *"Submarine No. 57"* and *"Kuroshio Maru No. 2"* to transport Andaman strength. These two ships had encountered with the three British Destroyers. Though one of them was hit and on fire, both of Japan's ships had to sink due to British torpedoes firing.

Thus, the NIGO exercise was a failure and the 7th Area Force ordered the postponement of transition of Andaman Strength. (Source of all information: *World History Chronicle*:

Burma, Dutch IndoChina area, Defence Research Bureau, Japan).

Air Raids

To explain the gravity of the situation, the war scenario of the Nicobar Islands can be described in details.

With the increase of the British Mobile Unit's manoeuvre, air raids in the Nicobar area particularly on Car Nicobar became frequent.

Lt. General Hashimoto Hidenobu took over the charges of the New 9th Air Force Division. Whenever he got chance, he would inspect the unit under his command as well as visited the concerned Units.

After visiting the 25th Force on 17 October, 1944 Lt. General Hashimoto flew to Singapore and on the way he got the news that enemy's Mobile Unit appeared in Car Nicobar area. He ordered the special manoeuvre "Se" 2nd Preparation. On 18th at dawn, an order was given for counter attack against British landing on Car Nicobar.

On 18th at 4 a.m. the Commander Marukawa selected the gallant fighters and the counter attack began. On 19 October 1944, black smoke was seen on southwest sea. The powerful fleet was protected by an escort aircraft, which was nearing Car Nicobar. Direct Defence Unit was circling over the battleship, which started firing from 8000m south at the aerodrome and the cruiser was firing at villages from west.

Nine fighters of the Marukawa Unit began resolute attack on the British Mobile Unit. Direct defence planes and half of the enemy planes were shot down. One plane dashed into the fleet and caused fire to the ship, which sank. One other plane came down low and crashed into the aircraft carrier. The plane blasted together with the ship that went to the bottom. Another fleet unit came to join the main fleet but due to desperate attack of Japanese fighters, rear of the ship blasted and started sinking. The battleship which was firing at the airport, started to retreat but the Japanese fighters would not let it flee. At the end, it caught fire by a bomb hit and blasted on the battleship.

On midnight 19th, the Japanese Commander received the news of British landing on Teressa Island. The Marukawa Fighters Unit took off from Medan at 9 a.m. on 19th and went to Nicobar at the height of 4000m. At about 12 hours, they watched a ship burning near 'No–man's land at Teressa. Just near Car Nicobar, they spotted an Aircraft carrier in the centre and 7 ships around it. The ships were sailing southwards. The Marukawa Unit immediately formed horizontal line and started machine gun attack from 300 m height. The British fleet gave fierce anti-aircraft attack while turning back and retreating.

As the unit was engaged in bombing on the fleets down on the sea, they were not aware of the other fleet firing the island. Suddenly, they noticed 20 planes of the Allies just in front of them at the same height. The unit's position was advantageous because the sun was at the back. Thus fierce air combat started and continued for 30 minutes. It was supposed that about eleven Allied planes were shot down after the fierce battle.

Anti-submarine Operation

21 October was the Anniversary Day of famous Nelson's Naval Battle of Trafalgar Strait. Japan expected enemy's attack so the vigilance and anti-submarine operation in the Andaman Sea and Malacca Strait increased. In the afternoon of 21 October, the report passed on by patrolling reconnaissance planes, " A floating submarine out of Teressa Island has been seen this afternoon." The 58th unit's Bomber planes were ordered to attack the submarine on return from Nicober. The bomber unit attacked the spot and it was presumed that the mobile unit had returned. No damage was done. (Source: *World History Chronicle*, Japan)

From this chapter we can have a clear war-time picture of these Islands and it carries the testimony that during the war, the Islands played a very crucial role and Japan exploited the strategic position of the Islands to fulfil her defence and offence objectives.

Source: *World History Chronicle*, Defence Block, Defence Research Bureau, Tokyo, Japan.

Notes

1. *Wars History Chronicle*, Vol III, Chapter 2. 'Drastic Air Manoeuvre After The Monsoon'

12 Surrender Leading to End of War

Operation Buccaneer

In August, 1943 at the Quebec Conference, code-named 'Quadrant', Rear Admiral Lord Louis Mountbatten was appointed the Supreme Allied Commander of South East Asia. On 22 November, 1943 in the meeting of the British Chiefs of Staff, Mountbatten explained his plan to occupy the Andaman and Nicobar Islands and it was code-named as 'Operation Buccaneer'. As to his plan, once Andaman was occupied, it would be possible to strike at Rangoon and attack Japanese Naval Traffic through the Malacca Strait. Besides, for the defence of the Islands, it would be possible to provide air and sea power from the nearest coast which is only 200 miles away from the Islands. Moreover, in the Islands, the Japanese man-power at the moment was estimated as only five thousands strong. So it was the right moment to invade the Islands which would be easily occupied.[1]

Mountbatten's 'Operation Buccaneer' appealed to Churchill who was a little jealous of the success of America's Pacific Operations and very eager to establish the superiority of British Navy. As to his intention, 'Operation Buccaneer' would be a proper repartee to America's success as it involved the intelligent exercise of sea power and was also the handiwork of a man whom Churchill favoured. Nevertheless, it would be possible to utilize Andaman as a launching ground for offensive manoeuvre towards Burma and Malaya under Japanese occupation.[2] Though the British Chiefs of Staff agreed to carry out 'Operation Buccaneer' by March 1944, the Chief of the

Imperial General Staff, Field Marshal Alan Brooke was against it. He pointed out that the cancellation of 'Buccaneer' would make available additional landing crafts for the Mediterranean invasion without which General Eishenhower could not get to the Pisa-Remin's line.[3]

Though Churchill himself was interested and the British Chiefs of Staff considered 'Buccaneer' the most promising operation to bring under control all the littoral countries and to exercise full power in the Bay of Bengal and Malacca Strait unchallenged, yet in the context of the Cairo Conference it seemed more imminent to deploy their full strength in Europe rather than in the South East Asia.

S.W. Roskill in his book *'The War at Sea' writes,* "Whereas the Americans were insistent that the Burma Operation and 'Buccaneer' should take place as planned, the British were equally insistent that any sea borne expedition in the Indian Ocean would undoubtedly lead to a diversion of strength from Europe", which might end in disaster, so apprehending the debacle, it would be wise to suspend 'Operation Buccaneer.'

On 5 December, 1943, Churchill received a cable message from the U.S. President Roosevelt, "Buccaneer is off" and indeed the operation was suspended in December, 1943, because the Allies were seriously conceiving a plan for an all –out offensive against Hitler which needed total mobilization of strength. But later on, it was felt, had the 'Operation Buccaneer' been carried out as early as December, 1943, the Andaman and Nicobar Islands would have been easily reoccupied and hundreds of the innocent islanders could certainly escape gruesome death, and the history of the Bay Islands would have been written in a different rhyme and rhythms. Besides, Allied attacks could have carried on against Japan advertently in Burma and Malaya from these islands.

Allied Attack on AndaNico

Though the plan to occupy the AndaNico Islands was delayed, the systematic aerial bombing on defence installations and other strategic locations in the Andaman continued. S.Woodburn Kirby in his book '*The War Against Japan*' writes, "—Power (Vice Admiral Arther Power) carried out a series of anti-shipping sweeps by destroyers in these waters, targets in the Andaman Islands were bombarded on 24th and 25th February, and again on 13th to 19th March 1945".

The Allied Bombers continued concerted aeriel attack on the targets in Andaman. On 30 April, 1945 the airfield at Car Nicobar was bombed by the naval artillery of the Allied flotilla including two battleships, four cruisers, two escort–carriers and six destroyers. In the evening, the fleet returned to the Andaman Seas and started shelling on the Lambaline airport, marine dockyard and other targets. The fleet spent 8 days in the Andaman Sea and carried on attacks on other strategic locations for the second time.

Meanwhile, the Allied Naval and Air offensive had started both in the Southern Pacific and the Northern Pacific strongholds of Japan. To counter the attacks, Japan was forced to transfer many of their air-squadrons from Burma to the South Pacific. By the beginning of 1944, the Japanese had begun to realize the magnitude of the Allied preparations for a counter offensive and were unsuccessful to stem the Allied advance. As a result of all these diversion, Japan lost the mastery of air over Burma and its surroundings. In the Andaman and Nicobar Islands, the Japanese Forces had been much depleted and their supply line was totally disrupted because of the Allied blockade.

In the Islands, Japanese defensive and offensive strength was dwindling, so their resistance to the Allied attacks was very negligible. The Japanese fighters could penetrate the Allied formation on rare occasions. Their flying heroes could only plunge into a suicide dive straightway to the master deck of the Allied ships and died a martyr's death. During 24 June, 1944 and 25 May, 1945, the extent of damage owing to the Allied attacks was summarized in one of the reports, quoted by Iqbal Singh, in his "*The Andaman Story*,. " The main item of interest consists of severe damage to the previously slightly damaged Saw Mill on Chatham Island which has now been rendered completely unserviceable. There is also some damage to the main wharf of the Island. The coal sheds at Hope Town Station have been completely damaged at the Marine Yard at Phoenix Bay. Throughout the various districts, a number of barrack type huts and identified barrack building have been damaged, destroyed or removed.

The total number of such buildings affected throughout the area is 17. On Ross Island, a considerable number of unidentified hut-type buildings, some of which may be barrack huts, have been destroyed in addition to even probable godowns in the vicinity of the Jetty. Throughout the whole area covering about 40 dwellings, mostly of a medium or small size, have been damaged or destroyed. At the Cellular Jail at Atlanta Point, a considerable amount of demolition and removal has taken place...".

Above all, the Chatham Saw Mill suffered enormously and it needs special mention. Even on 15 August, 1943 about 15 mill workers lost their lives due to Allied bombing. The southern end of the mill had been destroyed by a direct hit. The intake end of the old mill was wrecked. The rack bench machine had been blown into several pieces by an almost direct hit. There was a bomb hole at least 20 feet deep and 25 feet-30 feet across. Chatham, a small island, was struck by more than 74 bombs. After the old mill ceased to work, the Japanese opened a small make-shift saw mill in the west of India Match Factory building.However, the forest department is most fortunate in having lost no important member of the unevacuated staff during the Japanese occupation. Many notably, Durga Prashad (Exploitation Officer) and Akbar Ali

(Head Clerk) suffered terrible torture but survived. Despite being an important member of Peace Committee and his service to Japanese military authorities as the Chief Forest Officer, Durga Prashad was not spared, rather subjected to inhuman torture.

Retreat of Japan

Inspite of intensity of aerial bombing in 1944 Japan launched a major offensive on Burma-India borders. In March they began a very formidable movement into Manipur and Assam. The INA under the command of Netaji Subhash Chandra Bose was in high spirit to invade India in order to strike at the very roots of the British Imperialism. But the strategy of the Allies was more ingenious than that of the Japanese. When the Allies were gathering strength in the Burma front, the strength of Japan was diverted from Burma front to the Pacific to protect her hegemony in that region. Hence, in and around Imphal, it was a veritable blood bath and the Japan's defeat at Imphal had become fatal and suicidal. They were in disorderly flight closely persued by the Allied Forces. The Japanese were retreating fast towards the Central Burma where the decisive battle of 1945 was to be fought but the Japan's main army in Burma was so heavily defeated that it began to disintegrate.

Japan's hasty decision to retreat demoralized the Azad Hind Fauz and disappointed Netaji. Actually the surrender of Italy on September 1944 was a great blow to Japan. The American forces also recovered in the Pacific and Japan had to give utmost attention to home defence. The result was quite significant as Japan could not help the Azad Hind Fauz fighting in the Indo-Burma border. The Azad Hind Fauz lacked air cover and artillery and they did not possess even mortars and sufficient machine guns. At the magic of the clarion call of Netaji, the morale of the soldiers of INA was very high and nothing could hinder their heroic march. In conjunction with the Japanese, they captured Kohima and hoisted the tricolour flags at Moirang on mountain tops around on 14 April, 1944. In the last week of April, 1944, the INA was within ten miles of Imphal but the march was halted due to premature outbreak of the monsoon.

While the Indo-Japanese Forces had no air cover and their lines of supply were practically cut off, the Anglo-American had full command of air and poured reinforcements for the last ditch defence of Imphal. Unfortunate for the INA, besides the rigours of the monsoon, lack of ammunition and food, breakdown of communications, its ranks were stricken with malaria and dysentery. The Japanese army was fighting half heartedly whereas the British enjoyed superiority in armament-equipments and her war machine was so powerful that they fought a decisive war.

Mountbatten's aim[3] had all along been to capture Rangoon before the onset of the wet monsoon. In succession Prome was occupied, Pegu was seized on 1 May and on the following day Rangoon was reached. The advances were so swift that the plan for a sea borne assault seemed unnecessary. When the British force arrived, the Japanese had already evacuated Rangoon. At this juncture while Japan decided to retreat in April, 1945, for INA too there was no way out but to leave Rangoon and its retreat started on April 24. After this retreat the nemesis unwrapped its gloom as quickly as it had loomed large.

Surrender of Japan

In July, 1945, the Allied Powers met at Potsdam to draft their terms for the Japanese surrender. Indeed, this was the dictated peace but Admiral Sujuki Kantaro, the new Premier of Japan had been insisting to frame up the draft to avoid further loss of lives and wealth. Meanwhile the Allied Powers were busy in "the battle of Break-through" to fight out 10,000 Japanese soldiers under General Koba and it was only a matter of stamping out the resistance of outlying Japanese garrisons. The Americans were ready to invade Japan. Mountbatten was intending to sweep Malaya and Sumatra. Preparation to hit the last nail on the coffin of Japan's carcass was complete. On 26 July, 1945, the terms of Japan's surrender were announced but Japan did not respond so catastrophe befell on it.

On 6 August, 1945, the first atom bomb was dropped on Hiroshima causing total destruction of men and materials of that throbbing city. Perhaps Japan could not imagine the consequences of the onslaught and remained non-committant. On 8 August the Soviet Russia declared war against Japan. Nonetheless by astounding the whole world, the second atom bomb was dropped on Nagasaki on 9 August. Only after the devastation of it, Japan could conceive the magnitude of her follies and accepted the term of her surrender unconditionally.

On 13 August 1945, Netaji Subhash was called back to Singapore and informed that Japan had decided to surrender. Subhash had also realized the impending dangers and felt that nothing but a doom's day was awaiting. He too had no option but to agree.

In his last message to his countrymen, Subhash said, "A glorious chapter in the history of Indian's struggle for freedom has just come to a close and in that chapter, the sons and daughters of India in East Asia will have an undying place. Do not be depressed at our temporary failure. There is no power on earth that can keep India enslaved." He concluded with affirmation, "India shall be free before long".

Indeed, his prophecy came out true as on 15 August, 1945, India won freedom. On 30 Dec, 1943, Subhash standing on the soil of Andaman proclaimed the historic verdict, "Give me blood, I will give you Independence" and in reality, out of bloodshed, lifelong sacrifice and through struggle unto the death of this glorious son of India, we became independent.

However, on 14 August 1945, the Supreme War Council of the Japan Government and the Emperor consented on the terms of unconditional surrender. The terms set in the light of Potsdam Conference were signed by Japan on board a man-of-war, *'Missouri' in the Tokyo Bay on 2 September.* At last the Second World War was over. Though the sun in the land of 'the rising sun' set in, the history of the *'Kalapani'* is yet to unwrap.

Notes

1. *'The Uneasy Alliance'* by Robert Beitzell
2. Ibid
3. *A History of South East Asia* (Challenge to European domination Japanese impact) by D.G.E. Hall, p829.

13 Reoccupation Followed by Independence

Japanese Trickery

Though Japan had surrendered and accepted the terms of armistice unconditionally on 14 August, 1945, the Japanese military authorities at Port Blair received the news at night. Consequently on 15 August, they laid down their arms. All the detenus of Thokomohan and the prisoners in the Cellular Jail were set free and the release completed on 19 August. But the actual proclamation was made to the public by the Japanese Governor only on 21 August 1945. From 15th onwards, the Japanese were busy in incinerating all records and official papers in the headquarters of the Civil Governor. At the sea, all the mines plaited to impede the enemy's attack, were exploded. Many of the Japanese soldiers preferred death to surrender and committed suicide. The people though morosed and morbid, became cheerful at the helpless and woeful condition of one-time tyrant.

On 21 August 1945, in a public meeting the Japanese Civil Governor announced still cunningly that the war was over and it was peace everywhere. Japan agreed to it and accepted the truce. This was also published in the *Andaman Shimbun*. Though the people were happy at the end of war, they were at a loss at the sudden turn of events as neither they were told of the catastrophe in Hiroshima and Nagasaki caused by atom bombs nor they had any idea about the significance of the defeat and surrender of the Japanese. However, they became a little bold to express their discontents.

Next day, a group of women and children assembled near the headquarters and prayed for the return of their relations who had been rounded up by the Japanese. The Civil Governor yielded to their wailing and announced an ex-gracia payment of Rs. 500/-per head in-absentia. But this assurance did not pacify the lamentation and the women left the place cursing and abusing the Japanese without caring a fig for the money. Now it was the Japanese turn to bear with the public lynching, imprecation and malediction. Pride goeth before destruction!

But sin can never be suppressed. One morning.the people were delighted to see that a plane flew over the city strewing some leaflets. Befogging the Japanese, the people could collect a few leaflets and came to know that Japan was defeated in the war and forced to surrender.

It may however, be recalled that as early as November, 1944 the Supreme Allied Command of South East Asia had formulated an outline of prospective administration to be installed in the Andaman & Nicobar Islands after the surrender of the Japanese. On 11 November, the Government of India was informed that after reoccupation, the military administration would be kept under the jurisdiction of South East Asia Command but the Government of India would look after the execution of the civil affairs.

In April 1945, a Planning Unit was established under the Home Department and N.K. Patterson, the Chief Commissioner designate became the Chairman of the Unit. From May 1945 to August 1945, the Planning Unit made all arrangements to meet the urgent need of the supply of food and medicines to the famishing and dying islanders.

Operation Popcorn

On 15 August 1945 in a circular of Joint Planning Staff Committee, it was stated that the Commander-in-Chief should be invited to accept responsibility for the re-occupation of the Andaman & Nicobar after Japanese recapitulation. The operation to occupy the islands was code-named *'Operation Popcorn'*. As to the plan, 116th Independent Infantry Brigade under Brigadier J.A. Solomons and a Naval Brigade under Captain J.H. Blair were directed to occupy the islands. But the *"Operation Popcorn"* was delayed till the first week of October, 1945.

Meanwhile it was decided to send a mercy ship *'Bandra'* carrying civil supplies for the islanders and the prisoners of war at Port Blair. The *S.S. Bandra* sailed from Calcutta on 22 September, 1945 escorted by *INS Narbada* and reached Port Blair on 26 September with a civilian, Mr. Foster who had served in the islands as the Chief Forest Officer before the Japanese occupation.

The sight of Port Blair was in a state of suspense, roads were full of holes and pits, sweepings and rubbish were piled up by the roadside, even human excreta was not removed, houses were in a dilapidated condition. Due to lack of proper sanitation, the total atmosphere was morbific and the people were suffering from aneamia, beri-beri, scabies, phthisis and cholera. The whole population was in the grip of severe malnutrition.After visiting all the places, villages as well as convict stations, Foster was shocked to find most of the men, women and children naked, shabby and hunger stricken. The condition of the people was so pathetic that Foster immediately opened centres for free distribution of packed food, clothes and other commodities. He also made arrangements to provide medicines and vaccines to the ailing people.

In fine, while 'Operation Popcorn' was in action, the infantry and naval brigades left Calcutta for Andaman on 3 October, 1945. The reoccupation forces landed in command formation on 8 October, 1945 and took control of all strategic points and Japanese establishments. A peaceful landing was effected. The Japanese were rounded up on the same day and sent to different camps as prisoners of war.

S.S. Dilawara, being the flag ship under Brigadier J. Solomons not only carried huge quantity of food and clothes for immediate distribution but also to restore normalcy brought members of the Civil Administration who had worked in these islands before Japanese invasion.

Ceremony of Surrender

Meanwhile on 23 September, 1945, Admiral Louis Mountbatten became *'The Charge d'affaires'* of the AndaNico and issued a proclamation for the people of the islands:

> I, Admiral Lord Louis Mountbatten, Knight Grand Cross of the Royal Victorian Order, Knight Commander of the most Honourable Order of the Bath, Companion of the Distinguished Service Order, Personal Aide de camp to His Majesty the King, Honorary Lt. General and Air Marshal, Supreme Allied Commander, South East Asia, do hereby proclaim:
>
> Article 1 – The Japanese Occupation of the Andaman and Nicobar Islands is ended.
>
> Article 2 – Until such time as the lawful Govt. of India is once again functioning in the A.&N.Islands, I assume to myself full responsibility for the administration of the civil population and for the maintenance of good order in the islands.
>
> Article 3 – All persons will obey promptly all orders given by me or under my authority and must refrain from all acts which impede the Forces under my command, from all acts of violence, and from any act calculated to disturb public order in any way.
>
> Article 4 – I intend to fulfil my responsibilities for administration of the civil population through civil officers provided by the Govt. of. India and subject to my orders and I hereby delegate to the Chief Commissioner designate of the A &

N. Islands, full authority to conduct the administration of the civil population on my behalf, subject always to my orders and directions which I, or the Commander of the British Forces in the islands, may issue from time to time.

Article 5 – All laws and customs existing prior to the Japanese occupation will be respected in so far as military exigencies permit.

Article 6 – All proclamations and legistative enactments of whatever kind issued by or under the authority of the Japanese administration shall cease to have any effect.

Dated this 23rd day of September, 1945

Sd/Louis Mountbatten, Supreme Allied Commander South East Asia

On 9 October, 1945, the formal ceremony of surrender took place at 10 a.m. in the historical Gymkhana Ground at Port Blair. Among the local people, a few eyewitnesses who were present at both public meetings one in honour of Netaji Subhash Chandra Bose and the other in disgrace of the Japanese in the Gymkhana Ground, are still alive. Master Kesar Dass the oldest of all has recently passed away. Also Aafat Ahmed Khan who evacuated Port Blair in 1942 and brought back on board *S.S. Dilawara* to resume his duties, was another eyewitness of the surrender ceremony.

But the official version of the formal surrender was brought out by '*The Sunday Statesman*', dated 14 October 1945 as below:

"At 10 a.m a couple of ancient cars drew up. In them were the Japanese naval and army commanders. With a guard of Indian troops, they were conducted to a large table. Brig. J.S. Solomons, commanding our forces, then arrived and after inspecting the Guard of Honour, sat down at a table facing the Japanese and read out the instrument of surrender, the white-gloved Japanese listening intently.

Instrument of local surrender for Japanese Forces forming Garrison of Andaman and Nicobar Islands—

a. "The Commander, Japanese Garrison, Andaman and Nicobar Islands being fully aware that all Japanese sea, land, air, auxiliary forces have been already surrendered unconditionally by the Japanese Government to the Allied powers and by the Supreme Commander, Japanese Expeditionary Forces, Southern Regions to the Supreme Allied Commander, South East Asia, and that hostilities have ceased, does hereby undertake to ensure that the sea, land, air and auxiliary forces under his command or control, comply with the orders set out in the attached appendix and with all subsequent orders that may be issued from time to time by the Supreme Allied Commander or any of his subordinate Commanders. Disobedience of these and any subsequent orders, or failure to comply with them, will be dealt with in accordance with the accepted laws and usages of war.

b. This document takes effect from the time and date of signing.

c. The provisions of this document are complementary to and in no way prejudice or supersede, any general instrument of surrender that may be imposed, by or on behalf of the United Nations applicable to Japan and the Japanese Armed Forces as a whole.

d. The document is drawn up in the English language which is the only authentic version. In any case of doubt as to the intention of meaning, the decision of the Supreme Allied Commander is final. It is the responsibility of the Commander, Japanese Garrison, Andaman and Nicobar Island to make such translations into Japanese as he may require."

- Sd Vice Admiral Teizo Hara
  Local Commander, Japanese Navy, A & N, Islands.
- Sd/Maj.Gen.Tamenori Sato
  Local Commander, Jap. Army, A & N Islands
- Sd/Brigadier J.A.Solomons
  For Supreme Allied Commander, S.E.A.

Time 10.15.....Date 9 Oct.1945. Place .... Port Blair

The documents were then handed over for signature. Vice Admiral Teizo Hara signed and affixed his seal first and Lt. Com. Tazawa, Maj. Gen. Tamenori and a Staff Officer, Capt. Shimazaki, followed suit. For the Allies, the documents were signed by Brig. Solomons, Capt, J.H. Blair, the Naval Force's Commander, and Mr. N.K. Patterson, Chief Commissioner designate.

Immediately afterwards, the Japanese handed over the swords, saluted in turn and marched off towards their cars. They were driven away to the accompaniment of cat-calls and booing from the large crowd of delighted islanders who witnessed the ceremony".

The whole ceremony took only a few minutes. But the most remarkable event was that in the presence of the British Officers, the islanders and the Japanese, Loka, King of the Great Andamanese tribe was honoured with a cash reward for his valuable service to the cause of the British in the work-out of *'Operation Baldhead'*.

On 16th October, 1945 in a dispatch, a correspondent of the *Hindustan Times* on tour to Port Blair, writes, "The most hated men in the Andamans are the 300 or so of police whom the British left behind when they evacuated. They supplied the new ruler with details about each and every family or individual in the Andamans and that explains why the dossiers kept by the Japanese police which have now come in the hands of the British, are so rich in details about each individual.

These policemen, the population alleged, took prominent part in torturing people during the espionage trials. It is said that the property of those who were executed or tortured to death in these cases was shared between the Japanese Thokumohan and the Indian Police, This police force has now been disbanded and its men have been put in jail".

He further comments, "The fact that the morale of the people became so low during the Japanese rule that even children, a large number of whom had learnt the Japanese language, became informers."

However, the surrender ceremony was followed by a circular of strict instruction that every body of the Japanese forces should surrender arms and confine themselves in the periferry at least 4 miles away from the limit of Port Blair. Thus, their movement was totally restricted.

They were kept in barracks at Garacharma village. Their total number was 18,846. Among them only 186 were listed as war criminals. Later, the number was reduced finally to 112 who had to face the War Crimes Tribunal at Changi in Singapore.

For the local people, the most agonizing order of the British Headquarters was to arrest and shoot all the members of the Peace Committee as they were the collaborators of the Japanese. But Foster realized their helplessness so the shoot order was kept in abeyance and an enquiry was instituted to establish the fact. Later most of them were released except those who were *prima facie* culprits to be tried in a court of law.

Just after the formal reoccupation, military rules under the British laws were clamped for 6 months to cope with any untoward incidents and to restore normalcy. Later, on the civil administration was installed under N.K. Patterson, the Chief Commissioner designate.

About the deplorable condition of the population of the island, Patterson observed, that the population was obviously in extremely bad shape as regards nutrition, clothing and health, and the general deterioration and destruction was found to be very heavy in dockyard, saw mill etc. The population was suffering from starvation and malnutrition. The incidence of disease was very high. Clothing in most cases consisted of gunny sacking or old rags. There were literally no consumer goods of any kind available in the whole of Port Blair. The roads were in a shocking condition. The sanitary conditions were indescribable with drains blocked or destroyed. Buildings were in a dilapidated condition and in many cases partitions, ceiling and fittings had been removed or destroyed.

Abolition of Penal Settlement

Less than four months after surrender, on 7 February, 1946, Mr.N.K.Patterson took over the charge of the civil administration following sworn-in Ceremony.

Louis Mountbatten congratulated him by sending a telegram- *"I send my good wishes on the occasion of the resumption of civil administration of the Andaman and Nicobar Islands. I am sure that the islands may look forward to a new era of prosperity. My best wishes"*

One of the first decisions that the British government took after the resumption of the Civil Administration,was to abolish the Penal Settlement. This decision led in turn to the question of the future of convicts numbering nearly 6000 who had to remain on the Island at the time of the Japanese occupation in 1942. The Provincial Governments eventually all agreed to the proposal made by the Government of India that all convicts who had still some balance of sentence to serve should be given remission of that balance and should be allowed to return to their homes if they so desired.

Some four thousand and two hundred convicts were repatriated. All convicts of the Cellular Jail released by the Japanese were however approved but enroled in the labour force on condition to be repatriated as and when the shipping space was available. This created vacancies in the Labour Department, which were eventually filled by the local people. Before transportation a body of 10,000 Japanese soldiers were engaged in the labour force. In the Forest Department, considerable numbers of displaced persons, including Chinese, Malayans and Sumatrians along with the Japanese Army labour were also employed.

The condition of the whole population was very pathetic. All of them were just staggering to survive. They not only were mentally broken, but also had become easy victims of epidemics of scabies, beri-beri and malaria. Condition of health and hygiene was appalling. So the pressing need and the challenging task was to redress the woes and arrange speedy relief.

As to Patterson's instruction, "The whole energies of the civilian staff were directed to do the immediate tasks of relief." He engaged all government servants including those who had been living in the islands even during the Japanese period and the other old employees who had evacuated earlier and were brought back after re-occupation.

Patterson emphasized on, "... the close and easy co-operation of the civil staff with the Military Administration." Though the Military rule was to end after six months, in fact, it was handed over to the Civil authorities on 7 February, 1946. During this period, Patterson stated, ".. the whole of the Japanese forces had been repatriated, the evidence necessary for the trial of Japanese war criminals had been obtained and communicated to the appropriate authorities and steps for the repatriation of displaced persons had been taken."

After discharging his duties from October, 1945 to February, 1947, Patterson handed over the charge as the Chief Commissioner to Inam-ul-Majid, the first Indian I.C.S. ever appointed to the post of the Chief Commissioner. During Japanese occupation, hundreds of prisoners from Malaya,

Dutch East Indies and Singapore were brought in these islands as labourers and Majid made arrangements for their repatriation.

Visit of Mountbatten

Meanwhile, Rear Admiral Lord Louis Mountbatten, the Supreme Commander of the South East Asia Command and the architect of '*Operation Buccaneer*' had visited Port Blair on 28 November, 1945. He was received by N.K. Patterson, Brigadier Solomons, Group Captain Pope and Captain J.H. Blair. In this connection, it will not be irrelevant to mention that the meeting of Mountbatten and Blair was immensely significant for Mountbatten, the scion of Queen Victoria, became the last Viceroy to dissolve the British Raj in India which was founded by his great grand mother Queen Victoria and similarly Captain J.H. Blair, RNR was the great nephew of Archibald Blair who had first surveyed the islands in 1789 and founded the British settlement at the site which was later named after him as Port Blair.

About the sojourn, Mountbatten writes in his diary, "After inspecting the naval guard of honour, I visited and addressed practically the whole of 116 Brigade in groups and later went round the magnificent harbour with Blair and went on board H.M.I.S. '*Krishna*'. The population consists of some 12000 natives and 6000 convicts who have been released and pardoned. Wherever we drove, every single native, without exception, stood up and saluted as we passed, a relic from the Japanese who beat them if they did not salute. However, I think they were pleased to see us as they were being starved to death by the Japanese".

Visit of Wavell

Shortly afterwards, Field Marshall Lord Wavell, the Viceroy and Governor General of India along with his wife Lady Wavell paid a visit to Port Blair and took stock of the relief works and performance of the military administration. They visited the

Chatham Mill on 23 December, 1945, long before the beginning of any reconstruction of the mill which had been almost destroyed by the Allied bombing.

Tryst with Justice

Justice may be delayed but never be denied. Criminals are not only sentenced to punishment but also condemned to indignity if the crime causes wounds to humanity. During the Japanese rule it may sound natural for the occupation forces to inflict bestial tortures and implant atrocities to the people of the occupied islands in order to squeeze out confession of spying and to exercise domination over them. Hence, the mass murders in Homfraygunj may be admitted as tethering consequences owing to the charge of espionage but the gruesome killings of hundreds of innocent people in the sea of Havelock and in Tarmugli Islands who were not levelled with any charges and eliminated ruthlessly as they were human beings and needed morsels of food for mere sustenance, are utter denial and defiance of human rights and can universally be condemned as cognizable crime as genocide. So War Crimes Courts are usually set up to punish them who had indulged in the perpetration of treacherous crimes taking advantages of wartime uncertainties.

For the trial of the Japanese who let loose a reign of terror in the Andaman and Nicobar Islands and were responsible for the genocide, the War Crimes Court was established in Changi at Singapore and persons like Saudagar, HariKrishan, RamaKrishna etc. from the Andamans and Richardson, AbedNego, Ledie, Hussan, Wiliams, Koiny etc. from the Nicobars were sent to Singapore to give evidence for Japanese atrocities.

In that court, the eye witnesses gave their horried accounts explaining their own horrible experiences. Excerpts of a few are given below.

Witness Habibur Rahman, *Prosecution Document* (numbered 5114.) – "The document states that the Japanese

Excerpts from the Statement of a Witness, Hari Kishen at the War Crimes Court at Singapore: 25.4.1946

Prosecuting Officer: **Call Hari Kishen**

Hari Kishen

9th Witness for Prosecution: Examination in Chief

Witness duly made a solemn declaration.

Q. Is your full name Hari Kishen?
A. Yes.
Q. How old is this witness?
A. 17.
Q. Where was he living in 1945?
A. I was living at Tusanabad Thana where there was a forest camp.
Q. Is that near Port Blair?
A. It is within Port Blair.
Q. Did anything unusual happen to you in 1944?
A. Yes it happened.
Q. Can you tell us what happened?
A. Yes.
Q. (to Interpreter) Tell him to carry on.
A. On the 24th evening of October 1944 I was arrested by a Policeman from Thusanabad Thana and brought away under arrest from my Camp. I was taken to the gaol by the Policeman and brought inside to the Japanese. One of the Japanese, Tada, called me.
Q. Just one moment—you mentioned the name Tada. Can you see him in Court to-day?
A. Yes.
Q. Where is he?
A. He is number 2.
Q. Did you know why you were arrested?
A. I thought that the Japanese took me to be a British spy. They said when the planes came than I showed some light and signs.
Q. After that?
A. Where I was called in for interrogation, when being asked any questions, I was made in the room to sit down and put between my knees wood and another one on my thighs and hold a big wood in my hands.
Q. That was when you were being asked any questions?
A. Yes when being asked any questions.
Q. What happened when you were having this exercise?
A. When I was made to sit for five minutes I could not bear it and fainted and fell off. Tada came near me and put a Policeman near me and instructed that if I fainted or could not hold on to beat me.
Q. What language were these instructions given in?
A. Tada gave it in the Japanese language.
Q. And after he gave the instructions what happened?
A. I was sitting in that position for about 15 minutes after which I fell down. Then I was removed from that position and made to stand before Tada.

Azuma and his assistant beat a woman with heavy pieces of wood and burned her naked body. Azuma attempted to force Khaliq's wife to admit her husband was a spy and on her refusal said, 'Your husband shall never return home.' Khaliq was shot."

Witness Zaitoon Bibi, Prosecution Document (numbered 5116), "This document states that in January 1943, the witness's husband was arrested. She was taken to the gaol where she met her husband who was being beaten with a piece of wood until he became unconscious. Blood was pouring from wounds on his body. The Japanese on beating him threw hot and cold water over him to revive him.

The witness (Zaitoon Bibi) was then beaten in front of her husband after which she was taken to another room where she was forced to remove her clothes. She was tied up, hands raised above her head and legs apart, and a lighted candle was placed between her legs so that her private parts were burnt. Her husband was later shot."

Ramakrishna, who was the Deputy Commissioner in the Japanese Administration and later arrested on the charge of espionage, was put behind the bars and tortured by the Japanese. He went to Singapore to give evidence as an eyewitness. From his memoirs, we can have a vivid account of the trial in the War Crimes Court.

"A number of military tribunals were set up for the trial of these Japanese (who had been in the Andaman & Nicobar). The prosecutors were also military officers and the accused persons were defended by civilian lawyers from Japan. The one-time arrogant Japanese Officers were now submissive. They appeared in docks as criminals. They even stealthily approached witnesses who they had tortured, to be kind to them. The time had come for them to pay for their misdeeds"

"The Admiral who had ordered the mass murders was shot. Persons whom he least suspected, would give evidence against him, were those whom he considered dead as he had ordered them to be thrown into the sea to die. They were before him in flesh and blood, resurrected from Havelock Island. The Japanese Supply Officer who had p omised them food and the Chief of Thokomohan (Intelligence Department) who had been personally responsible for their arrest and carriage into the sea were hanged. The Civil Governor Jyochi Renusukai was sentenced to 25 years of hard labour. The Chief of the Police Mitsubashi who had manufactured all the so-called spy cases and who had perpetrated tortures and killed people mercilessly from 1943 onwards with the help of his colleagues, was hanged. There were no other death sentences. All others were sentenced to various terms of imprisonment ranging from seven to twenty five years hard labour for taking part in atrocious deeds".

"Indian collaborators and mischief mongers who had overdone their legitimate duties and who under the protection of the occupation forces, had inflicted tortures, were tried by criminal courts of the Andamans and sentenced to various terms of imprisonment. By and large, it were the officials of the Police Department who had now to face prosecutions for the tortures inflicted by them on their brethren, under the orders of the Japanese illegal government. Deciding these cases was, however, not a simple matter. Even if it was conclusively established that the accused persons had been responsible for atrocities, the courts could not lose sight of the fact that the Indian officials working under the order of the Japanese, were themselves in a precarious position and a single wrong move on their part could have been fatal for them".

In one of the Judgments, I Majid, Chief Commissioner and Sessions Judge observed, "... further it has to be taken into account that the position of persons serving either in the police force or in any other capacity under the Japanese, was extremely difficult and may be even said to be precarious at times. Nevertheless, in judging each case, it will be necessary

List of Persons persecuted in the torture chamber inside the Cellular Jail by the Japanese authorities – List submitted to the War Crimes Court at Singapore.

a. *List of Persons who were kept in the Cellular Jail and awarded rigorous punishment by the Japanese—*

1) Nasar Mullah 2) Brojendra Lal 3) Ram Gobind 4) Gurmurthy 5) Het Ram 6) Banta Singh 7) Shakar Kandi 8) Nawab Ali 9) Kesar Kaur (Female) 10) Pandoo 11) Labh Singh

b. *List of Persons who were arrested on so-called 2nd Spy Case, succumbed to bestial tortures executed by the Japanese—*

1) Bhikam Singh 2) Diwan Singh 3) Sangara Singh 4) Bakshis Singh 5) Chiranji Lal 6) Pati Ram 7) Farman Shah 8) Mohammed Khan 9) Dalip Singh 10) Nasib Singh 11) Ahmed 12) Moti Ram 13) Faizal Hussain

c. *List of Persons who were sentenced to death and executed in the 1st Spy Case, tried in jail on 30.3.1943*

1) Narayan Rao 2) Attar Singh 3) Surender Nath 4) Abdul Khalik 5) Suba Khan 6) Chota Singh 7) Gopal Krishna.

d. *List of Persons died of torture in the first Spy Case*

Muthuswamy and others.

to see whether the accused, if proved to have committed an offence, did not do it, having reason to fear instant death".

In another case, Mr. M.J.K. Sullivan, the Deputy Commissioner and Addl. Sessions Judge remarked, "... to start with, the Japanese tended to keep on the officials in those posts, in which they found them, under Japanese Heads of Departments, but sooner or later, they grew suspicious of them and involved them in fictitious spy cases, to appoint others temporarily in their favour, in their stead. There were in all 5 five main spy cases and many brave and innocent men met their death or were imprisoned through them. What then were the police to do? We cannot blame them in the least for taking up service under the Japanese. They had no alternative. It was a question of starvation and possibly worse or serving once more in the Police Force."

But the courts did find a number of Indian collaborators guilty of various charges and asserted that there were no mitigating circumstances in favour of the accused persons.

In conclusion, Ramakrishna further remarks, — " .... The conduct of the Japanese occupation forces in these Islands was abominable. It can however, by no means, be said that the Japanese Government or the Japanese people or the Japanese law recognized such inhuman conduct".

Again I. Majid, Chief Commissioner and Sessions Judge commented, "It was a well known fact that the Japanese proved themselves to be an extremely cruel people and in their attempt to subjugate the Islands, resorted to extreme forms of cruelty but it can by no means be stated that their laws countenance such treatments".

Shri Sullivan, Additional Sessions Judge also endorsed the comment, " It is interesting and revealing to note however and of this fact also I take judicial notice that later on in the Japanese occupation, the Japanese judges came from Singapore who put an end to this practice and torture and false confession, thereby showing that this procedure was not accepted by the Japanese Judicature. It was no universal practice of the Japanese to torture. A good Japanese Commander in North Andaman tolerated no such thing".

The nefarious reign of terror unbridled by the Japanese military authorities in the Andaman & Nicobar Islands ended in world wide indignation and opprobrium, and it remains ever as a bleeding and dolorous memory even in the hearts of the generations to come.

Compton Mackenzie has rightly remarked in his book, *All Over The Place*, (p154) "I dare say when I reach Japan and see the gardens, I shall begin to wonder of what their makers did in war, might not have been due to temporary rabies. Then I shall see it again with the mind's eye of the eyes of those people in the Andamans when they told me their horrifying tales and I shall remind myself that forgiving should no more be the equivalent of forgetting than tolerence should be the equivalent of laziness".

14 British Conspiracy Agony & Ecstasy

Since the beginning of the Penal Settlement, the fate of the Islanders was twice betrayed, once by the British and next by the Japanese. On the eve of Independence, they had to make again a tryst with destiny. It was so agonizing and uncanny that it seemed at times very precarious and unspeculative to guess what was to befall on the islanders while their brethren in the mainland of India would be celebrating the Independence Day.

During the Japanese occupation, Netaji Subhash Chandra Bose landed at Andaman and spent three nights there considering it a place of pilgrimage as hundreds and thousands of freedom fighters were transported there and subjected to severe tortures but their indomitable spirit could not be cowed down and they continued to struggle for freedom until the last breath.

In his own words, " while we were in the Andaman Island, we visited the notorious Cellular Jail in Port Blair and paid homage to those patriotic countrymen of ours who suffered indescribable persecution and torture in the past and some of them even laid down their lives as victims of British tyranny and brutality".

To pay a glaring tribute to the eternal memory of the glorious freedom fighters, Subhash renamed the Andamans as 'Shaheed' and the Nicobars as 'Swaraj' after they had been handed over to the Azad Hind Government.

After the re-occupation by the British, they were brought under the rule of the British Crown and on 15 August, 1947, with the independence of India, these islands got freedom and became an integrated part of India. India achieved independence, through bloodshed and sacrifice, but to achieve freedom, the islanders had neither struggled nor shedded a single drop of blood. Instead, their fate was put on trial of stake and bait time and again in the eerie bargain of the impudent British. In that foul game, the Andaman & Nicobar Islands happened to be a wretched pawn and almost ceased to be a part of India, but only due to the providence of God and for some intrigue in the deal, this calamity did not cudgel and the fate of the islanders was not sealed.

Announcement of Attlee

On 20 February, 1947, Clement Attlee, Prime Minister of Great Britain announced that India's Independence would be granted by June, 1948. Since then a queer drama encompassing the fate of these islands was looming large. The British tried by tooth and nail to stop cession of these islands to India and to keep them under her possession.

Objection of Chiefs of Staff

First objection came from the British Chiefs of Staff Committee. On 7 March, 1947 Pethick Lawrence, the Minister of State (India) wrote to Lord Wavell, Viceroy of India that in the opinion of Chiefs of Staff Committee, the Andaman & Nicobar Islands must be retained under the hegemony of Great Britain. At least for defence and security, Joint Command might be installed in collaboration with India.

On 18 March, 1947, the Chiefs of Staff Committee expressed their plan to build up airbases at Port Blair and at Car Nicobar and to keep them under their control.

On 19 March, 1947, Wavell replied that last year on 13 July, 1946, British Military Authorities in India had advised to develop a military base in these islands in order to extend securities to Malaya and Burma. Of course, Wavell did not forget to mention that this archipelago was a part and parcel of India and India would never renounce her claim over these Islands.

When Lord Mountbatten became the Viceroy of India, the British Government sought his opinion. On 1 May, 1947 he commented that after independence, if India joined the Commonwealth, it would be better not to discuss the fate of the islands. If India refrained to join, the issue whether the islands ceded to India or remained as a part of Britain might be solved tactfully.

Actually, the period was very crucial and critical, as Mountbatten had already drafted the plan twice for the momentous transfers of power to India as well as to Pakistan giving them the dominion status.

On 16 May, 1947 Jawaharlal Nehru expressed the acceptance of the Congress to the plan and cited that as the Andaman and Nicobar Islands had not been shown as a separate state in the plan so it must invariably merge to India.

Movement for a United Bengal

In the meantime, another question stormed the political sphere. At that time, a movement for a sovereign, United Bengal got momentum and the Government of Bengal, under Sir Frederick Burrows wrote to the Viceroy that he favoured the Shaheed Suhrawardy – Sarat Bose - Kiran Shankar Roy group proposal for an independent Bengal. Naturally, the British Secretary of State for India pointed out that Calcutta being the main port of transport and communication with the islands, if ceded to Hindustan (India), obviously the islands would merge to India. On the other hand, if Bangladesh was formed as an independent country, Calcutta would naturally merge with it. In that case, the fate of the Islands would be decided as to the situations.

The British Secretary of State further enquired if the Andaman & Nicobar Islands were ceded to either India or Pakistan and later on if the country decided to recede from Commonwealth, what the plight of the islands would be in relation to Great Britain. Hence, it would be better to accept the proposal of the Chiefs of Staff Committee considering the strategic importance of these islands, that they should be brought under the direct rule of the British Government.

Opinion of Cabinet Committee

On 28 May, in the meeting of the Cabinet Committee on India and Burma, Mountbatten stated that Nehru and Patel were worried of the controversies concerning the Andaman & Nicobar Islands as they believed that there should be no confusion on the right of India over the islands as it had clearly been indicated in the Govt. of India Act, 1935.

On the contrary, Stafford Cripps in a meeting remarked that Krishna Menon was of the opinion that India would agree to relinquish her claim over the islands in due course.

It's really surprising how Krishna Menon could pass such a misleading remark at this level because he was always taken as the spokeman of Nehru and his remark would only imply Nehru's opinion and might create confusion.

However, the Cabinet Committee on India and Burma being inspired by Cripps' remark, took the decision that British Government had never accepted India's right over the islands so their merger with India could not be a decided fact.

Role of India Office

London's India Office was always an anti-India coterie. On 10 June, 1947, Frank Turnbull, Assistant Secretary of Draft Committee stated that the Committee had taken decision to retain the Andaman and Nicobar Islands with Britain. This would be a gain in exchange of liquidation of British India.

Turnbull further wanted that Viceroy would negotiate the matter with the Indian Leaders and convince them. Meanwhile, the communal atmosphere of India deteriorated gravely and tension prevailed everywhere. The political tug of war concerning the Punjab and the North-West Frontier Province acquired the ugly turn of an incipient civil war. The interim government run by the Indians became callous owing to inner tussle and the people were in ferment on account of the communal trial of strength.

Joint Meeting of Indian Leaders

Earlier on 2 June, 1947 at the joint meeting of the leaders of the Congress represented by Nehru, Patel, Kripalani, and those of the Muslim League by Jinnah, Liaquat Ali, A.R. Nishtar and the Sikhs by Baldev Singh, Mountbatten reminded them that a terrific sense of urgency had been pressed upon him by everybody to whom he had spoken. They had wanted the present state of uncertainty to cease. Therefore the sooner power was transferred, the better for all. In that meeting for the first time, the viceroy officially indicated that power may be transferred much earlier than June, 1948 as declared by Attlee. And Jinnah had to accept a moth-eaten, corridor-less Pakistan.

In the meantime, Lord Listowel took charge as Secretary of State in place of Pethick Lawrence. On 12 June, 1947, in a memorandum to the British Cabinet, Listowel suggested seeking Viceroy's views regarding the retention of the Andaman & Nicobar Islands by the British for a naval base. Since this was already leaked to the Indian Press, Mountbatten advised, "..... there was no question of raising this controversial subject at the present delicate stage of our political negotiation and this should be settled separately in a treaty or agreement".

He further warned that if the archipelago was retained with Britain, there would be wide-spread discontent and commotion in India and it would spoil the whole atmosphere. Hence it would be wise to be refrained from creating chaos by either exercising Britain's claim or refuting India's right over the islands. In his report, Mountbatten made up for his egotism by sensitivity to Indian concerns and strongly opposed London's move to retain the Andamans. It would, "cause an absolute flare-up throughout the length and breadth of India," he wrote, 'My own position would be undermined.' But the British Chiefs of Staff were insistent.

Inspite of this advocacy, on 16 June, in the meeting of the Chiefs of Staff Committee, Major General Ward emphasized on the Britain's claim not only on the Andaman & Nicobar Islands but also on the Laccadive Islands and they should be retained for air transport route to the Far East.

Issue of Military Requirements

Moreover, Joint Planning Committee had already recommended to develop Navy and Air bases in both the Islands and if necessary, proper act might be passed to seize the Laccadive Islands from the Madras Presidency.

The Chiefs of Staff Committee further pointed out that the draft legislation bill for the transfer of power did not take due care of their military requirements and suggested that provision might be made for this purpose.

London's India Office in forwarding copies of the draft resolutions to New Delhi stressed on the need to keep the secrecy of the clause on the Andaman & Nicobar Islands. But the Secretary of State in a note to the Cabinet while recognizing the delicacy of the matter recommended that the draft legislation might be shown to the Indian leaders before it was introduced in the House of Commons to avoid controversies.

However, in response to the Viceroy's advice and the suggestions of the Secretary of State, the Chiefs of Staff Committee in London emphasized on the safeguard of the air route to the Far East and commented, "...it was of utmost importance to us to retain possession of Andaman, Nicobar and Laccadive Islands. It would not be sufficient to ensure ... that we should merely be allowed to use the islands as naval or airbase but essential to retain sovereignty over them."

In a note to the Ministry of Defence of His Majesty's Government, it was pointed out that above were the minimum requirements of these islands and therefore essential that the islands were ceded to the British while the method and timing for raising the matter was a matter for political decision.

Already in the Article 2(1) of the draft proposals, there was the provision to exercise the British suzerainty on those islands. Even Turnbull pointed out that as to the Article 16(1) of the Council of India Act, the Andaman and Nicobar Islands ceased to be a part of India.

The Viceroy received the draft Bill from London and expressed his amazement to find the provision that "Andaman and Nicobar Islands should cease to be a part of India after August 15."

Though the Minister of Defence quoting the Chiefs of Staff's opinion stressed on the importance of the islands as an essential link in the chain of Commonwealth air and sea communications in view of Viceroy's personal objection, the cabinet decided not to include this item in the legislation and seek separate negotiations with India.

Comments of Mountbatten

On 18 June, 1947 in a telegram to the Secretary of State, Mountbatten sent his comments on the draft bill for transfer of power by 15 August, 1947 and therefore insisted that this date be adhered to instead of 1 October as indicated in the bill. He further stressed that the clause which sought to delink the Andaman and Nicobar Islands from India, should be omitted and instead enquired if it would be enough if the Congress gave a firm undertaking that India would later enter into an agreement with His Majesty's Government giving them all facilities, perhaps on a "joint user" basis of the naval and airbases in the islands.

Almost at the same time, Secretary of State informed the Viceroy of the tenor of discussions in the Cabinet meeting on the Andaman and Nicobar Islands. The India-Burma Committee of the British Cabinet, however, approved the suggestions of Mountbatten and decided to drop the Article 16(1) from the draft bill. The advice of the Chiefs of Staff Committee to seize the Laccadive Islands was also turned down.

Claim of the Muslim League

Taking advantage of the political uncertainties that added fuel to the controversies, was the sudden claim of the Muslim League over the Andaman & Nicobar Islands. Over the issue, Jawaharlal Nehru reacted vehemently. In view of Pakistan's claim to a share in the Islands, Secretary of State thought that it would be wise to keep the decision on the islands in abeyance till further discussions. He also suggested that "till then, a clause could be inserted in the draft bill in the sense that the islands should continue to be governed by the Chief Commissioner under the Governor General".

Claim of Burma

On 20 June, 1947, another unexpected claim was put forth by the Burmese Press over the Andaman & Nicobar. All of a sudden, it urged the Government of Burma to claim the ownership of the islands since geographically the islands were in close proximity of Burma. Moreover they had been administered from Burma before they were transferred to the Government of India.

Mountbatten became very worried of the turn of situations and reiterated to drop the article that would separate the islands from India.

But the Chiefs of Staff Committee did not stop in pursuing the matter and insisted to capture the islands to meet its defence requirements. On 25 June, Lieutenant General Hollice wrote a letter to Alexander, Minister of Defence explaining the strategic importance of the islands and emphasizing on the British interest to build up Navy and Air bases.

Joint Control of Indo-Pak

The Cabinet Committee realized the importance of Mountbatten's suggestion and on 25 June told him to convince the Indian leaders on the point that so long the fate of the islands was not decided, they would be controlled jointly by India and Pakistan and if the Indian leaders did not agree, the question of the islands would be dropped from the draft bill so that they could easily be brought under direct rule of the British Government.

The scheme might be followed till the two dominion states, India and Pakistan would come to a consensus about the future of the islands. It was as follows—

a) The Andaman and Nicobar Islands would be controlled jointly by both the dominions.
b) The administration of these islands would be run by the Chief Commissioner to be appointed and guided by the Governor General.
c) To maintain peace and to run the administration properly, the Chief Commissioner might enact laws and introduce regulations under his jurisdiction.

But Mountbatten did not yield and informed Listowel that the Congress would not agree to the scheme and the attempt would be futile.

However, Prime Minister Attlee supported Mountbatten and instructed the Cabinet Committee to review the whole scheme and drop the disputatious articles.

Protest of Nehru

On 2 July, 1947, the Andaman and Nicobar Islands propped up once again. The Muslim League on finding the islands mentioned as part of India in the Bill got upset and claimed them for Pakistan. Underlining the importance of the islands for Pakistan to move troops from West to East Pakistan, the League said that the islands constituted an essential calling station for a voyage from Chittagong to Karachi.

On 4th July, Jawaharlal Nehru strongly objected and refuting the claim of the Muslim League outright argued strongly by citing data from the Census of 1941 that out of total island population of 34000, only 8000 were the Muslims so the claim of the League on these islands as Muslim dominated area was utterly wrong. Besides, for the security if the possession over these islands was necessary for Pakistan it would be more important for the defence and security of India to possess them.

Jinnah perhaps being fanned by the Torry members tried to put up the claim of Pakistan over the islands time and again but failed. Obviously, he was aggrieved.

Conveying the League's comments, the Viceroy was told that the League had stressed on the need either to give the Andaman and Nicobar Islands to Pakistan which were needed by her as a link between the two wings (West and East Pakistan) or to specifically exclude them from the scope of the present bill "to be dealt with later separately". The Viceroy however, did not advise any such change.

On 5 July, 1947, considering the political situation and objection of Viceroy, Secretary of State rejected Pakistan's claim over the Andamans on geographical considerations as well as demand for joint control as impracticable. A dissatisfied Jinnah protested to the Prime Minister as well as to the leaders of the opposition in London against the rejection of Pakistan's claim on the ground that the islands were historically neither a part of India, nor their population connected with India by "ethnic, religious or cultural ties" and pressed his claim again on the ground that " the islands were an important communication link between the two parts of Pakistan". Earlier on 21 May, Jinnah issued a statement demanding an 800 mile corridor through India to link the western and eastern halves of his proposed Pakistan. The demand was, however, rejected but again his claim on the AndaNico testified to his ability to retain the initiative.

The question of British defence requirements was again the subject of animated discussion at the Chiefs of Staff Committee when a note prepared by the Chief of Naval Staff of UK was discussed. There was overwhelming consensus that the right time to negotiate concessions was before 15 August when the British still had authority and not later when the authority would have passed into Indian hands. The members were critical of the Viceroy for seeking concession now, otherwise could vitiate the atmosphere of goodwill. In their discussions, the question of exercising sovereign authority over the Andaman & Nicobar Islands was raised time and again but it remained as it was.

On 14 July 1947, Prime Minister Attlee told the House of Commons that there was nothing in the wording of the Indian Independence Bill to modify the complete independence and autonomy of the two dominions. Listowel, the Secretary of State with the approval of Clement Attlee sent a brief note giving details of the British defence requirements in India and Pakistan after 15 August prepared by the Chiefs of Staff to the Viceroy to get them solved by negotiations with the leaders of two dominions.

The note further expected India to establish defence facilities considered essential by the British in the Andaman and Nicobar and Laccadive Islands. British interests were also involved in Hyderabad. On July 15, the Ministry of Defence discussed a letter received from Air Chief Marshal, Sir Christopher Courtecy that he had been approached to raise an airforce for Hyderabad and argued that it might be in the best interest of Britain to retain a foothold in India. But the plan was turned down.

Concern of Australia

Even the Australian Government expressed its great concern on the stand of UK to facilitate the defence requirements. On 4 August, 1947, it further requested His Majesty's Government to keep Australia informed of the negotiations with India for defence facilities on the Andaman and Nicobar Islands and to take into account the vital concern of Australia in the Indian Ocean line of communications, in view of the strategic importance of the islands.

It also advocated long–term lease of the islands' facilities since the sovereignty had to pass to India. The facilities should also include right to station troops and maintain naval and air facilities.

The Chief of the Viceroy's Staff, Ismay discussed in the meeting of the Joint Defence Council in details of long-term defence arrangements. He said that the objective of such arrangement was two fold. The first objective was to ensure that the necessary assistance could be provided to the two dominions in the event of either of them being victims of aggression and secondly to give both India and Pakistan as full and free members of the Commonwealth, "the opportunity to offer assistance to any other member or members of the Commonwealth, if they themselves should so desire". Hence, the islands would play a crucial role to ensure security and defence of the country, it belonged.

What the Chiefs of Staff emphasized and some of the Commonwealth countries expressed in their correspondences, was focused on the strategic importance of the Andaman & Nicobar Islands. It was admitted that the archipelago is situated at the epicentre of geo-political arena where to keep surveillance on any movements by the air and the sea, and to take the stock of political vicissitudes in the littoral states are very vital for the defence and securities of the Commonwealth countries.

But the game of ducks and drakes with the fate of the Andaman and Nicobar Islands ended in a grand finale in favour of India with the clear declaration by Prime Minister Clement Attlee in the House of Commons long back on 14 July, 1947 that the Andaman & Nicobar Islands would be an inseparable part of India. Indeed it was an unforgettable gift and gesture of goodwill of Attlee. The islanders are also thankful to Nehru who was adamant not to yield to Jinnah's shrewdness and overruled his plea by means of arguments and sagacity. But the people of the islands should be grateful to Lord Louis

Mountbatten, the last Viceroy of British India for his deliberate persuasion, indomitable spirit and presumptuous gesture to negate all attempts to retain the islands under the British suzerainty or to share with Pakistan. He did everything to prove that the Andaman and Nicobar should be a part and parcel of India.

To pay a glowing tribute to him his historical deliverance should be recalled in which he foretold, — ".... Any attempt by His Majesty's Government to claim the Andaman Islands as colonies will cause an absolute flare up throughout the length and breadth of India..." and in fine, His Majesty's Government admitted to let the islands cede to India.

These are the factual events of the drama played by the British inconspicuously behind the screen and the islanders all through remained ignorant of the sequences which had ultimately decided their fate favourably.

15 Epilogue

While in Delhi, the people were jubilant in celebrating the freedom week which had started with the rehearsal of unfurling of the national flag at Gandhi Ground by Dr. Rajendra Prasad, the sky was rent in the chorus recital of 'Bande Mataram' but the milieu in these islands remained as monotonous as ever and days passed by in the beaten track with no novelty or excitement.

Even on 14 August, 1947, while the people of the mainland were waylaid with emotions and heartened with the exuberance of sentiments in the prospect of freedom, in these islands, there was no such exhaultation or exhibition of hilarity.

On 15 August, 1947 when the whole India was mad with all round excitements and ecstasies, and while all eyes were set on the horizon looking at the new dawn of the birth of a free India,When Nehru's poetic rhetoric was still ringing in the hearts of millions, " **At the stroke of midnight hours when the world sleeps, India shall awake to light and freedom,"** the islanders spent the night in slumber and sluggishness. But how did the people remain unconcerned? Were they aware of the Day? Did they awake of their somnolence and dissolution? Who witnessed that historic moment? When was the sun of the free India rising on the horizon of the Andaman sea, how many paid homage to it?

That day in the Gymkhana Ground, Inam-ul-Majid, the then Chief Commissioner hoisted the national flag and the people in numbers took part in the ceremony in "orderly way". But the *First Independence Day* was not celebrated with that spontaneity and splendour as it should have been. The people really did neither care nor realize the great significance of the Day so their participation was casual and enthusiasm on their part was absent.

The condition of the Nicobars was even more disdainful and miserable. In July, 1949, Shri A.K Ghose, ICS who took over the charge of Chief Commissioner from I. Majid, visited the Nicobars and was surprised to notice that the Union Jack was still fluttering high in the sky at Kondul. On enquiry, he came to know that the people did not hear of the Independence and had no idea about India on the whole. This was really a deplorable condition of the islands. Even two years after independence, the people remained ignorant of the freedom of the country and were accustomed to unfurl the Union Jack as usual.

The causes of such inertness and numbness, despondency and indolence on the part of the islanders were known to all and it's obvious that it will take time to come out of the trance. During the British rule, they did neither care for the welfare of the people nor take any interest to explore the potentialities of the islands rather the islanders were left much to themselves. During Japanese rule, the land and the people of the islands were exploited only to meet Japan's wartime purposes. The British made the islanders physically callous and mentally impotent but the Japanese waved a wand of horror to make the people terror-stricken and moribund. After independence, fortunately for the people, these islands were ceded to India.

In the Constitution of India, these islands were placed under 'D' class states. In 1952 the Administration of the AndaNico was placed directly under the President of India. In the re-organization of States, the designation of these islands was changed to Union Territory from 1 November, 1956 and since then the islands are governed by a Chief Commissioner under the direct control of the Central Government. Later, in 1982, the designation was changed from the Chief Commissioner to

Lieutenant Governor and Shri M.L. Kampany became the first Lt. Governor of this Union Territory.

After independence , people of all communities from the mainland have settled here. In 1949, the Government of India decided to let the refugees, mostly farmer refugees from the erstwhile East Pakistan settle here under the rehabilitation scheme in order to increase the population of the islands and to make the islands self-sufficient in food production. They were followed by the settlers from Kerala and Tamilnadu under the colonization scheme. Even the ex-servicemen were settled in the Great Nicobar considering the security and defence of the islands. In course of time, a cosmopolitan character of the population has developed and the territory is rapidly taking shape of a mini-India where people of all communities, of different caste, creed and language live in unison having no contention owing to the diversities.

The next volume of this book will deal with the phases and prospects of settlements. In that volume, the dangers from known and unknown quarters are also to be discussed elaborately so that Chief Commissioner, A.K. Ghose's Open Door Policy of settlement and the recent trend 'Destination Andaman and Nicobar', much publicized and sellable slogan floated by the Department of Tourism, destined to fetch whether foreign money or international malign are to be viewed and explained whether "no more influx" should be the policy of this Mini-India.

A Select Bibliography

Unpublished Records in the custody of National Archives of India, New Delhi

1. Proceedings of the Government of India in the following branches of the Home Department :
   (a) Port Blair Branch from 1873 to 1947.
   (b) Political Branch from July 1907 to 1947.

Unpublished Records with the Defence Ministry

1. "History of Japanese Administration in the Andamans", File No. 601/76524 containing information regarding Japanese Rule dispatched by the Allied Intelligence Bureau.
2. 'Andaman Interlude',— Unpublished diary of Major Danis McCarthy.
3. 'The Andaman Islands under Japanese Occupation :1942-1945', unpublished memoirs of Shri Ramakrishna, Retired Deputy Commissioner who witnessed the onslaught of Japanese Rule.

Published Reports of the Government of India

1. Census Report, Andamans and Nicobars, 1901 by Sir Richard Temple.
2. Census Report, Andamans and Nicobars, 1911, Vol. II by R.F. Lowis.
3. Census Report, Andamans and Nicobars, 1921, Vol. II By R.F. Lowis.
4. Census Report, Andamans and Nicobars, 1931, Vol. II by C.J. Bonnington.

5. Census Report, Andamans and Nicobars, 1951, Vol. XVII by A.K. Ghose.
6. Census Report, Andamans and Nicobars, 1961, Vol. V by S.K. Sharma.
7. Appendix B to Census Report, 1910, Ossuary Feast by V.J. Solomons.
8. Appendix K to Census Report, 1921, page 43-44, A Festival in Car Nicobars by W.R. Park.
9. Appendix N to Census Report, 1921, page 47, Nicobarese Folklore by G. Whitehead.
10. Appendix O to Census Report 1921, page 48-50, Nicobarese Folklore by E. Hart.
11. Appendix E to Census Report, 1951, On the Origin of the Andamanese by Dr. Lidio Cipriani.
12. Appendix F to Census Report, 1951, On the Shompen of Great Nicobar by B.S. Chengapa.
13. Appendex P&Q to Census Report, 1921, p51-52, "Religious Ceremonies in Nicobars." By John Richardson.
14. Indian Antiquary : January- December, 1819, Vol. XXVIII. "Papers relating to the Settlement in the Andaman Islands in the 18th Century" by Richard Temple.
15. Selections from Records of Government of India, Vol. LXXVII
    (a) A Short Description of Nicobar by G.B.Hamilton.
    (b) On the Islands of Nancowry and Camorta by R.H. Colebrooke.
    (c) Extract from 'Voyage of the Austrian Fregate Nobara', Nicobar Islands –23 Feb. to 26 March, 1858.
16. Journal of the Royal Geographical Society- F.J.Mouat : "Narratives of an Expedition to Andaman Islands in 1856-62".
17. M.V. Portman: "Exploration and Survey of Little Andaman", 1888, Vol 10.

18. Imperial Gazetteers of India
   (a) "Hell on Earth" by Colonel Wedge Wood,
   (b) "Andaman and Nicobar Islands", by W.S. Molesworth, 1909
19. Journal of the East India Association "Andaman Penal Settlement", 1914, p159-81.
20. The Andaman and Nicobar Information, 1957-1990.
21. Report on the Administration of the Andamans and Nicobars and the Penal Settlement of Port Blair from 1864 to 1866
22. Yojana, Vol. XX, Number 13 & 14, Pub. 15 August, 1976.
23. Report on Special Areas Development Programme, its Schemes and Implementation; Deptt. Of Rehabilitaion in Andaman & Nicobar Islands, March, 1972, Port Blair.
24. Reports of a Commission on the Organisation of the Indian Army, 1959.
25. Social Panorama of Andaman and Nicobar Islands and prospect of Anthropological Research- A&N Information, Vol.1965, V.K. Kochar.
26. A note of Insanity, Convict, Marriage- Census, 1911 Vol. 11, Part \I—II, Woobey.

Bibliofile

- 'Land and People of the Andamans' Sen, Prabhat Kumar – Kolkata, 1962.
- 'Andaman and Nicobar Islands'- Chak, B.L, Publications Division, New Delhi, 1971.
- 'Pen Pictures of the Andaman and Nicobar Islands'. – Hussain, S. Yusuf, Lucknow, 1954.
- 'The Andaman Islanders',— Cipriani Lidio Weidenfield and Nicolson, 1966.
- 'Andaman Islands – A Social Study',— Brown, A. Radcliffe, Illinois, 1922.

- 'A History of Our Relation With the Andamanese'-M.V. Portman.
- 'The Long Afternoon: British India 1601-1947' — Golant William, Vikas Publishing House, 1975.
- 'The Andamans and Nicobars' -Kloss, C. Boden, Vivek Publishing House, New Delhi, 1971.
- "A Collection of Voyages, 'Captain Dampier's Voyage Round the World', Craddock, Eginald A, London,1729 .
- "The Nicobar Islands" Man, Edward Horace, London, 1933.
- "The Story of the Victoria Cross", Smyth, Sir John, London, 1963.
- "Penal Settlement in Andaman"—Majumder, R.C, Delhi 1975.
- "History of Exploration",— Sykes, Sir Percy M, London,1950.
- "History of the Andaman and Nicobar Islands", — Mathur L. P. ,Delhi 1969.
- "Islands of the Marigold Sun"—Vaidya, Suresh, London, 1966.
- "The Andaman Story"— Iqbal Singh, Vikas Pub, 1978.
- "Disciplining Punishment" – Sen, Satadru, Oxford, 2000.
- "Reconstructing the Criminal – Culture, Law and Policy in England, 1830 – 1914", Weiner, Martin, Cambridge, 1990.
- 'My INA Days in the Andamans' – Avasthi, R.L.
- 'The War in the Far East' – Collier Basil, Heineman, London, 1969.
- 'The Forgotten Army, India's Armed Struggle for Independence, 1942-45, Rupa & Co,1994.
- 'Andaman Ke Itihas Ka Safar' – Sivram Shakuntala, Confluence International, New Delhi, January 2003.

- 'At the Feet of Mother India' – Avasthi, R.L. 1995, Pub: 'The Rest', B.3/33,Shivala, Varanasi- 221001.
- "Cellular Jail—Cells beyond Cells"—Chowdhury, Swapnesh and Roy, Priten, New Delhi.

PART – II

- "The Unification and Division of India"—Misra, B.B. Oxford University Press, 1990.
- "A Short History of the Second World War",— Collier, London, 1970.
- "A History of South East Asia", Hall, D.G.E., Macmillian, 1968.
- "History of Modern World"—Nanda, S.P., N. Delhi.
- "The Springing Tiger", Toye, Hugh., London, 1959.
- "The War in the Far East"—Collier, London, Heinemann, 1969.
- "In Andamans, the Indian Bastille"— Sinha, Bejoy Kumar, Kanpur, 1939.
- "Countdown to Partition, The Final Days", Bhattacharya Ajit, Harper- Collins, 1997.
- "Netaji Subhash Chandra Bose: His Great Struggle and Martyrdom", —Hayshida, Tatsuo., Allied Publishers, 1970.
- "History of the Second World War", — Kirby, S.Woodburn, Vols. II & IV, 1972.
- "The Proudest Day" – Read, Anthony & Fisher, David, Pimilico, London.
- "My Life and Times:Octave Nine(1946-1953)"-Mackenzie, Sir Compton Mackenzie, Chatto & Windus, London, 1970.
- "All Over the Place" – Compton Mackenzie, Chatto & Windus, London, 1949.

- 'The War Against Japan', Vol III, Woodburn Kirby S.United Kingdom Military Series.
- 'Quit India Movement – British Secret Documents' – Dr. P.N.Chopra, Interprint, New Delhi,1986.
- The Diary of Col. Ishii Akiho, Staff. Southern Command.
- The Diary of Maj. Gen. Sugahara Dodai, Commander-in-Chief , The IIIrd Air Force, Japan.
- Recollection : Captain, Yoshimoto Seishi, The 7th Combat Unit, Japan.
- War History Chronicles – Pub. By Asagumo Shimbun Sha, Tokyo, Japan.
- "A Matter of Honour: An Account of the Indian Army,- Its Officers and Men", Mason, Phillip, London, 1974
- "Freedom at Midnight", Lapierre and Collins, Vikas Pub. N/Delhi.
- "The Great Divide Britain – India- Pakistan",- Hadson, H.V., London 1965.
- "Divide and Quit"—Moon, Penderel, Oxford University Press, Delhi, 1998.
- "Memories of Jinnah"—Hasan, Khalid, Oxford University Press, Karachi, 1990.
- "Mission with Mountbatten", — Campbell –Johnson, A., London 1951.
- "The Transfer of Power in India", Menon, V.P. Bombay, 1968.
- "Escape from Empire: The Attle Government and the Indian Problem", Moore, R.J., Oxford, 1983.
- "Prelude to Partition",— Page, D.J.H., New Delhi 1976.
- "Churchill, Cripps and India, 1939-1945", Oxford, 1979.

Index

Aberdeen jetty - the point of embarkation for the ferry to Ross Islands

Aberdeen Bazaar in the late 50s. Not much changed from the days of the Japanese occupation.

The remaining portion of the old Deputy Commissioner's office, where the Japanese housed their Intelligence Department.

Japanese Bombs being removed from somewhere in South Andaman. Bombs meant to be dropped on British India from these shores, but the plan did not get off the ground

A Japanese anti aircraft gun, one of the many left behind by them.